# ARTLESS

## THE ODYSSEY OF A REPUBLICAN CULTURAL CREATIVE

# ARTLESS

## THE ODYSSEY OF A REPUBLICAN CULTURAL CREATIVE

A MEMOIR BY

## GARY D. COLE

OOLIGAN PRESS

PORTLAND STATE UNIVERSITY

*Artless: The Odyssey of a Republican Cultural Creative*
by Gary D. Cole

Copyright © 2006 by Gary D. Cole.
All rights reserved.

ISBN 10-digit: 1-932010-12-2
ISBN 13-digit: 978-1-932010-12-1

Cover photo by Laura Howe.
Cover design by Laura Howe and John Kimball.

This publication is the product of Ooligan Press and the Publishing Program
of the Center for Excellence in Writing at Portland State University. It was produced entirely by the students of this program. For credits, see back matter.

Ooligan Press
Center for Excellence in Writing
Portland State University
Department of English
PO Box 751
Portland, OR 97207-0751
ooligan@pdx.edu
www.publishing.pdx.edu

Library of Congress Cataloging-in-Publication Data

Cole, Gary D., 1960-
  Artless : the odyssey of a Republican cultural creative : a
memoir / by Gary D. Cole.
    p. cm.
  ISBN-13: 978-1-932010-12-1 (alk. paper)
  ISBN-10: 1-932010-12-2
  1. Cole, Gary D., 1960- 2. Politicians--United States—Biography. 3.
Dramatists—Oregon—Biography. 4. Oregon—Biography. I. Title.
  CT275.C67725A3 2006
  979.5'043092--dc22

                                                    2006004903

Ooligan Press is engaged in a marketing experiment.
Please test the following site to see if enhanced mate-
rials are available for this book. If so, enjoy! And don't
forget that you can go to www.publishing.pdx.edu
for the latest on this and other Ooligan Press books.

# WASHINGTON (NEARLY)

I was about to start the perfect job. All my friends said they could not imagine a better fit. After two decades of laboring in the trenches of the performing arts and Republican politics, I had been offered the position of Deputy Chairman for Grants & Awards at the National Endowment of the Arts (NEA) in the administration of President George W. Bush. I would be in charge of a program that annually awarded over $60 million to arts organizations all around the country—a miniscule sum in the overall federal budget, but an enormous amount relative to total arts funding. I would have the chance to apply on a national scale what I had learned in Portland, Oregon, co-founding and shaping two innovative theater organizations and working for years on the political front lines. I was the right guy in the right place.

The offer came on a Monday in early June '03 while I was at my parents' home outside of Chicago. Our family was still giddy in the wake of my brother's wedding that weekend, ending a long bachelorhood that my mother feared would be everlasting. There happened to be some champagne in the fridge, and we toasted a fabulous opportunity that had come along after a period of bitter struggle. A few years before, I had left a successful law practice to launch a company that captured outstanding new theater on digital video and to manage the construction of a new performance space for the nonprofit theater I headed. Both projects had taken a far greater toll on my marriage, emotional state, and pocketbook than anticipated, and we celebrated an office that offered a graceful transition from the strains of arts entrepreneurship and brought my wife and two young children closer to family in the East and Midwest.

This job was also the ultimate validation of my belief that I could be both a devoted arts professional and a dedicated Republican. I was well aware that the arts and Republican politics were an unusual combination, but in my view a valid one. I understood that the Republicans had traditionally been the party of the Establishment—of conventional success in society—and that artists more often than not were outsiders and outcasts. I knew, painfully, that virtually no one I worked with in the theater world was registered Republican and that their reaction to my politics was usually some mixture of amazement and contempt.

But I was a Republican because I subscribed to two fundamental values: personal liberty and responsibility and skepticism of government. These I also considered—and still consider—to be at the heart of artistic creation. To me art is undiluted, uncompromised individual expression. The artist cannot hide behind the corporate veil or organizational cloak, but is laid bare through direct communication with those who experience the art, whether it be a viewer standing before a painting or an audience member awash in the sounds of a musical composition. The artist has no choice but to accept responsibility for the work of art. Government's corresponding obligation is to offer the freedom that allows artists to create according to the dictates of their art, which is why a healthy skepticism is always in order. Governments—good, bad, or indifferent—have a tendency to support those who support them and attach strings to their patronage. Undue reliance on governmental largesse tends to produce art that is a captive of that government, rather than a product of the robust and unflinching independence that is the hallmark of great art.

The writer David Brooks wrote in the *Atlantic* that "any Republican who contemplates a career in academia these days is both a hero and a fool." I will admit to occasional feelings of both heroism and folly as a lone Republican in the theater, a sea of those otherwise registered. Despite the comparable political imbalance, however, academia is not the arts. Art by its very nature tends to be decentralized and dispersed, not institutionalized into the massive edifice that is the modern university. An artist does not need to be a card-carrying member of a thought-conforming faculty in order to make art. Art tends to exist at the margins of society, and at the margin it is possible to take risks and defy orthodoxy in a manner academics would brave at their peril.

On an admittedly small scale, I had practiced in the arts what I had preached in politics. I had shaped a nonprofit performing arts organization that reflected my values, and the result was one of the rising theater companies in Portland. Through entrepreneurship I had sought to expand the audience for the arts by putting great new theater on digital video, and my company had achieved national recognition (if not yet, alas, profitability). I had demonstrated that not only was there no contradiction between my devotion to the arts and Republican politics, but that the two could flourish in tandem.

Or so I thought, as I sipped champagne and basked in a congratulatory glow that June afternoon. I soon found that I had been sadly, and utterly, mistaken. The divergent strands of art and Republicanism that I had woven into the fabric of my identity over the past twenty years came wildly unraveled. I was left holding the frayed ends, numb at what proved to be a short-lived tenure as a senior Bush administration official. Very short-lived.

It took me month after excruciating month to come to grips with the demolition of my personal mythology. Not only had I not proven myself to be that singular being, a Republican artist (or at least an artistic Republican) able to reach the top rank of both pursuits, but I was now jobless and directionless. I regrouped as best I could, selling our home in Portland and resettling in the Carolinas, where my wife's family has deep roots.

At first I clung to my hurt and my anger, both boon companions who, unlike my former Republican comrades, had not deserted me. I was devastated by my treatment at the hands of the Bush gang and prepared to denounce the administration as the intolerant, pandering, brutal, cowardly, reactionary regime that roughly half the country believed them to be. I could not bring myself to watch the news programs to which I had formerly been addicted, but when I did see images of the President I beheld not the tough, decisive leader I had campaigned for but the smug, narrow-minded jackass so many of my colleagues in the arts saw in the White House. The nation's bookshelves were groaning with weighty tomes blasting the mendacity of Bush and his fellow travelers, and I found myself primed and ready to add to the chorus.

Then, as I settled into a routine in my new home—taking my children to sports and dance practice, discovering different regional rhythms in the local press, finding new runs through the woods—the bitterness began to subside. Perhaps, I thought, I'll just walk away from it all and, though not a Christian, simply turn the other cheek. I immersed myself in a childhood memoir about my years as a paperboy for the *Chicago Tribune*, my first effort at writing since the completion of the play that had led to the founding of my theater company. The memories of once beloved customers along my old paper route were a balm to my wounded spirit.

But I hadn't walked away from much in life, and even after a few months of emotional convalescence, I could tell I wasn't going to be able to do it here. What a little distance from the fray enabled me to see, though, was that my disastrous turn in the Bush administration had forced a choice of paths, a choice I had been unable or unwilling or uncalled upon to make in over twenty years of straddling the contrarian and the conformist, fringe theater and the CIA, Judaism and Christianity, and (to borrow once again from David Brooks) the bohemian and the bourgeois. I felt compelled to retrace the steps of my odyssey as a Republican cultural creative, both to arrive at closure over the ruin of my grand aspirations and to give a personal account of one man's rugged hike along cultural fault lines.

I have by no means relaxed my views of the Bush administration. I do believe my story, the story of a Republican insider and grassroots arts entrepreneur whose bid for high-ranking office tumbled into our country's yawning culture gap, has something to offer to the debate over the character of this administration, and I will gladly air my opinions.

But I have come to believe that I owe George Bush and his confederates a debt of gratitude, as they did me a great service in dictating a choice in my life. The arts are where I belong, at least as much family obligations, available resources, and creative talents will allow. Had I remained in a senior position at the NEA, I am convinced I would have been called upon to act as a censor of the arts, charged with ensuring that potentially controversial grant applications were buried deep in the bowels of the bureaucracy. I have come to realize that I had spent far too long championing liberty both in the arts and as a Republican to compromise myself as Bush & Co. would have had me do.

So I lost the perfect job. But I found that after years of driving on both sides of the center line without incident, a spectacular crash had guided me to the right, or perhaps I should say the proper, side of the road. I may not have been the right guy, but after slipping off the high wire of a balancing act that had opened back in college, I had finally landed in the right place.

# BERKELEY

My odyssey begins as it ends, in an attempt to serve a Bush. I was standing on a street corner in Berkeley, California in '80 trying to persuade passersby to register as Republicans. St. Jude must have been smiling somewhere. If ever there were a cause more lost than this one, it had escaped my notice.

I was in Berkeley attending the University of California during my junior year abroad. Berkeley was technically still part of the United States, I knew, but for someone who had grown up in a placid, conventional suburb outside of Chicago and spent his first two years in college at a leafy campus in rural New England this was a lot more abroad than the south of France. "Berserkley," as it was fondly known, was celebrated/notorious for its People's Park demonstrations against the Vietnam War in the late sixties. Many of the radicals and rabblerousers had never left town. They could be found—graying and fraying—among the gaggle of alternative/organic/holistic establishments off Telegraph Avenue that bore no resemblance to any downtown I had ever set foot in.

I had come to Berkeley to find something that was missing in my sheltered collegiate life. My school, Williams College, was a wonderful place: a picture postcard campus full of bright, motivated, well-rounded star students who wore their elite status with casual grace. I had found great friends, academic challenge, and terrific sweaters.

But not fulfillment. The provincial nature of Williamstown, an isolated village of 1,500 in far northwestern Massachusetts, had begun to wear by my second year. Diversity was not then the household buzzword it has since become. Despite some efforts on the college's part, the greatest mark of differentiation within the student body was whether you had gone to a rural, donor-enriched prep school or a suburban, property tax-enriched public school. Williams seemed the beaten path, and I needed a detour. I craved the pulse, the rough-and-tumble, of a big city, major university campus.

I figured Berkeley was about as far as I could go in the opposite direction—geographically, culturally, socially—and still get a first-rate education. The University of California system was regarded as one of the best in the country, and Berkeley (aka Cal) was its flagship school. Thinker of big thoughts that I deemed myself to be, I had chosen philosophy as my major, and the university had an internationally acclaimed department. The Bay area still held the promise of romance and redemption that had bewitched so many, including my own parents when they fled Cleveland for San Francisco in the late fifties and had contrived to conceive me there.

Cal accepted me as a transfer student (they sadly didn't consider themselves a junior year abroad location), and I arrived in town during the summer of '79. A family friend had wangled me a job as a busboy in a coffeehouse/restaurant in San Francisco's bustling Union Street district, and I commuted via bus from a frat house in the Berkeley hills that rented dirt-cheap rooms over the summer. As the new guy, I invariably drew the worst shifts, sometimes closing the restaurant well after midnight on Saturday night and then opening it for brunch early on Sunday morning. Several times I just brought my sleeping bag, pushed back the tables, and slept on the floor—a little fitfully, as the restaurant next door was operated as a halfway house for ex-convicts. When I did take the bus back to Berkeley after a late shift, I found walking up Bancroft Way after midnight to be a scene out of *The King of Hearts*— wraith-like figures darting across the street and disappearing into the mist, faint whispers and muffled echoes, distant laughter.

I soon discovered I was not in Williamstown anymore. After I'd been at the restaurant a few weeks one of the older waiters came up to me with the weekend section in hand. He said he had a date Friday night with someone about my age and wondered if I could make any movie suggestions. I looked over the listings and pointed out two or three films that looked good to me. He chose one, thanked me, and said: "I'm sure he'll love it!" I somehow managed to stifle my gasp. Guys dating guys was well beyond my social ken. When I shared this news with one of the cooks, he welcomed me to San Francisco and said that he and I were probably the only straight guys working at the place. He then flashed a lecherous, conspiratorial grin and remarked that the waitresses, most of them very pretty and in their twenties or thirties, knew the lousy odds for women in this town and needed to be consoled from time to time.

My Williams background did come in handy in one respect. I had taken Music 101 my freshman year and by the end of the term could distinguish Bach from Brahms with some regularity. The restaurant featured Baroque music as its soundtrack, and I was amazed at the number of times patrons would motion me over and ask me to identify the composer of whatever was then playing. I often knew the answer, but even when I didn't I was amazed at how often "It sounds like Vivaldi" would command a nice extra tip (if the waiter deigned to share it with me).

Once school started, I was both thrilled with the novelty of it all and petrified by knowing virtually no one in this sea of humanity so far from my moorings. I wound up living in a group house a mile or so south of campus that turned out to be across the street from the local Hare Krishna Temple. Occasionally I would be awakened early in the morning by the sounds of chanting and drum-beating coming from our saffron-robed neighbors. I sometimes answered in kind in the heat of the day by shouting epic utterances from Nietzsche's *Thus Spake Zarathustra* from our roof deck, stripped to the waist and sporting mirror shades. I found the Krishna local color more amusing than annoying until federal authorities seized a submachine gun from the back of the headman's Porsche, after which I kept the Nietzsche to a dull roar.

Williams students are always busy, the result of years of relentless résumé building, and I was chafing at the relative inactivity of just hitting the books and people-watching. I had run track at Williams, but I figured that the Berkeley team was not in dire need of a mediocre sprinter from a Division III school. I had also served on the Williams Lecture Committee, where my signal achievement had been helping to land a speech by celebrity alum George Steinbrenner (which he then proceeded to cancel the day before the event after publicity had been out for weeks), but there seemed to be too much bureaucracy in the comparable organization at Cal. I decided to sign on as a reporter for the *Daily Californian*, the university's student newspaper. I lucked into a plum first assignment, covering a reported plutonium leak at the Lawrence Livermore Laboratory operated by the university system, but soon found myself on an obscure campus finance beat with articles well below the fold and well after the front page. I actually enjoyed my little niche of bond issue and financial aid stories, as it gave me an upfront look at the massive underbelly of the school and produced useful information for students about how they could afford to pay for college. But like any cub reporter, I craved the limelight.

It soon found me, in spite of myself. The *Daily Cal* was run largely by journalism grad students with sandals and beards who had been around in the glory days of Berkeley anti-war activism and saw the newspaper as an instrument of social change. We were in a presidential election cycle, and they devoted a healthy chunk of the paper to savaging the Republican presidential candidates, particularly former California Governor Ronald Reagan. This outraged the student government, which was dominated by conservative, Southern California, polo shirt and khaki-clad fraternity types who wanted the *Daily Cal* to cover campus activities. This sparked a delicious confrontation—rock-ribbed Orange County versus tie-dyed Berkeley—in which the student senate threatened to cut off the paper's funding unless they curtailed their national political coverage and shifted their focus to the campus. The editors railed in high dudgeon against totalitarian censorship, but they finally capitulated.

Which meant they needed to find someone who was actually covering campus affairs. Which meant me. In a glorious stretch of four days, I had no fewer than five front-page stories, most dealing with threatened changes to federal student loan programs. I could barely contain my excitement as I pulled the top paper out of one of the campus kiosks to find yet another above-the-fold byline.

My enthusiasm was not shared by the editorial staff. I strolled into the newsroom one afternoon to find the paper's political editor, who could have passed for Che Guevara, glaring at the day's front page and cursing: "Who the @#$% is Gary Cole and what the %$#@ is this *&^% doing on the front page again?!!"

After a week or so, the student government relented. The paper got its appropriation, the editors went back to castigating Ronald Reagan, and my stories went back to page twenty-three.

The incident, however, had helped to pique my interest in the '80 presidential campaign. I was accustomed to following politics as a blood sport, raised as I was outside of Chicago in the heyday of Mayor Daley, but this would be the first election where I was actually old enough to give a thumb's up or down to the gladiators. I had a deeply rooted cynicism toward the Democratic Party, the product of soaking up years of manipulation and corruption on the pages of the *Chicago Tribune*. I had grown up viewing Republicans as good government reformers trying to make democracy function in the face of the dirty tricks of the Daley machine and its allies in organized labor. I felt little affinity for the congressional wing of the Democratic Party, which seemed dominated by Southern Dixiecrats like John Stennis of Mississippi, Herman Talmadge of Georgia, and Robert Byrd of West Virginia—hugely powerful masters of pork barrel politics with questionable records on civil rights.

The GOP, of course, was also the party of Abraham Lincoln, a demigod in my home state (its slogan is still the Land of Lincoln). The youth of Illinois were all schooled in Lincoln's courageous facing down of slaveholding Democrats in order to preserve the Union. Lincoln embodied the image of a progressive, reformist, freedom-loving party arrayed against the feudal Democratic forces of prejudice and exploitation.

There was an element of youthful revolt in my choice of party. My mother had rebelled against the reflexive Republicanism of my grandmother and was an unabashed liberal who had first exposed me to politics at a Eugene McCarthy "Clean for Gene" rally during the '68 presidential campaign. I had never set out to poke Mom in the eye as such, but I had prided myself on my independence since I started making my own walking around money at the age of eight as a *Tribune* paperboy. I was determined to chart my own course politically, and it suited me fine if our trails should fork.

My poor opinion of Democrats had not been helped by the performance of President Carter. He struck me as a nice, well-meaning man who was hopelessly out of his depth dealing with an international crisis in Iran and an economy wracked by gasoline shocks and double-digit inflation and interest rates. I understood why the voters had responded to the cesspool of Watergate by electing a total outsider untainted by the scandals in Washington, but I thought the result was an overmatched administration that was woefully short on credentials.

And credentials meant a great deal to me. I may have been the product of a privileged background, the son of a children's heart doctor and a Wellesley-educated educator, the beneficiary of one of the nation's best public school systems in the Chicago suburb of Winnetka, but I had worked hard to build the record that got me into Williams. I had strived to punch the right tickets—the grades, the after-school organizations, the community involvement—and I had a natural affinity for those who had taken the route of well-rounded achievement.

So when I went to size up the field of potential Republican opponents to Jimmy Carter, I quickly settled on George Bush. He seemed to have done it all—congressman, ambassador, CIA head, war hero—and preserved a certain grace and dignity throughout. He was the perfect successor to the hapless Carter, a seasoned hand who could restore order and confidence in Washington. He had formidable competition in the Republican primaries, but Ronald Reagan struck me as a Hollywood B-movie lightweight, Bob Dole as a dark hatchet man, John Connally as a slick Texas operator, Phil Crane (my former congressman) as nice hair/little substance, John Anderson as a principled no-hoper, and Howard Baker as a captive of the legislative branch.

I beat a path to the Bush volunteer corps, which landed me— shiny campaign button on blue oxford shirt and all—on that Berkeley street corner urging passing pedestrians to register Republican so they could vote for Bush in the primary. I might have stood a chance had I set up my table on Prospect or Piedmont where the fraternities had their houses, but off Telegraph I was mercilessly heckled. The only comparable abuse I had witnessed was of visiting team outfielders by the bleacher bums in Wrigley Field, and at least the players were paid for their pains. I stuck by my man, however, through that dismal exercise in futility and the hard slog of the primaries. Once it became clear that Reagan would gain the nomination, I naively assumed that my candidate would obey his own admonitions about the former movie star's dangerous inexperience and lack of substance and spurn any offer to serve on his ticket. I was devastated when Bush agreed to become Reagan's running mate. I grasped at some intuitive level that a man with a first-rate résumé should not turn down another impressive credential, but I was left with a sickening feeling of betrayal and little desire to watch two men with big smiles and small track records duke it out in the fall.

# WILLIAMSTOWN

I needed tangible evidence of the transformation I had undergone in Berkeley. As I contemplated my return to Williams and my old friends, I felt compelled to demonstrate that I was not the shallow sophomoric suburbanite they'd known before. As I couldn't very well wear my *Daily Cal* clippings around my neck, I did what countless generations of men had done before me to display their manhood: I grew a beard (or rather a wispy collection of reddish whiskers that made for an untidy tangle around my chin but left an almost Lincolnesque void above my lip).

Despite its mustache-challenged appearance, my new foliage served its purpose. As I passed my classmates on campus, I would get those quizzical looks that said, "This person looks familiar, but who the hell is he?" This was exactly the effect I had sought to produce. I'd spent a year at the intellectual and cultural powerhouse that was Berkeley, after all, not gawking with tourists in Provence.

The beard soon came in handy in other respects. Shortly after school started I saw an audition notice for the Drama Department's fall play, George Bernard Shaw's classic *Major Barbara*. I had served as the equivalent of a spear carrier in the chorus of a few high school musicals and had been roped by a friend into playing the Third Shepherd in the Medieval Club's Christmas pageant, but I had never attempted serious theater before. My year away from the track team had left neither I nor the team in desperate need of each other, however, and working a beat on the *Williams Record* held little appeal after my flirtation with the big time at the *Daily Cal*. More critically, I felt that taking a part in a play would showcase some of the flair, the new dimension, the added stature, that I had gained at Berkeley. I checked out the script and prepared to audition.

Thanks in large part to the beard, I believe, I was cast as the broken-down old Cockney Peter Shirley. Peter is ministered to by the aristocratic Salvation Army Major Barbara Undershaft (played by Carolyn McCormick, who went on to minister to the criminally insane as a psychiatrist on *Law & Order*). I struggled as a well-fed child of privilege to reach the impoverished despair of this failing man, but thrived on the wit of Shaw's dialogue, the immediacy of the interaction with my fellow actors, and the intensity of the rehearsal process. Not to mention the cast party, which was a marked improvement on most of the keg-centered festivities on campus.

Socializing with the theater crowd, however, had its perils. One night after a few post-performance drinks with the cast, I headed back to the dorm around eleven thirty to find one of my classmates shooting baskets out back. Perhaps spurred by my slight inebriation and gray hair and beard (I had yet to remove my make-up), he challenged me to a game of one-on-one. Basking in the glow of my performance and emboldened by a five-inch height advantage, I took the bait. I did not reckon on my diminutive adversary driving to the hoop and then unexpectedly stopping and bringing his head up into my chin, which sank my teeth right into my lower lip. Blood flowed freely. My opponent, who was pre-med, decided to put his march to victory on hold and escort me to the infirmary. The expression of the nurse on duty at the sight of this twenty-year-old student—grizzled beard stained with blood, gray-sprayed hair wild and unkempt, rivulets of wrinkle make-up and perspiration streaming down the nose— had nothing on Macbeth seeing Banquo's ghost.

Above all else, I relished those performances where Peter Shirley and I flowed into one another, when I had no consciousness of playing a part and no awareness of the audience beyond the lights. This happened on only a few nights during the run of *Major Barbara*. Most of the time I could not rid my mind of the distractions of my day, of the presence of my girlfriend in the audience, of another actor's inability to use deodorant. During these performances I delivered my lines competently, but I knew I had left something on stage.

I was exhausted after the play closed, but I felt a tremendous sense of loss. I had never been part of a group that had labored so intensely and melded so cohesively, only to go our separate ways after a few short months. It wasn't so much that the cast and crew were to be my lifelong friends, but that we had made a huge mutual commitment that so quickly dissolved into nothingness. Even sports had not produced this sense of shared sacrifice for me, in part because a track team is pretty much a collection of individual competitors, but also because of the element of artistic expression that somehow charged me spiritually more than any physical competition ever had. I longed to recapture that unity, that merging of self and character, which had occurred on stage during those few fleeting performances.

The Drama Department had other thoughts in mind. They decided to stage Harold Pinter's Old Times as their winter show, a dark comedy that featured three actors, exactly one of whom was a man. My kinship with my fellow *Major Barbara* performers soon gave way to ruthless competition for the one male part, which did not appear to require a beard. I made the callback round of auditions, but when the cast list was posted on the bulletin board of the department, my name was not on it.

I was certainly not shocked by the outcome, but I was surprised at how disappointed I was. My career on stage had consisted of one production, but already I had a sense of expectation and even entitlement. I railed at the Drama Department for selecting a college play that had so few opportunities for students and determined that I would not be denied in the spring.

In the meantime, I had accepted an invitation to move in with some friends to a converted farmhouse a few miles from the college. They had asked me to join them when I returned from Berkeley, but I was hesitant to go off campus after being away from the school for a year. A few months of dorm life soon cured me of my reluctance.

This house was notorious. During my time in Williamstown it had been the lair of a succession of hockey and lacrosse players, hard-partying seniors who had hit the social apex of a hierarchical small college and played it for all it was worth. These were still Williams guys, of course, so they cared about their careers to come, but they knew that the die had largely been cast by senior year, most certainly by the second semester.

My housemates were the in-crowd. They were successful athletes from prestigious prep schools. They had money, looks, and girls. Everyone knew who they were. They captained major sports teams. They drove Saabs. Williams College had officially banned fraternities in the sixties because they had effectively monopolized the school's social life, but this ersatz farm was for all intents and purposes a frat house in exile.

I felt at home there. Several of my housemates were good friends, and I got on well with the rest. While admittedly not at their level, I had been an athlete, so I did not feel out of place in a jock house. After the relative asceticism of Berkeley, the jam-packed parties, the six-pack croquet competitions under headlights after dark, and the impromptu five-iron competitions over the pond out back were a hell of a lot of fun.

But I was a Jew in a house of WASPs, and I felt it keenly. Not because I wore my Jewishness on my sleeve. My family had done much to assimilate, including punching that surest of tickets to the American mainstream: sports. My paternal grandfather, a third baseman on the Case Engineering college baseball team in Cleveland, had changed his name from Cohn or Cohen to Cole early in life to improve his job prospects. My maternal grandfather had gone to Washington & Lee University in Virginia, one of the bastions of the South's Protestant aristocracy, and went on to become one of the original owners of the Cleveland Browns football franchise. My father had been an outstanding swimmer in high school and at the University of Michigan and had been rushed by a number of Gentile fraternities who had no idea he was Jewish.

While my parents had both grown up within a Jewish social circle in the upper middle class Cleveland suburb of Shaker Heights, neither family was religious. As a teenager my mother had gone through some sort of confirmation ceremony, but not a bat mitzvah, and my father had almost no religious education. Our short-lived efforts to celebrate the Sabbath when I was a boy had been aborted because my mother couldn't stop snickering at my father's atrocious Hebrew pronunciation. I had attended Sunday school for a year or two, but stopped going one weekend and never went back.

My parents had chosen in the early sixties to buy a home in the upscale Chicago suburb of Winnetka, which had a small Jewish population, rather than in the more traditional Jewish enclaves of Highland Park and Glencoe. This had a huge impact on my upbringing. Most of my friends growing up were not Jewish, and I developed very little sense of Jewish identity. I knew my ancestry, of course, and at some unspoken level was proud to be part of a people who had survived and accomplished so much, but my ethnic heritage and religion came to be topics I preferred to avoid. When the conversation would turn in this direction, there was a slightly sickening sensation in the pit of my stomach. I usually managed to escape outright lies about my background through a deft facility in changing the subject or by simply naming the countries from which my ancestors had emigrated—Austria, Germany, Russia, France. I found it easy with a WASPy last name to blend in with non-Jews, and I did.

Life on the frat-house farm was of a different order of magnitude, however. I had always lived in a setting where there were other Jews around, in Winnetka or in the dorms at Williams, not to mention the radicals of Berkeley. This was the first time I had gone solo in the rites of assimilation, and I felt the self-inflicted sting of stereotype—I'm the brainy one, the one with the hooked nose (at least as much a product of a boyhood collision with a line drive as heredity, but there it was), the one whose thick black hair furled instead of flowed. My newfound enthusiasm for the theater only added to the sense of otherness. My housemates didn't quite know how to place my love of the stage; nor did I, for that matter.

Which didn't stop me from going full-bore in the auditions for the spring show *Ondine*, Jean Giraudoux's fanciful tale of a water nymph that had been a vehicle for Audrey Hepburn in the fifties. The beard came through once again. I landed the plum role of the King of the Sea, which allowed me to clap my hands and conjure up all sorts of whiz-bang special effects. It was tremendous fun and offered a higher billing in the program than the relative bit player Peter Shirley. Most of my housemates attended and had far more to say about the sheer costume of the well-endowed actress playing Ondine than my stirring performance.

The close of the show brought the now familiar sense of letdown, although less severe with second semester senior festivities in full swing. I drank prodigious quantities of beer and whiled away the days until graduation whacking golf and croquet balls on the lawns of the farm. My maternal grandmother, a staunch Republican like her industrialist father before her, had never seen my Berkeley-inspired facial growth. I was slated to pick her up at the Albany airport and drive her to Williamstown for my graduation. I found I couldn't face her sporting my current foliage. On the spur of the moment I cut off the beard and felt that delicious tingle of newly unsheathed skin as the June breeze rustled through the lowered windows of my Honda Civic.

# LONDON

I couldn't decide what to do for an encore. The theater had been an exhilarating excursion, but supporting roles in two small college productions did not appear to make a career. I suffered from the achiever's complex of expecting predictable returns from optimum efforts, and the contingent life of a struggling actor living from audition to audition was just too speculative for me. And frankly, I was hardly God's gift to acting.

As I neared my graduation from Williams, I hit on the notion of a year in London. I had spent a year in grade school there with my family during a sabbatical my father had taken and had become a confirmed Anglophile. Our family had sidestepped its heritage, so a country that so zealously embraced its own was startling and intoxicating. Good Jewish boy that I was, I had considered enrolling in law school, but I was tired of the familiar cycle of class/homework/exam that had been my daily grind for fifteen years. The nation was mired in recession in '81, and the job market was dismal. I figured if I were just going to wind up in some stop-gap position, it may as well be in London.

I got lucky. It turned out that a family friend had strong ties to a prominent English law firm and arranged an interview with their New York partner. I was amazed when they offered me a one-year internship in their home office in London. My amazement was tempered a bit when I learned that the offer was for £5,200 for the whole year, about $8,000 at the current exchange rate. My needs were modest, however, and the mother of another family friend was willing to provide room and board at her flat in west London at a reasonable rate.

I was treated like all of the English law graduates, which meant poorly. My paltry excuse for a desk was in the same office with a more senior attorney. Under the English system, lawyers generally study law at university for three years, then attend law school for a year before doing a two-year apprenticeship called pupilage for barristers (the bewigged and berobed lawyers who write briefs and argue in court) or articled clerkship (pronounced "clarkship") for solicitors (basically all other lawyers). My firm were solicitors, so I was thrown in with a group of some thirty Oxford and Cambridge graduates who were "doing their articles."

My innocence abroad vanished rapidly. One of the first cases I worked on featured a munitions manufacturer who had terminated one of their agents in South America. The agency contract called for a commission of fifteen percent, of which one percent was actually to be paid to the agent and the remaining fourteen percent was to line the pockets of various generalissimos. The terminated agent was apparently not as adept at bribery and graft as his successor, who managed to land a major arms deal a few months after his appointment. The terminated agent had the effrontery to claim that he was the one who had greased the skids for the deal and brought suit in English court demanding that he receive the full commission. The manufacturer, a public company, had no intention of letting the lawsuit see the light of day and touch off a major scandal, but they were concerned that settling the case and paying off the disgruntled agent would violate the English version of the Foreign Corrupt Practices Act. We consulted an eminent barrister, who in the paneled majesty of his chambers reasoned this way and that in his plummy upper class accent before finally concluding that, on balance, the payoff could be supported. The client breathed a sigh of relief and cut a check.

My boss was swallowed by a huge case involving a swindle of the ruling family of a wealthy Middle Eastern country to the tune of several hundred million dollars. The malefactors blew mind-boggling sums on the international commodity markets, some days commanding more than half the trading volume in certain precious metals on major exchanges. The investigation occupied a squadron of lawyers in our department, including one mild-mannered solicitor who was feted extravagantly during one of his trips to the region. At the end of one evening of feasting, he was reportedly offered the services of a beautiful young woman. A happily married man, he respectfully declined and retired to his room. After he'd gotten ready for bed he heard a knock. He opened the door and found a boy who couldn't have been more than nine or ten. His hosts had assumed that if he were not interested in the attentions of lovely young girl...

These high-stakes, globe-spanning cases, and others involving Iraqi gun-running and currency speculation, were heady stuff for a callow, now beardless twenty-one-year-old fresh out of college. My adventures in international intrigue by day were accompanied by an orgy of theatergoing by night. I was astounded by how central the theater was to English culture. Major stars appeared in West End plays, openings were grand events, and reviews (which I'd never paid much attention to as a *Tribune* paperboy) were matters of serious consequence. I was captivated by the palatial London theaters, with their multi-tiered balconies, gilded ceilings, and plush seats—a far cry from the presentable but modest venue on the Williams campus. Theater was a force to be reckoned with in London, and it took me by storm.

I confess to having retained my student ID, which I justified by my intention to return to school the following year and by the poverty imposed by my lordly $8,000 annual salary. Thus armed, I roamed the streets of London on an underpowered moped, darting into the narrowest of parking spaces and dashing up just before curtain for student rush tickets to the hottest shows of that season (and a number of others less celebrated): the breakthrough performance of Rupert Everett in *Another Country*, Julian Mitchell's ode to the British public school, communism, and cricket; Trevor Eve's brilliant lead in Mark Medoff's groundbreaking *Children of a Lesser God*; Brian Friel's moving take on Ireland and British colonialism, *Translations*.

But the shows that packed the greatest punch for me that year were revivals of two classic British comedies: Noel Coward's *Present Laughter* and Shaw's *Arms and the Man*. Wit, sparkle, repartee, retort—the elegance and effortlessness of expression were exhilarating, although as I left the theater I sensed the relative poverty of my own vocabulary. I felt a particular kinship with the *Arms and the Man* production, as I was, of course, in some small way a recent Shaw veteran myself.

Shaw's musings on the perilous romance of war took on a special relevance that spring, as the Falklands crisis erupted off the coast of Argentina. The Argentine government invaded the Falkland Islands, which were occupied by fewer than 2,000 inhabitants of mostly British origin. Britain then appeared to be wallowing in a mire of self-loathing, the product of years of imperial shrinkage, class warfare, and economic stagnation. The Falklands affair looked to be another exercise in defeatism, as the initial military assessment was that these remote islands in the South Atlantic were too far off to recapture.

Margaret Thatcher, at that time only a few years into her first term as Prime Minister, saw things differently. She rallied public opinion in favor of launching a task force to repel the Argentine aggression. I followed the conflict intently and saw the collateral impact firsthand at my firm, as a number of our clients were stymied by the British government's decision to freeze Argentine assets.

For me, the Falklands crisis was a powerful lesson in national pride. Whatever the merits of their claim, the Argentines had used military force without apparent provocation and in clear contravention of the wishes of the Falklands inhabitants. Though I was conscious at some level of the tinpot nature of the affair—dispatching gunships to regain tiny sheep-dominated specks of rock thousands of miles distant—I was struck by the collective lifting of spirit in a nation that so desperately needed it. I hadn't seen much national pride in my own country in recent years—the legacy of Vietnam, Watergate, oil shocks, stagflation—and it was refreshing to see a patriotic outpouring in support of a just cause. It wasn't lost on me that it was a conservative government that had shown such bold leadership.

The Falklands also provided a striking illustration of personal responsibility. Lord Carrington, the distinguished Foreign Secretary in Prime Minister Thatcher's cabinet, resigned because he felt he had not prepared Britain sufficiently to deter the invasion. No one else seemed to fault him severely, but he believed that someone had to accept responsibility for the fiasco, and he was the man in charge of the relevant ministry. I was floored that someone would sacrifice his own career when he was not directly at fault, which contrasted so dramatically with President Nixon's refusal to resign until Watergate had reduced the nation to a stew of partisan vitriol.

I flirted with the prospect of remaining at my firm and becoming a British lawyer, but I was not an expatriate at heart. I had taken my detour and felt ready to return to the main road. I left London with rich memories of honorable conservatives in government and fabulous plays in the theaters.

## PALO ALTO

I decided that if practicing law in America could be anything like the dizzying rush I had experienced in London, that was the profession for me. I applied from England, was accepted at Stanford Law School, and arrived in Palo Alto in the fall of '82. I soon achieved a certain notoriety as the very first person called on in my section's very first class. I never did live down my slightly stuttering summary of the facts of that first case, *Vosburg v. Putney*: "One Putney kicked one Vosburg in the shin..." I was thereafter and forever dubbed: "one Cole."

In the pressure cooker of the first year in law school, I was astounded to find an audition notice posted on the school bulletin board for a series of one-act plays by the legendary Bertholt Brecht. I had assumed my career as an actor was over. I had not reckoned with a rumpled, roly-poly, gay, Jewish theater junkie who ended up in my class. Marc Fajer, the notice-poster and director, had directed numerous plays as a Stanford undergraduate but failed to gain admission to the prestigious graduate directing program at the University of Washington. He had, however, managed to get himself into Stanford Law, where he decided to take out his frustrated thespian ambitions on the rest of us.

The response to the audition notice from his risk-averse, career-driven fellow law students was underwhelming, so Marc brought in a few ringers from elsewhere on campus to fill out the cast. He cajoled the law school administration into letting him use a classroom as our theater, which prompted some quizzical looks from passing library-bound students as we belted out our lines in rehearsal. Marc somehow devised a rehearsal schedule that worked around the cast's class schedules, exams, and job interviews, although love of the greasepaint and the roar of the crowd was not going to stop a cast member paying a healthy five-figure tuition from accepting a flyback to New York for a top-dollar job. His rehearsals included time devoted to touching exercises and physical game-playing, which may have gone down well in the bohemian Drama Department of his undergraduate days but were viewed askance by the more buttoned-down law student types.

Our production of Brecht did not make anyone forget Marlene Dietrich in *The Three Penny Opera*, and it felt peculiar performing by night in a room where we law students had been grilled by day, but we acquitted ourselves respectably and emboldened Marc to expand our repertoire. Our second year featured productions of Shakespeare's *The Merchant of Venice* (a natural for a law school crowd with its "pound of flesh" trial scene), starring a brave professor as Shylock and a type-cast dean as the Duke, and Lanford Wilson's *The Hot L Baltimore*, where I returned to my crusty codger acting origins playing the checker-wielding old coot Mr. Morse.

Our law school plays introduced me to some graduate students in the Drama Department, where I was also cast in a few shows. The most memorable of these was a medieval French farce called *Master Pierre Pathelin*. The grad student who directed the play claimed it would originally have been performed by roving theater troupes that would have rotated the parts among the various company members. Accordingly, she rehearsed the show so that each of us would play different parts in turn. This proved to be an androgynous nightmare and was nixed by the Drama Department powers that be after a few weeks, but the experience came in handy one Saturday night when an actress failed to show up for performance. As her character, a busty French peasant woman, appeared only in the first act of the play and mine (a malicious judge) appeared only in the second act, I was asked by the director to strap on her yellow wig and enormous hook-on breasts and do my best. I somehow made it through the evening, although the gorgeous French folk song sung by the absent actress (whose parents were from France) became a raucous version of "Frère Jacques," the only French song I knew.

Despite this frenetic acting schedule, I did manage to make it to most of my classes and keep up a grade point average that would not disgrace a Jewish mother. I had discovered by my second year at Stanford that what I enjoyed about the law was not poring over cases, but dealing directly with flesh and blood clients and the endless variation of fact patterns that human nature could produce. It was an easy decision not to go out for the Law Review, which left me time for theater and my other chief pastime, the Stanford Law Forum. The Law Forum was the law school's public events organization and had traditionally focused on high-minded speeches by judges and eminent practitioners. I was a more shameless huckster than my predecessors as president and—despite a limited budget—deployed the prestige of Stanford to attract a motley crew of personalities, including: the celebrated trial lawyer Gerry Spence (who arrived from Jackson, Wyoming clad head to toe in buckskin), Antonin Scalia (before his ascension to the Supreme Court), the loathsome McCarthy-era hatchet man Roy Cohn (a tiny, reptilian man who crawled from the back of the largest stretch limousine I had ever seen), divorce lawyer to the stars Marvin Mitchelson, and Communist Party USA head Gus Hall (whose mammoth Mesabi Range miner's paw engulfed mine when we shook hands).

I had little time in my schedule for politics, but the Law Forum did extend an invitation on a non-partisan basis to all of the presidential candidates to speak on the Stanford campus during the '84 campaign. We had no takers during the primaries, but the Mondale campaign decided after the convention in San Francisco that they would do their first joint appearance with the vanquished insurgent Gary Hart at Stanford in the fall. The campaign had enlisted the support of the usual suspects among the area Democratic groups, but they needed a bona fide student organization to serve as host because the university event staff who would set up lights, sound, and seating could only be paid through transfers from a university account. Somehow, the Law Forum ended up as the campus host for this marquee appearance, and I spent over a week dealing with oily advance men and earpiece-dangling Secret Service types.

The cost of the event far exceeded the Law Forum's annual budget, and I had received solemn promises from the Mondale campaign that we would have cash in hand to cover virtually all expenses well before the scheduled date. Days passed, and despite repeated assurances, no funds arrived. I was accustomed to shady dealing by Democrats as a boy growing up on the outskirts of the Chicago political machine, but not this close and personal. Finally, I was summoned to a dingy motel room near the San Francisco airport the night before the event and told that there had been a snafu and that no money would be available until after the joint appearance. With the beady, bloodshot eyes of the advance team trained on me, I said that I would have to consider canceling the event, as the Law Forum couldn't cover the cost itself. They called my bluff. They knew I would be crucified on campus if I pulled the plug.

The weather soon avenged their treachery. An unrelenting downpour started several hours before the event and forced us indoors. The capacity of Stanford's Memorial Auditorium was far less than the campaign had expected outdoors and the spirits of the drenched crowd were low. Walter's daughter Eleanor Mondale was up on stage with me, however, and she looked terrific. Perhaps predictably, Vice President Bush campaigned in San Francisco the following day under brilliant sunshine. Months after the election, we finally got our payment thanks to an advance man who had stashed away some campaign funds for us in case we got stiffed.

My final year as a law student also brought the plum codger role of Polonius, sadly not in *Hamlet* but in Tom Stoppard's *Rosencrantz & Guildenstern Are Dead*, Marc's last law school production. I felt born to say Polonius's celebrated line, "Though this be madness, yet there is method in it." This seemed an apt slogan for my job search, which was then in full swing. I had spent the summers after my first and second years at Stanford at large firms in Chicago, San Francisco, and Washington, DC (splitting my second summer between two cities). I thought the fall of my third year would be a leisurely process of elimination, as all three firms had made me attractive offers for a permanent job.

Then I saw a notice on the placement office bulletin board for interviews with the General Counsel's Office at the Central Intelligence Agency (CIA). This gave me pause. I had been a trifle bored with my summer clerkships. The money was great, the lawyers sharp, and the offices top-drawer, but the work had given me nothing of the rush of international intrigue that had thrilled me in London. I had no idea what a lawyer for the CIA would do, but it sounded alluring and mysterious at a time when my other options seemed predictable and uninspiring. I signed up for an interview, figuring that at least I could tell my grandchildren I'd had a meeting with "The Agency."

I arrived at the scheduled time only to find Marc Fajer stationed at a table near the interview room, protesting the CIA's presence on campus on behalf of the Gay & Lesbian Law Students Association. I was taken aback. I knew the CIA was a controversial agency, of course, but I'd not heard about any brouhaha over sexual preference. Marc was a close friend, as well as my long-time partner in theater, and the thought of crossing his impromptu picket line was troubling. At the same time, I was mighty curious to hear what these spooks had to say and see whether it was even worth considering a detour from the conventional law firm path. I hesitated briefly, then told my friend I would have to speak with him later about the CIA's policies and went on through the door.

The interviewer—a gray, unassuming man in a dark suit and red tie—was low-key, but he knew his pitch. He understood his competition at a school like Stanford were the big-time law firms, and he deftly undercut them at every turn. He could tell he was dealing with a young and impressionable prospect who wanted something more out of his career than just status and money, and he managed to blend foreign adventure, patriotism, and top-secret missions into an enticing concoction that was much more subtle than "Be all that you can be."

I walked out of the interview thinking, "Why the hell not?" I was single, and while the money was far less than the law firms were offering ($26,500 versus as much as $60,000), I could still afford to service my student loans. The economy had roared back from the doldrums of the early eighties, and law firms were snapping up bodies out of schools like Stanford willy-nilly. I figured that I could try it for a few years and if it weren't to my liking, I could always head back to the private sector and find something worthwhile. The Agency made me an offer later in the fall, and I leaned strongly towards accepting it.

I still had to deal with two influential figures in my life: my mother and Marc Fajer. Mom, true to her bleeding heart, was convinced that the CIA and their fellow rogues at the FBI were a plague on Western civilization and sent me the grassy knoll conspiracy books to prove it. I loved my mother, but I was just as prepared to rebel against her as she had been to revolt against my rock-ribbed conservative grandmother.

Marc was in some ways a tougher challenge. I learned that the CIA's policy was to consider a person's sexual orientation in the recruitment process if the applicant were not out of the closet. The rationale was that sexual orientation could be a basis for blackmail if not previously disclosed to family members, friends, or business associates. While this struck me as supportable, if not compelling, Marc contended that this was just a smokescreen and that the real policy was to bar homosexuals altogether.

Curiously, Marc had a lot more evidence about discrimination by private firms than he did about the CIA. He had conducted an informal survey by sending some firms a résumé that highlighted his involvement with gay and lesbian organizations and other firms a résumé that made no mention of this aspect of his life. The rejection rate for the "gay" résumé was substantially higher than for the "straight" one. I argued to Marc that, whatever the sins of the CIA, they were not guilty of hypocrisy. At least they had the guts (as well as the legal responsibility) to articulate their policy publicly. The law firm discrimination struck me as more insidious, as they maintained a public face of tolerance while privately ensuring that gays and lesbians did not enter their workforce.

Many of my friends at Stanford had no time for Marc or his activism. These were my teammates in intramural sports and my golfing buddies on the Stanford course—essentially the Stanford Law School equivalent of my jock housemates at Williams, although more diverse. I understood their reaction to Marc, as he was easy to stereotype: a militantly gay, Jewish, artsy, non-athletic liberal from Long Island. I did not defend his politics, as they were not my own, but I felt a kinship with him as a co-conspirator in this strange and wonderful process of creating theater productions in the halls of Stanford Law School.

Marc's objections to the CIA's hiring policies, however, seemed speculative and short on data. The lure of involvement in clandestine operations and foreign travel was real. I accepted, to the supportive bemusement of my friends and the derision of a number of left-leaning classmates. The contempt was mutual. I felt that those who derided my public service talked a good game about going to law school to make a difference and then ended up accepting a fancy law firm job for big bucks. I resisted asking them how they planned to change the world billing 2,500 hours a year on Wall Street. As it happened, I—the Republican—was the only person in my class of 175 or so at Stanford to take a federal agency job right out of law school.

But first I had to run the security clearance gauntlet. This meant, among other things, passing a lie detector test, which made me queasy. I wasn't worried about being fingered as a foreign agent; it was the youthful inhaling I was concerned about. I came of age in the seventies, and virtually everyone I knew had smoked pot at least a few times and experimented with harder stuff. Suffice it to say that I was no better or worse than my peers. I checked with some family friends, and the advice that came back was that it was far worse to conceal the indiscretions of youth and register false answers on the polygraph than to just make a clean breast of it. The key, several people said, was how frequently and how recently you had taken drugs. The answer to avoid was the one given by one of my classmates who had interviewed for a State Department job: asked how long ago he had taken illicit drugs, he had responded, "Uhh…last night." He'd apparently had a very happy birthday the day before.

The Agency flew me back to the DC area and put me up at a nondescript hotel in Northern Virginia. On the appointed day I was ushered into the main reception area at CIA headquarters in Langley, complete with the celebrated seal, the inlaid floor, and the hush of a sacred site. I felt like an extra on a very familiar movie set. I went through a fairly benign physical examination, then the scene shifted from body to mind. Some very earnest-looking psychologists administered a battery of tests apparently designed to ensure that my psyche fell within the standard deviation of non-deviancy. I resisted the temptation to take the tack of an old high school friend, who in his disgust at being subjected to a Rorschach test in order to gain admittance to a Texas university responded to each ink blot by saying "tree" until faced with a drawing that had red dots, to which he declared "apple tree." I seemed to pass muster, although I could tell nothing from their expressions. Then I was told that my lie detector test had been scheduled for the following day to ensure they had enough time. This put my already jangled nerves in a state of disarray. Were those funny mushrooms ingested in a burst of post-graduation exaltation going to come back to haunt me?

I spent a restless night and returned to headquarters the following day. The polygraph room was dark, quiet, and clinical. The operator was polite, but his expression betrayed even less than the shrinks' of the day before. He strapped me into the machine and began the familiar litany of obvious questions. Suddenly we moved from my mother's maiden name to contacts with foreign nationals. I would think we had exhausted a particular subject, then a few minutes later he would come right back to it. I seemingly relived every moment I had spent abroad before he finally turned to the fateful subject. As a Jew I was unfamiliar with the ritual of confession, but I felt a certain electrified catharsis as I poured out my sorry tale of summer camp counselor nights off, red-lit college dorm rooms, and that one night of nasal passages poised over somebody's cracked mirror. I held nothing back. At one point I thought I caught a gleam in the operator's eye, as if to say, "Is that all you've got, buddy?" The better part of four hours later, he released me.

Then came an agonizing wait. My offer from the CIA had arrived in early December and was contingent on clearing security. I was told that it usually took three months or so to complete the clearance process, but that mine might take longer because of my time overseas. March and April came and went, and I still had no confirmed offer. My friends had long ago locked up their jobs and spent much of their time on the Stanford golf course. The law firms where I'd spent my summers had graciously extended back-up offers, but they could not keep these open indefinitely.

Amidst the uncertainty, I had the theater. Marc's last hurrah as a Stanford director was an outdoor campus touring production of *A Midsummer Night's Dream*, and he forgave my employment transgressions sufficiently to typecast me as the aged windbag and stickler for Greek legal strictures, Egeus. This was my eighth and final play in three years as a Stanford law student. My clearance finally came through during the run of the show, and I celebrated at one marathon cast party. It was a little peculiar sitting in a hot tub explaining to undergraduate actors who had heard me on stage declaiming the virtues of the laws of Athens that I was off to become a CIA attorney, but they had just witnessed stranger wonders in the Athenian wood.

# (NEAR) LANGLEY

I loved the ceremony of becoming a CIA employee. I took my oath in October '85. Others may have resented the solemn briefings, the regulations reviews, and the new badge rituals, but to me it was all part of the wonder of being admitted to a secret society.

My affiliation with the Agency, however, was not a secret. As a CIA attorney, I was an overt employee, which meant that I could publicly acknowledge my employer. This was not to be advertised, though. If questions about my employment were to come up in conversation, I was initially to say only that I worked for the government. If asked what branch of the government, I was to say only that I was in the national security area. It was only if a direct question were put to me about my agency that I was to let non-employees know that I was with the CIA.

I fell afoul of secrecy regulations my third day on the job. When I was a clerk at a Washington, DC law firm reveling in the relative leisure of the summer program, I called up a Stanford classmate who was working at another firm. As he and I were both from Chicago and die-hard Cubs fans, I thought I would be cute and leave a message that Ernie Banks—the legendary Cubs slugger—had called. His secretary was evidently not a baseball fan, as she dutifully wrote down the message without batting an eyelash. This led to a series of messages back and forth throughout the summer, with each of us leaving the names of increasingly obscure Cubs players.

My friend had accepted a position at the law firm where he'd spent the summer, and I decided to call him from my new CIA office. He was out, so I left a message that Rich Nye had called. Nye was an undistinguished pitcher who had been with the Cubs during their notorious collapse in '69. His most notable distinction was being traded to the Montreal Expos for the immortal Boots Day. Nye was obscure, but my buddy was a Cubs fanatic and I figured he would surely recognize the name.

I was wrong. He called my office number and got my secretary, as I was doing research in the library. He asked for Rich Nye. My secretary said, "Who?" He asked again for Rich Nye. She told him that there was no Rich Nye at this number. He asked what company this was. Our staff were trained to answer the phone "Office of General Counsel." He predictably asked "Office of General Counsel of where?" She just repeated "Office of General Counsel." At this point the light finally went off above his head. He said "Is this the CIA?"

I returned from the library to find my boss sitting in my office. He shut the door and with a grim expression asked, "Who is Rich Nye?" I couldn't believe this was happening to me, particularly not in my first week on the job. I stuttered out an abject explanation of our little inside baseball message charade. He said, "I hope you understand, Mr. Cole, that this agency has very strict rules against the unauthorized use of cover names." I was about to dig a hole under my desk when he burst out laughing, as did my secretary, who was listening outside the door. She had told the whole story to my boss, who thought this was a capital opportunity to yank the chain of the new kid. My heart left my throat, and I felt like I had survived some sort of weird hazing ritual.

My boss's boss was the General Counsel, Stanley Sporkin. Stan was an unusual choice to be the Agency's top lawyer. He had been the hard-charging head of the enforcement section at the Securities & Exchange Commission (SEC) when William Casey was the chair. After President Reagan rewarded Casey for his service on the '80 campaign by naming him Director of Central Intelligence, Casey tapped Stan to be his General Counsel. An SEC enforcer needs to be aggressive, pugnacious, and bombastic. As I soon learned, a CIA General Counsel needs to be conciliatory, self-effacing, and low-key in an agency not celebrated for involving lawyers in its day-to-day affairs. Stan's style had not endeared him to the Deputy Directors who ran the four directorates within the Agency: Operations, Intelligence, Administration, and Science & Technology.

The result was internal exile. The General Counsel's office had been banished from headquarters to an outbuilding near the suburban shopping enclave of Tyson's Corner. I had looked forward to the glamour of roaming the storied hallways of Langley. Instead, I found myself in what seemed to be an annex of Bloomingdale's, which would have made for great shopping on my lunch hour if I could have afforded it on my government salary.

To be fair to Stan, part of the unneighborly response of the Deputy Directors could be attributed to envy. Because of their time together at the SEC, Stan enjoyed a unique personal relationship with Director Casey and was granted a level of access that the other brass could only dream about. Also, the Office of General Counsel had grown at a rate that far outstripped most other Agency components. For years, it had been a small, low profile shop staffed largely by CIA careerists from other Agency divisions who had gone to law school at night on the company's nickel. My boss had been one of those, the office's ninth or tenth attorney who had started his career as an intelligence analyst.

Watergate and other Vietnam Era scandals changed all that. The regulatory and compliance burden imposed on the Agency increased dramatically, and there was a corresponding explosion in the number of lawyers hired by the General Counsel's Office. Stan beefed up the recruiting program in an effort to attract outsiders from top law schools who, like me, were looking for an alternative to law-firm servitude. This growth spurt occurred at a time when other Agency components, particularly the Operations directorate, had suffered through a brutal housecleaning under President Carter and his Director of Central Intelligence, Stansfield Turner.

The lawyers in our office were not actually barred from headquarters, of course. Shuttle buses ran there on a regular schedule, and we were called on to attend our fair share of meetings and briefings. But much of the business of an agency like the CIA is conducted in whispers and nods along the corridors of headquarters. Most of that whispering and nodding was taking place beyond our earshot.

Stan tried to make the best of it. He pushed a program of placing General Counsel lawyers within Agency divisions, where they effectively served as in-house counsel. In some cases this succeeded in getting our office in the loop. In other cases the out-placed lawyer "went native" and took his cues from the head of that division, not his superiors in the General Counsel's office.

Despite a long career spent in government service, Stan was not bureaucratic, which was both a virtue and his undoing. When faced with a tough problem, he would gather his chief lieutenants in his office, lean back in his swivel chair, join his fingertips in an A-frame just below his chin, and close his eyes while they debated the prudent course of action. Just when you thought he had nodded off, he would vault forward in his chair, bark out a course of action, and send everyone packing. If he thought one of his section chiefs had a bright idea, he would tell him to run with it, even if the brainstorm encroached on the traditional turf of one of the other chiefs. The result was sectional warfare and barely controlled chaos. The five or so top managers in the office were constantly jockeying for position and looking to pick off client accounts that would expand their fiefdoms. They were outwardly civil to one another, but behind closed doors there was constant scheming for targets of opportunity.

One afternoon a few months after I arrived at the Agency, my boss called his assistant chief and me into his office. It was clear from the cat-ate-the-canary grin on his face that he thought he had pulled off a major coup. Stan had asked him to prepare a draft finding. I looked puzzled. The assistant chief explained that a finding was an authorization signed by the President approving the use of covert action. Covert action, I knew, meant activities conducted or sponsored by the government in support of friendly states or groups, or against hostile states or groups, in such a manner that official US involvement was not apparent and could be disclaimed. The vast majority of the CIA's operations consisted of intelligence collection in some shape or form, using human sources or technical devices to gather information overseas. Covert action was different. Covert action was intended to secretly influence events abroad, not simply find out what was happening or likely to happen.

It was covert action, not intelligence collection, that had touched off many of the major scandals affecting the CIA.

Most intelligence gathering by the CIA and other national security agencies was not particularly controversial, as long as it was directed against foreign nationals and conducted overseas. But assassinations, coups, and insurrections have a way of jangling the nerves, especially among legislators who don't learn about the actions until after the fact. As a result of perceived abuses in covert action by the CIA, Congress had fashioned legislation requiring the President to issue a written finding of national security need before a covert action program could be undertaken. In fact, virtually all of the controversial covert actions that had earned the CIA a reputation as a rogue agency had been approved by the President, who had found it convenient to use the Agency's clandestine capabilities to conceal official US government involvement. But the legislation now required a paper trail, Capitol Hill's preferred means of exercising oversight.

The problem for my boss was that this paper trail was not typically handled by our section of the General Counsel's Office. Our division's stock in trade was intelligence collection directed against US nationals, who were entitled to constitutional protections that the rest of the world did not enjoy. We worked primarily with operations and technical types who wanted to search the house, tap the phone, or open the mail of US citizens or permanent residents overseas suspected of collaboration with unfriendly foreign governments. This was exactly the sort of work I had hoped to do in signing on as a CIA lawyer—sensitive, top level, plenty of cloak (if not dagger). But it had nothing to do with covert action, which was customarily handled by another division within the General Counsel's Office. My boss chortled that there was something big cooking involving assistance to friendly elements in Iran and that he had managed to cut his chief rival in the office out of the loop.

So it was left to the assistant chief and me to cobble together a finding authorizing, in vague and general terms, some sort of covert assistance program to potential allies within Iran. I was new at this game, but even I knew this was big stuff. At that time, Iran was running neck-and-neck with the Soviet Union as "Foreign Enemy Number One." Memories of the '79 seizure of the US Embassy and American hostages by Khomeini's regime were still vivid. Iran was thought to be behind much of the terrorist activity in the Middle East, including the truck bombing of the Marine barracks in Beirut that killed over 240 servicemen and the kidnapping and execution of CIA officer William Buckley, also in Lebanon. The Iran-Iraq War had been slogging on for over five years, and although the US was officially neutral in the conflict, it was well known throughout the intelligence community that the President did not intend to let Iran prevail.

The difficulty facing us was one encountered by any lawyers taking on a new type of matter: we had no form. All of the findings within the General Counsel's Office were kept in safes controlled by the hated rival division. The assistant chief knew there was no way he could coax samples out of the other division, as he would be immediately suspect as a confederate of our boss. He devised an operation that called for me—an innocent newcomer to this long-simmering civil war—to play dumb and ask a fellow foot soldier in the rival division if I could have a look at a few findings out of curiosity. To our amazement, the stratagem worked. I was able to hold on to a couple of old findings long enough to work up a draft that looked like it had been prepared by somebody who knew what he was doing. It was long on ends and woefully short on means, but we had only the few scraps fed to us by our boss and figured the powers that be could fill in the gaps.

Our boss was thrilled with our work product and took it up to Stan. Over the next month or so our boss, a grizzled CIA careerist, gave us wide-eyed reports of meetings he had had downtown with a Marine lieutenant colonel named Oliver North. He expressed astonishment at the degree to which North had managed to wrap senior CIA operations officials around his finger. He also gave salivating descriptions of North's secretary, a luscious blonde named Fawn Hall.

Part of the wrangling over this period was whether our finding could authorize prior covert action. I was not given much detail, but it appeared that some of the assistance to friendly Iranians had already taken place. Stan and my boss asked me to research the doctrine of *nunc pro tunc*—an ominous sounding legal doctrine (from the Latin meaning "now for then")—under which certain judgments can be given retroactive effect. It struck me as a stretch to invoke a doctrine in the context of a highly sensitive presidential finding that was supposed to apply to ministerial court actions, and I said so. I later learned that my superiors took a different view.

I happened to be in Stan's office one day when Stan's secretary announced that Oliver North was on the line. Stan picked up and said, "Hi, Ollie, this is Stan." He paused for a moment and then quipped, "Stan and Ollie—what a team!" He little knew how prophetic his reference to Laurel and Hardy would prove to be.

# DC (ONSTAGE)

The daytime drama of national security had not curbed my appetite for theater. I saw an audition notice for a little known David Mamet play, *The Water Engine*, to be produced near the Palisades area of DC where I was sharing a house with some law school friends. I badly missed the camaraderie of a theater cast. My CIA employment barred me from all sorts of extracurricular activities, in particular partisan politics, but I saw no restriction on being in a play. I worked hard, usually from eightto six or six thirty, but my evenings and weekends were generally free for rehearsal or performance. I auditioned and was cast in the ensemble.

This was my first acting venture outside of university theater, and I was in for a nasty shock. I was accustomed to rumor and innuendo—which are rife in any show—but not to bold-faced lies. The producers made promise after promise—about the production budget, actor pay, technical capabilities, marketing—each of which they proceeded to break. I think they meant well, but they were so intent on appearing as big shots in front of their admiring cast that they could not own up to any shortcomings.

The cast consisted mainly of naïve recent college graduates who were just thrilled to be in a show. A few quit in disgust, but most of us just rolled with the broken promises, even when the producers could not deliver a heated rehearsal space in the dead of winter. The Mamet play was supposed to mark the launch of a new company, and some of the stalwarts hoped that by sticking it out through the hell of this production they would get in on the ground floor of the company. I wanted no part of the producers after the project, but there were some good people in the cast and the show itself—set as a radio play about the undoing of an inventor of an engine that runs on water—was well worth the chapped lips and ego. An incidental benefit was the opportunity to learn the state song of my own Illinois (actually written into the script by Mamet).

The cast bonded in the face of common adversity, and several members became friends. One invited me to the opening of a late night show he went on to direct at the Source Theater. He said it was called *Batman Versus The League of Doom* and was basically a theatrical send-up of the old sixties TV series, which had been a staple of my childhood after-school viewing. I didn't see how it was possible to parody the over-the-top antics of Adam West, Burt Ward, Cesar Romero, and the rest, but I was keen to find out. The Source was a gritty, no frills black box theater in a tough neighborhood on DC's NW 14th Street corridor. My actor/director buddy had told me that Walter Mondale's son Billy had been cast as a henchman of one of the villains. As it turned out, the henchmen were subtly dubbed "Dumb" and "Fuck," with Billy cast as "Fuck." As we filed into our tattered seats after eleven thirty, we noticed none other than Walter and Joan Mondale seated a few rows from us, bewildered frozen grins locked on their faces, hoping that no one would recognize them as the parents of "Fuck" (who, to his credit, delivered admirable *pows* and *bifs* in the obligatory fight scenes).

The production was uneven, to put it mildly, but I loved the energy and intensity of the small space and the immediacy of the actors just a few feet in front of me. I hadn't seen much "fringe" theater; most of my theatergoing had been in London at major West End venues made affordable by my ersatz student ID. My parents had taken me to a few small theater shows in high school, most memorably a production by Steppenwolf Theatre (long before they hit the big time) of Pinter's *The Caretaker*. The production starred Gary Sinise and was put on in a basement space so cramped that an actor inadvertently whacked me in the leg with a golf club in the middle of the performance. The offender bowed in my direction during the curtain call, but it still hurt like hell.

I soon became a regular at the Source, which offered a wildly varied season at prices I could afford on my government salary. Their productions ranged from Clifford Odets to Shakespeare to late night shows even more outrageous than *Batman Versus The League of Doom*. Their crowning achievement during this period was a madcap, Monty Python-esque production of *Titus Andronicus*, with body parts flying off at a clip reminiscent of the celebrated "Anyone for tennis?" sketch. My appetite whetted, I started venturing to some of the other small theaters in the DC area, including The Studio and the Woolly Mammoth.

It was a delicious life, roaming the hushed corridors of the CIA by day and the dingy lobbies of fringe theaters at night. I was conscious of mingling in utterly different worlds, and yet I felt no sense of contradiction or crossed purposes. I took my job seriously and subscribed fully to the critical mission of the Agency. The Soviet Union had not yet crumbled and was still vigorously recruiting agents in the US; I was proud to have served my country on some of its most sensitive counterintelligence cases. But my patriotism didn't keep me from appreciating great theater that poked and prodded authority figures, whether from hundreds of years ago or last week, or from performing with actors whose political views might have been diametrically opposed to my own.

My colleagues at the CIA were bemused rather than threatened by my involvement in theater. They were mostly conservative suburbanites who rarely ventured into DC after dark and viewed my bohemian nightlife as endearingly exotic. They couldn't imagine themselves rehearsing in unheated halls in winter or venturing to a crummy neighborhood for a midnight show, but they got a kick out of the fact that one of their own was actually doing it.

I heard little about the Iran finding after my boss's fevered reports regarding his encounters with Oliver North and Fawn Hall. There was a buzz all around the office, however, about the Contras. The CIA had formed a major task force dedicated to Central America, with the primary aim of destabilizing and ultimately overthrowing the Sandinista regime headed by Daniel Ortega. There was a mobilization of bodies from all over the Agency for the Central American Task Force, including several lawyers from our office. My boss bewailed these developments, as the Task Force account had gone to a rival chieftain.

Our division focused on the narrow intersection between foreign intelligence collection and the Constitution. Most intelligence gathering overseas is directed at foreign nationals who do not enjoy the benefits of constitutional protection against unlawful search and seizure. The CIA can tap their phones, open their mail, and search their homes with impunity under US law. US citizens and permanent resident aliens (called, in the trade, "US persons") do not, however, lose their constitutional rights just because they happen to leave the country. If the CIA wanted to wiretap or search the residence of a US person overseas, it had to follow certain procedures laid out in a presidential executive order requiring a determination by the Attorney General that the person was an agent of a foreign power. Our job was to work with our operations clients to make the case that the target of the tap, search, or other surveillance met the agent of a foreign power standard.

This could be electrifying work, particularly when the opportunity for an operation arose suddenly and we had to dash down to the Department of Justice and make our case orally to the Attorney General's chief intelligence advisor. Our division also had the choice assignment of traveling to CIA stations all over the world and briefing operations types about the executive order and its procedures. The rogue agency scandals of the seventies resulted in a mandate that stations be briefed every several years, so the lawyers in our area were regularly criss-crossing the globe spreading constitutional good cheer.

I had to pay my dues for the better part of a year before landing one of these plum foreign tours. The European circuits were the most popular, for obvious reasons, and the more senior lawyers had a monopoly on these. As the junior guy in the division, I drew an Asian trip. When traveling outside the country, CIA employees were entitled to a daily allowance, which was set on a country-by-country basis. If the employee spent more than the per diem, it came out of his pocket; if he spent less, he could keep the difference. The officer I was traveling with decided that we would share a room on the road in order to save money. He was considerably more senior than I, so I had no choice but to go along with his economizing.

This arrangement worked fine until we hit Bangkok. My roommate decided that he wanted to visit Patpong, the notorious red light district. He corralled me and a third person traveling with us to join him. It soon became clear that his interest in the area was not merely cultural. The third guy and I left him to his courtship rituals and headed back to the hotel for a nightcap. We closed the bar, and I wearily took the elevator up to my room only to find a "Do Not Disturb" sign on the door, obviously placed there by my solicitous roomie. I went back to the lobby, but there was nothing open and I was not up for braving the heat and humidity of steamy Bangkok for a nocturnal promenade. I returned to the room to find the sign still hanging in the door. I finally tumbled into a chair and dozed off until my thoughtful fellow traveler roused me well after three in the morning and announced that I could now enter the bedroom. I had been briefed on many occupational hazards of serving in the CIA, but not this one.

The saving grace on this tour was a visit to Australia, where we stopped over in Sydney for a weekend after briefings in Canberra and Wellington, New Zealand. I noticed that a production of Mamet's *Glengarry Glen Ross* was playing at the celebrated Sydney Opera House, and I had to see how the Australians handled one of America's finest contemporary plays. They did a creditable job, although it was painful for a Chicago boy to hear Aussies trying to imitate the speech patterns of Mayor Daley.

One of the other major accounts of our division was the War on Drugs, which was just starting to gather force in Washington under the patronage of Nancy Reagan. Intelligence agencies were reluctant players in these hostilities because of concerns about compromising sources. If a CIA source on foreign intelligence matters in a country involved in drug trafficking also provided information about drug dealing, he might have to testify at trial if his information led to a prosecution: the US Constitution mandates that the accused in a criminal trial have the right to confront those testifying against him. Having a source testify in open court would obviously expose his cooperation with the US Government and destroy his future usefulness to the CIA. Of course, this sort of exposure could also occur in the context of an espionage trial, but those prosecutions were rare and more closely related to the mission of the Agency.

We were tasked to develop ways to share intelligence information with other agencies while still protecting the identities of sources. Despite the bureaucratic infighting, this was heady stuff that involved highly classified intelligence and helped get me out of the shabby confines of our Tyson's Corner annex. I was usually asked to accompany the National Intelligence Officer for Counternarcotics, the intelligence community's point person on drugs, to monthly meetings with other War on Drugs big shots, including the Justice Department's chief criminal lawyer, William Weld, and FBI Director William Webster.

I was impressed by these upper-echelon political appointees, in particular by Weld, who had been the US Attorney in Boston before coming to Washington. The caliber of some top-level appointments like Weld had helped to build my enthusiasm for the Reagan administration. My '80 candidate George Bush had denounced Reagan's "voodoo economics" during the campaign, and the deficit-defying manipulations of budget boy wonder David Stockman had done little to prove him wrong. I was a true fiscal conservative and was appalled at the explosion in federal debt during Reagan's first few years in office. But after the initial supply-side orgy, it seemed that the administration had hit its stride and let grown-ups like James Baker hold sway. Carter had been a notorious micromanager and appeared to view the role of President as administrator-in-chief. Reagan's style of setting broad policy outlines and then letting seasoned professionals do their jobs was a welcome contrast and seemed a more effective conception of the presidency.

And then it all started to collapse. In the fall of '86 the Nicaraguan army shot down an American cargo plane whose surviv-

ing crew member claimed he was working for the CIA. Shortly afterward an obscure Middle East publication reported that the US
had sold arms to Iran. Attorney General Ed Meese then disclosed
that proceeds from the Iranian arms sales had been used to fund
the Contras, and the feeding frenzy erupted.

Our office was engulfed by the scandal. We were bombard-
ed by requests for information and document production by the
newly appointed independent counsel, Lawrence Walsh, and by
the congressional committees investigating the affair. CIA lawyers were constantly on call to squire panicked operations officers
to interviews with investigators. The senior lawyers in the office
seemed to be in perpetual meetings with the new General Counsel (Stan had since been appointed a federal judge) and usually
emerged from these marathon sessions with dazed looks.

I soon figured out from reading the *Washington Post* exactly
what I had worked on just a few months after joining the Agency. The CIA had engaged in covert action by facilitating, at the
behest of Oliver North, the shipment of arms to Iran. There had
been no presidential finding to authorize this action as required
by law. When Stan learned what had happened, he rightly concluded that a finding was necessary, preferably one that approved
the shipment that had already occurred. That's what had led to
my little drafting project.

I became a person of interest to the independent counsel and
the congressional committees. I was interviewed at length by investigators who went over in minute detail whom I had spoken
to and when. The experience was simply gut-wrenching. I knew
I had done nothing wrong—on the contrary, I had worked to secure a presidential approval required by law. But as careers were
being destroyed right and left by the scandal, I wondered whether
I would be forever tainted as a lawyer, even though I had been only
twenty-five when given the fateful assignment. Some old hands

were saying that this was the worst crisis at the Agency since Watergate, perhaps even including Watergate. The fact that CIA Director Casey had conveniently died of brain cancer before the investigations got fully under way only added to the furor. My personal agony was compounded by the fact that I could not discuss my situation with anyone other than my colleagues at the Agency, each of whom was scrambling to cover his own backside.

In the midst of the madness, it occurred to me that there might be the germ of a play here. I was drawn not so much to the scandal itself, which despite its titillating facts I found in many ways depressingly mundane, particularly as the gears of the Washington scandal machine ground on. What intrigued me most was the Contra cause that was the root of the matter, one of a host of insurrections in developing countries that had been the playground of CIA operatives for decades and the chief battlegrounds of the Cold War. Ideological purity and naked power lust, socialist rhetoric and the harsh realities of race and class, the rule of law and the redress of colonial inequities—all of these bubbled up out of the Agency's involvement in Nicaragua (and Honduras, and Guatemala, and a multitude of other countries around the globe) in a simmering stew that I savored.

But I was acting, not writing. The arctic production of *The Water Engine* had not cured me of the bug to perform. I answered an audition notice for *The Merchant of Venice*, an old favorite from my law school days, and was stunned when I was cast as Bassanio, one of the leads and a far cry from my usual crusty codgers and other line-limited character types. I soon found out why I had risen to such prominence. The cast of the Mamet production had been replete with bright young things who, if asked their profession, would have responded "actor/actress," even though they hadn't come within hailing range of making a living at their chosen craft. That show had been a way station on a journey that may have led them to New York or Los Angeles or Chicago in a quest for stardom. They took movement classes, method classes, dialect classes, anything offered by charismatic thespian gurus who might lead them to better things. Some of them were quite good (far better than I), although almost all would likely have to pack it in a few years hence.

My compatriots in *The Merchant of Venice* were retired civil servants, bored housewives, doe-eyed collegians, and boozing sybarites, all drawn together in that strange and wonderful pageant of deluded grandeur known as community theater. The company was presided over by a delightfully daft couple who squabbled constantly but held on for dear life to the modest franchise they had created. An able-bodied male in his twenties with most of his hair and some semblance of acting chops was a rare thing in these parts, and I was rewarded for my relative virility. My deft portrayal of Bassanio begat a role as the blazing youth Damis in *Moliere's Tartuffe*, in which the absent-minded retiree playing the title character was so manifestly inept that those of us on stage with him often had to grit our teeth to keep from bursting into laughter.

And yet, despite the mangled dialogue, indifferent production values, empty fraying red plush seats, and addled director/producer spousal unit, there were performances when I felt amazingly privileged to be up on a stage somewhere speaking the lines of two of the greatest writers who had ever lived. Those evenings I was somehow able to suspend my own disbelief, although I suspect the audience was not similarly affected.

I sensed a creeping addiction to these proffers of plum roles amidst mediocrity and decided to kick the habit before it was too late. I landed the part of Richard the Lionheart in the classic *The Lion in Winter* with the St. Mark's Players, who performed in a lovely Episcopal church on Capitol Hill near the condo I had purchased after my housemates moved away or married. This, too, was community theater, but the beauty of the church setting and the sense of mission born of association with a congregation (some of whom participated in the productions) gave it an entirely different feel from the Guffman-esque sensibilities of my prior venue. The St. Mark's folks viewed their plays not simply as a pleasant diversion for the audience or a nice hobby for the performers, but as an instrument of self-exploration supported by faith. This lent a gravity and spirituality to the process of creating theater that I had not previously experienced, although thankfully it did not stop the cast from going out for the occasional beer. As a non-practicing Jew I felt a little out of place in a company with this Christian theological dimension, but it was not as if they tried to convert me at every rehearsal.

My evening plunges into community theater were a welcome escape from the daily turmoil of Iran/Contra. As the sordid details of the affair appeared on the front page of the *Post* (far and away my best source for information, even as an Agency insider), it became clear that Oliver North, a Marine lieutenant colonel in a town where lieutenant colonels were a dime a dozen, had bewitched many of the top brass in the CIA Operations directorate into enabling his wild schemes to keep the Contras afloat at whatever cost. Whether these seasoned Agency clients of ours—a number of whom either lost their jobs or were indicted—danced to his tune because they thought Director Casey had supplied North his flute or because they shared his maniacal devotion to the Contra cause, I could not tell.

It also became evident that my office had served as North's lawyers because the legal department of the National Security Council where he worked had no clue regarding the legal requirements for covert action. We paid a heavy price for taking on this account, in demotions, man-hours, and loss of morale. Stan, then a sitting judge, spent the better part of an excruciating day testifying before the congressional committees about our involvement. I was too small a fish to be mentioned by name in his testimony, but I felt the taint.

I began to think it was time to move on. The Agency seemed paralyzed. William Webster, a former judge, had been brought over from the FBI to right the ship and project an image of propriety, but the CIA was neither the FBI nor a federal court and he seemed to be starting from scratch. Ironically, the advent of his regime gave me my best access to the Director's office, as he decided to keep to the tradition—started when he was a judge and continued during his tenure at the FBI—of hiring young lawyers to serve as clerks. His callow clerks, of roughly my age and educational background, were viewed askance by the steely-eyed CIA veterans they were supposed to be monitoring and welcomed a friendly face from familiar territory.

My division was finding it hard to get our requests for searches and wiretaps through the Department of Justice. Even time-sensitive applications could languish for weeks. Attorney General Meese was heavily implicated in Iran/Contra and appeared to spend most of his day fending off the independent counsel and the hounds baying on Capitol Hill. His top lieutenants—Lowell Jensen and Weld—also seemed consumed by the scandal and ultimately decided to resign before their own careers went up in flames.

It was profoundly disillusioning for an idealistic twenty-something to be serving in an agency and administration in such a state of dysfunction. Those who might have been my mentors were obsessed with saving their own skins. And at a far higher level, the Reagan mystique of remaining above the fray, setting broad guidelines and leaving it to capable deputies to fill in the gaps, had been exposed as a yawning vacuum filled by grasping subalterns like Oliver North.

I also discovered an allergy to bureaucracy. I was still fascinated with the CIA and loved the one-on-one contact with operations and technical types who had foregone lucrative careers in the private sector for the singular world of clandestine activity. But in many ways it was just another huge Byzantine edifice, hidebound by innumerable layers of management and crippled by the inevitable turf battles. Lack of turnover made things worse, as the lubricant of ever-changing political appointments that greased the operations of other agencies oiled few of the Agency's gears. Sadly, one of the few positions in the Agency that was subject to political appointment was the General Counsel, which meant that it was highly unlikely that an ambitious young lawyer like me would ever rise to the top spot in the office, barred as I was from involvement in political activity under the federal Hatch Act.

The crowning bureaucratic blow came one holiday weekend spent at the beach. I was scheduled to fly back from the coast very early on Tuesday morning, which still would have allowed me to get into work at a decent hour. Unfortunately, major storms grounded air traffic, and I ended up having to drive back to DC. I didn't get into the office until about one pm. Despite the fact that I worked at least an hour or more of uncompensated overtime every business day and sometimes on weekends, my boss still felt compelled to dock me a precious vacation day.

That did it. I flirted with working as a staffer on one of the congressional intelligence oversight committees, but the only available position there was filled shortly after I applied by someone on the chairman's personal staff who had no intelligence-related experience. I joked bitterly that I had one serious drawback for a job on Capitol Hill: I was qualified. I decided shortly afterward to start contacting DC law firms about a lateral move. I figured if I were going to head into private practice I'd better do it soon, as it wasn't like I was a Justice Department lawyer bringing marketable courtroom skills or an IRS maven with saleable tax expertise. Mercifully for society at large, there wasn't much call for a background in wiretaps and counternarcotics assistance in the private sector. The same family friend who had helped me land the position in London steered me in the direction of one of the major DC firms, Covington & Burling, who were known for valuing governmental backgrounds in the hiring process, no matter how exotic. After several rounds of interviews, they made me an attractive offer that gave me full credit in terms of partnership track for the time I had spent at the Agency. The offer was particularly satisfying because Covington had passed on my bid to join them for a summer clerkship while I was at Stanford. I accepted over a sumptuous lunch at the Cosmos Club that I roguishly concluded by announcing, "You have hours to bill and I have people to kill." Thankfully that bit of youthful bravado did not result in their withdrawing the offer.

I wasn't looking forward to breaking the news to my boss, but I didn't think he would give me too much heat. I'd worked damned hard for a lot less than I could have made elsewhere and had lived through the hell of Iran/Contra courtesy of an assignment he had seen fit to give me. I was very wrong. He berated me for what seemed like an eternity. The Agency had devoted untold sums to my training and had lavished foreign travel opportunities upon me, he screamed, and this was how I repaid their generosity. At some level I had to admire the depth of his attachment to the institution that had been his life, but it also laid bare the tunnel vision that had been the Agency's undoing in Iran/Contra. I knew in my heart that my account with the CIA was square. I left with a clear conscience and a hope that I had not been tarred for life.

## ABROAD

I hadn't experienced much of an interior creative life as an actor of modest talents. I plumbed the depths of my assigned roles as best I could, but most of the time I was striving to project an external appearance that would be passable for an audience of hopefully limited discrimination. Every once in a while I would strike an emotional chord that surprised me in its reverberation, but mostly I contented myself with a command of language that came naturally to a lawyer.

To my surprise, the trauma of Iran/Contra sparked an internal dialogue that germinated the seed of a play about revolution in the Third World. In the waning months of my time at the CIA, I began to shape the contours of a script that took as its point of departure the bitter colonial legacy and deep social fissures the Agency had been called on to exploit in Central America and beyond. To me, the high water mark of playwriting had been those productions of Shaw and Coward I had seen in London, and I wondered if I could somehow present this rich subject with wit and sparkle rather than ideology and dogma.

I knew from my law school classmates in private practice that the jolly outings and catered parties of the summer clerkship programs had given way to the merciless grind of the partnership track. While I thought that the experience of working with aggressive CIA officers would serve me well in dealing with demanding private sector clients, I understood that I would have a lot of catching up to do in learning new areas of the law and grasping the inner workings of a law firm. I concluded that if I wasn't going to have the time to grow as an actor, it was time to put acting aside. I didn't see how I would have much chance to develop my meager dramatic talents while billing the expected 2000 plus hours hours a year. It had been hard enough moonlighting on stage while working government hours.

But I wasn't prepared to let go of the theater. Part of this need was preserving my own self-image. I couldn't accept that I was just a lawyer, just as I couldn't accept that I was just a Williams undergraduate or just a Stanford law student. I knew there had to be something more to me than that, some special dimension made manifest through the performing arts. Part was simple stress reduction: I needed an outlet away from the pressures of a busy law practice, and I could lose myself in theater in a way that no amount of running or tennis could achieve. And part, I dared to hope, was the presence of a genuine creative spark within me that made me more than just an artistic dilettante.

I decided it was time to write. Writing offered a way to remain engaged in the theater at my own pace and on my own terms. I could work when it was right for me. I would not be dependent on the casting and scheduling whims of some director. But I could still with justification view myself as a theater person with skin in the artistic game.

I was painfully aware, however, of the reality that I had never written a play in my life, or for that matter anything else that had not been assigned to me in school or by my superior at work. I was at a loss how I would ever begin, particularly when faced with the prospect of launching my career in private practice at a major national law firm not known for treating its associates with kid gloves.

The only way this play was ever going to be anything other than a glorious ice-breaker at cocktail parties was to stave off the servitude of law firm life a little longer and just start writing. My new employer, Covington & Burling, had prospered without my services for the better part of the century, so I asked if they could manage without me a few months more. They graciously agreed.

I didn't fancy hanging around Washington, DC. I needed to put some distance between me and the Iran/Contra-ravaged Reagan administration. I also didn't feel like staring at the walls of my 540-square-foot condominium for months on end. The steamy heat of a DC summer was just around the corner, and the clatter of my cheap wall unit air conditioner did not seem conducive to the creation of great theater.

I had to go abroad. The glamour of nursing a cheap glass of red wine at a fashionably shabby sidewalk café, several days' stubble on my cheeks, pensively poised over my writer's pad, simultaneously savoring and deflecting the admiring glances of smoldering beauties at nearby tables wondering at my masterpiece in the making, was irresistible. While I was hardly flush after several years of civil service salary and student loan payments, I figured I could rent my condo for a few months, cover my mortgage, and have a little money left over. I mapped out an itinerary that was fanciful, picturesque, and relatively cheap: Spain, Portugal, Egypt, and Israel.

But first, I decided, I needed to draw together my two key formative influences as a theater artist: London and Marc Fajer. It would be a major splurge, as I could not in good conscience deploy my Stanford Law student ID three years after graduation, but I needed inspiration and companionship before embarking on my playwriting adventure. We drank in the West End to the dregs, hitting seven shows in as many days, including a stirring revival of Sondheim's *Company* and the opening of Stoppard's *Arcadia*.

The week was exhilarating, but intimidating as hell. As I saw Marc off and prepared to make for the Continent, I wondered how I would ever come close to the caliber of writing I had just witnessed. Anal lawyer that I was, I had prepared an outline for the play (yes, on a yellow legal pad) so that I would not face the torment of a blank page without a clue as to where to begin. I was a great admirer of the classical structure of Shakespearean comedies such as *A Midsummer Night's Dream*, which often opened in the ordered world of a court, then shifted to the wilds of the forest as some crisis shattered the familiar order, then returned to the court as the growth of the characters conferred a wisdom and self-knowledge that restored the former order, but richer and deeper than before.

The central characters in my play were to be the members of a British expatriate family in some unnamed developing nation embroiled in civil unrest. The father, Rupert Pudgethorpe, is the canny executive in charge of a major multinational's operations in the country. He is a bluff, hearty, cunning man of middle age whose workaholic tendencies leave his long-suffering wife Rita alone and afraid amidst the increasing violence of the capital city where they live in comfort. Their clever, trendy daughter Nancy is back for the summer from her studies at an upper-crust British university, where she has picked up a lot of clever slogans and a stylish black leather wardrobe. Rupert decides to play Cupid by matching Nancy with his earnest young assistant Wilkinson, a dogged up-and-comer in the company. Nancy finds Wilkinson too corporate for her bohemian tastes and blasts her father and the company for propping up a corrupt regime. He, in turn, reproaches her for her ignorance of a complex political environment that offers no genuine democratic alternatives and in which their company makes a healthy profit but also provides desperately needed employment.

I had laid things out this far when I arrived in Madrid. I knew I wanted to introduce a cell of revolutionaries into the plot and somehow devise a kidnapping conspiracy in which the rebels would prey on Rita's loneliness and Nancy's naiveté. The action would then shift to the rebels' den, where the two women would confront their captors and come to grips with the contrast between the dark reality of the country in which they were interlopers and their own sheltered lifestyle. They could then return to their former lives, chastened but endowed with new perspective. Rupert and Rita would reconcile, of course, and Nancy would be smitten with the worthy Wilkinson.

I pictured the first act as almost a drawing room comedy, with quick-witted repartee among the members of the Pudgethorpe family playing off the sincerity of Wilkinson as a comic foil. Slowly, almost imperceptibly, the wit and elegance that kicks off the play would give way to the rage and confusion of rebellion until the audience—by the second act—genuinely has no idea whether the third act will bring total chaos or restoration of the comfortable order that began the play.

I was well aware of the irony of rambling through Spain and Portugal, two of the most egregious colonial powers, as I tried to fashion my First World meets Third World script. I knew that Spain, in particular, had foisted an extractive aristocracy on its colonies in Nicaragua, Honduras, and other sites of CIA covert action in which a tiny percentage of the population controlled almost all of the wealth and land.

But what a country in which to write and travel on little money—a languid pace, gracious restaurants offering sumptuous paella washed down with a bottle of local vintage at modest prices, rich history and dazzling Moorish and imperial sights offered with minimal hype, refuge in the genius of Zurbaran and Velasquez. I soon slipped into an easy rhythm of travel in the morning hours after a late breakfast, a light beer-dappled lunch followed by several hours of longhand writing at the table, a little post-siesta sight-seeing followed by feet up and a good book at the pensione or hostel, then a hearty dinner over wine at a budget restaurant I had spotted during the day. If inspiration exceeded intoxication, I would write for another hour or so after dinner before turning in or, on rare occasion, trying a Spanish disco, which didn't seem to hit its stride until after midnight even on a weeknight.

I began to find a voice. It was halting at first, and annoyingly pedantic. My greatest struggle was to introduce my themes—the imbalance of socialist ideology and post-colonial reality, the potential of capitalism to be reformist or reactionary, the power of the individual to make choices even under great organizational pressure—without reducing my characters to mere mouthpieces for a particular point of view. This was my only serious criticism of Shaw, whose brilliance in dialogue in my view occasionally strayed into propagandizing. I found I had a good feel for the British characters, who were more familiar to me in class and attitude, but lost my way in developing the rebels. Rightly or wrongly, I had made the decision not to identify the country in which the play occurs. I wanted to avoid easy stereotypes and point up the universality of the themes I was exploring. The lack of an ethnic identity, however, made it more difficult for me to picture the rebels in my mind and give them flesh and blood.

I passed from Spain into Portugal, which offered many of the traveler's virtues of Spain at even more reasonable prices and with comparatively little tourist fanfare. I soon discovered the meditative powers of port wine, which certainly endowed me with a sense of enhanced artistic sensibilities (if, as I later re-read my Portuguese period, little in the way of additional substance). My only complaint about Portugal was that I was mugged at knifepoint in Lisbon near the train station. I made the likely ill-advised decision to utilize my college sprinting skills and dash across the street. I got away, but spent the next several days looking over my shoulder, nerves too jangled to write. I chuckled at the random violence featured prominently in my play rendering me unfit to work on it.

I had planned to fly from Lisbon to Cairo to begin the Middle Eastern leg of my travels, and I had been told that it was far cheaper to buy a Lisbon-Cairo ticket in Portugal than to purchase in advance in the United States. Wrong. The major airlines were quoting around $700 for a one-way ticket to Egypt, which would have strained my bohemian budget. I came across one little-advertised alternative. Czechoslovakian Airlines, the national Czech carrier, offered a bizarre package that featured a morning flight on Monday from Lisbon to Prague, then had you cooling your heels Monday and Tuesday night and all day Wednesday at the airport hotel before flying from Prague to Cairo after midnight on Wednesday and arriving in the wee hours of the morning on Thursday. Total cost charged by this hard-currency starved Eastern bloc country: $220, including two nights accommodation. I was at one of those precious moments in life where I had more time than money, so Czechoslovakian Airlines it was. I had sampled the pleasures of Pilsner Urquell in London and figured I could hang out at the airport hotel with a nice buzz on and attempt to come to terms with those elusive rebels.

I left Lisbon early Monday in the company of a motley collection of ill-tailored, stony-eyed Soviet apparatchiks and Third World satellite-dwellers clad in improbable combinations of Western and traditional dress. Neither the plane nor the crew inspired much confidence, but we somehow made it to Prague, where I made inquiries as to the location of the airport hotel. I was advised by some humorless desk clerks that I would not be lodging at the airport hotel. Mildly alarmed, I pressed for details. I would be taken by bus to downtown Prague, I was informed, where I would be put up at a hotel in the city center. Would I be able to look around Prague during my stay, I asked? But of course, came the huffy reply.

I was dumbfounded. Not six weeks before, I had been a full-fledged, top-secret–clearance-carrying employee of the CIA. This was the summer of '88, well over a year before Havel's Velvet Revolution and the fall of the Berlin Wall. If I had applied in the United States for a tourist visa to see the sights of Prague, I would have been laughed out of the embassy. And here I was, the guest of the Czech Government for over two days on their nickel with the run of the capital. And they threw in free meals, for good measure!

The rebels started to take better shape in my rambles past the Austro-Hungarian palaces of Prague. I came up with the plot device of inserting a pair of rebel girlfriends as maids in the Pudgethorpe household. They used their position to play on the vulnerabilities of Nancy and Rita and introduce them to two rebels, a dashing young romantic (A) and an urbane old socialist politician (B), who served as the instruments of the kidnapping. The conspiracy was masterminded by a third rebel, a hard-core, jargon-spouting ideologue (C), and enforced by a gun-toting brute (D), who is rewarded by the movement for his violent propensities. I still struggled to move these characters (who were identified by letter only, not by name) from mere types to well-delineated individuals, but the action of the play was gathering a nice momentum.

I survived the midnight flight to Cairo but found it difficult to concentrate in the thick of the dust, heat, and unending stream of humanity of the Egyptian capital. I was a little ashamed that I could not write a play set in the Third World in the face of Third World conditions. I didn't hit my stride creatively until I took a creaking passenger train south a long the Nile to Luxor, where I ventured out with mad dogs and Englishmen in midday 120 degree heat to view the celebrated tombs, and in particular Aswan. I lounged for hours in a riverside café sipping delicious tropical fruit drinks, fanned by the Nile breeze, the lilting rhythms of Bob Marley playing gently in the background of this oddly endearing Afro/Arab city, and filled page after yellow legal page. I was in such a groove that I almost passed on the long bus ride to the temples of Ramses II at Abu Simbel. Thankfully I had the sense to take a break and witness one of the most awe-inspiring sights I shall ever see— massive marvels of ego and engineering.

The tension of the second act builds as the rebels find the Pudgethorpe women to be a far cry from the docile victims they had expected. There is no response to their ransom demands until Rupert and Wilkinson suddenly arrive at the rebel den with a suitcase containing far less than had been demanded. The rebels are about to reject this out of hand until Rupert advises them that the rebel chief himself had clued him in to their whereabouts. It turns out that he had been paying off the rebel leader for years (to the dismay of the priggish Wilkinson, who had no idea there was a corporate slush fund). The other rebels are aghast to learn that the chief had rejected the kidnapping plot (because of the threat to Pudgethorpe's payoffs), and that the mastermind (C) had decided to go ahead with it anyway in the hopes of making a big score and boosting his stock in the movement. (D), the gun-toting brute, decides to take charge at this point. Things turn ugly as he brandishes his gun and grabs Nancy. The act ends in a sudden blackout and the sound of gunfire.

I was sorry to leave the soothing cafes of Egypt and take the bus across the Sinai Desert to Jerusalem. I wasn't sure why I had included Israel on my itinerary. It seemed a place—as a Jew—I should want to visit, but I felt out of place as soon as I arrived. I knew I was in denial regarding my own ethnic identity, but denial was easier to sustain in the melting pot of the United States, where everyone had to some extent turned his back on the old country in order to become an American. For the first time in my life, I was in the midst of Jews who, unlike me, were entirely at home in their own skins. In Israel I should have been at ease as a Jew among Jews, but instead I felt even more alien than in Czechoslovakia or Egypt, where I had been just another American tourist. It was stirring to witness a strong, vibrant nation built by a people who had been shunned and slaughtered for so long around the world, but I struggled to accept these people as my own, despite the obvious physical similarities.

My grandparents had not been devout, but their civic and social lives had revolved around the Jewish community of Cleveland—membership in a Jewish country club, service on the board of the Jewish hospital, leadership in Jewish charities—they knew who they were and from whence they had come. My parents had deliberately moved away from this environment, joining an integrated pool and tennis club in the Chicago suburbs, socializing with non-Jewish friends (although most of their circle were Jews), and embracing Christmas in our household. They identified themselves as Jews, but had broadened their sense of community. I was one generation further removed from my roots, a gap widened by a set of WASP childhood friends, a traditionally WASP college, and an Anglophilia born of my years in London. Judaism to me was an inconvenient heirloom, one which I knew I should find room for in my house but preferred to leave boxed in the attic.

I reached the height of my ambivalence on an intense day trip to the desert fortress of Masada, where Jewish zealots during the revolt against Roman rule committed mass suicide rather than submit to capture. I rose at dawn and reached the fortress, a desolate rock rising above the Dead Sea, before the temperature reached intolerable levels so that I could take the steep ancient access route to the summit known as the "Snake Path." For reasons I could not explain I felt an urge to run the path once I began my ascent and managed to keep my legs churning over almost the entire stony, serpentine route. Spent and drenched with sweat as I scoured the ruins, I pictured the stark contrast between the gaudy luxury of Herod's palace built by the Romans and the desperate poverty of the starving, besieged zealots who later occupied it.

As I looked on at this awful site of collective self-sacrifice, I wondered why Jews had been fated to two millennia of isolation and persecution. I viewed Masada as a terrible symbol of the separation and suffering that seemed a constant in Jewish history. At the same time that I felt a kinship with the indomitable Jewish fighters who had resisted valiantly against impossible odds, I also saw this lonely rock as a monument to the wisdom of assimilation—my assimilation.

I left Israel both more proud and more ashamed to be a Jew. The intensity of coming to grips with Israel hampered my output somewhat, but I was able to work out the basic contours of the third act. The scene shifts from the rebel den back to the Pudgethorpe home, where we learn over a celebratory dinner that Wilkinson had leveled the sadist D with a shot from a disguised gun. In the ensuing melee, the mastermind (C) is knocked cold by Rupert, Nancy finishes off one of the maids, and the other maid is left sobbing by her fallen boyfriend, D. The two remaining rebels, A and B, had been coerced into participating in the kidnapping plot and are only too pleased to let the Pudgethorpes escape. Wilkinson's bravery is not lost on Nancy, who had previously found him unprepossessing. Rupert is chastised by both his daughter and Wilkinson for paying off the rebels, which he not only defends as necessary to corporate survival amidst chaos but also reveals to have been part of a grander strategy authorized by the board that included bribes to the government as well. Shortly after this confession, Rupert receives word that news of the bribery scheme has hit the papers in England and that the board has made him the public scapegoat. Rita rejoices at the news of his firing, which will enable them to leave the strife-filled country and retire to more congenial surroundings. Rebels A and B then return in something of a coda to express their regrets to Nancy and Rita for their complicity in the kidnapping, and all who deserve to live happily ever after do.

I flew back to DC with the tanned self-assurance of a globetrotting writer and a sheaf of scrawled yellow legal pages to support my conceit. Before submitting to the will of Covington & Burling I had a few weeks, which I spent fleshing out my plot lines and filling in gaps. I hit a couple of shows at the Source and the Studio and found myself entering the theater with an extra bounce in my step that announced my new status as a bona fide playwright.

# DC (OFFSTAGE)

Covington & Burling, while an admirably eclectic firm, was unimpressed by my literary attainments. They were paying me a fourth-year associate's salary to work in two legal practice areas, corporate and real estate, in which I had precisely zero years of experience (my work in London having been entirely focused on litigation). I had cleverly contended in the interviewing process that my work at the CIA would serve me well advising on business deals, as an intelligence operation (I suggested) was essentially a transaction for which necessary resources, approvals, and documentation had to be drawn together by a skilled attorney. The argument was a trifle specious, but they accepted it and placed me accordingly.

The adjustment from life at the Agency was jarring. On the positive side, I had resources at my disposal I could not have dreamed of as a civil servant: a secretary who actually did my work instead of saying she might get to it if she ever reached the bottom of my boss's out-basket, an in-house word processing center open nights and weekends, overnight and courier services at my beck and call, reimbursed meals if I had to work late, catered training lunches, a real leather office chair. The setting was magnificent. Covington had a wonderful collection of Oriental rugs lining the corridors, not to mention mahogany grandfather clocks and other client confidence-inspiring antiques.

On the negative side, I was now a slave to the billable hour. The pressure of tracking every moment of my day in five-minute intervals was intense, particularly when I already felt far behind the other associates in my class regarding practice area knowledge. When I left the office at the CIA, I literally left my work behind me, as it was prohibited to take classified material out of a secure area. In private practice, the projects seemed always with me, through evenings, weekends, and holidays.

I had looked forward to getting involved in Republican politics, an activity forbidden as a federal civil servant, but found I had little time. I did join with a few Stanford classmates to host a fundraiser for our former professor Tom Campbell, who was running for Congress in Pete McCloskey's old Silicon Valley district. I didn't know much about Tom's politics, but he was without question the most impressive person I had ever met: bachelor's and master's degrees in economics from the University of Chicago, law degree from Harvard (where he edited the Harvard Law Review), clerkships on the D.C. Circuit Court of Appeals and with Justice Byron White on the U.S. Supreme Court, private practice with a major Chicago law firm while earning his Ph.D. in economics from the University of Chicago, White House Fellow, Director of the Federal Bureau of Competition at the FTC, and Stanford Law School professor at age thirty-one. Tom always reminded me of the humorist Tom Lehrer's line about Mozart: "When he was my age he'd been dead for six years."

Tom had been a great mentor to me at Stanford while I weighed the CIA offer. When I reminded him of his counseling me to take the Agency job over the objections of my mother, he told me of a conversation with his father just after he'd made the decision to run for Congress. His father, a Democratic stalwart from Chicago's heavily Catholic South Side, had been the longest serving federal judge in the country, appointed by FDR in the thirties. When Tom told his father that he planned to run as a Republican, Judge Campbell stared at him for what seemed an eternity before finally hissing, "And do you plan to become a Protestant too?"

Even if I'd had time, there were no meaningful opportunities to become involved in local politics as a Republican. I lived in the District of Columbia, where George Bush had barely reached a double-digit share of the vote during the '88 presidential election. I learned that being involved in Republican politics in DC meant hosting fundraisers for politicians from somewhere else—something that was unappealing to me. About all I had time for outside the practice of law was tinkering with my play, which I had dubbed *Bodyhold* (a riff on the kidnapping conspiracy). I became an overnight authority on playwriting competitions, of which there were an amazing variety, all with slightly different requirements as to synopses, excerpts, cover letters, et al. At first I was a passionate serial applicant, firing off weighty packages all over the country. As rejection letters began to stream in, I became more selective in the contests I chose to enter, but my acceptance ratio remained dismal. The pain of rejection in these competitions was compounded by the lack of feedback on my script. Form letter after form letter would arrive, with no comment on the quality of my work.

As the stars began to fade from my eyes, it occurred to me that I might fare better trying to build relationships with local theater professionals, who were better situated to help me develop my script. I made a list of the artistic directors at the smaller theaters around the area, many of which I had been frequenting for several years—the Source, the Studio, the Woolly Mammoth, the Olney Theatre in suburban Maryland—and began a relentless cultivation campaign. No one knew who I was, however, as my leading roles in community theater had not translated to reviews in the pages of the *Washington Post*. Also, *Bodyhold* featured ten actors (the three Pudgethorpes, Wilkinson, four rebels, and two maids), which I learned is a daunting number for all but the major regional companies, who were out of my league. The fact that *Bodyhold* was in many ways a traditional play, in essence a classically structured drawing room comedy, didn't help. It did not cry out as new, trendy, or cutting edge.

About the only useful purpose my playwriting served at this time was as a novel ice-breaker at cocktail parties. When people learned of my theater background, almost invariably they would ask why I was not doing courtroom work; they assumed that an actor would make a crackerjack trial lawyer. I—with a self-deprecating shrug—would reply that they might reach a different conclusion had they actually seen me on stage. More earnestly, I would point out that acting for me was a form of artistic expression, and while there was considerable craft in trial lawyering, there was little art. If my interlocutor had not yet left for the restroom or a refill on the Scotch, I would close my rejoinder by observing that there could be as much drama in the negotiation of a business deal as in any courtroom potboiler.

Fortunately I was never pressed on this point, as I had only one anecdote in my storeroom of dramatic business negotiations. Shortly after I arrived at Covington, I was assigned to be the junior associate on a massive real estate transaction in which our client, IBM, was contributing two huge parcels of land in suburban DC to joint ventures with a prominent New York developer. My job, as the low man on the totem pole, was to review the property management and marketing agreements used in previous joint ventures between our client and this developer, who had done a number of projects together. I closeted myself with a sheaf of these bulky and tedious documents and was well armed when the time came to negotiate this aspect of the deal. We gathered in the breathtaking Park Avenue offices of the developer, in soft leather armchairs around an enormous marble conference table overlooking Central Park. There was an entourage of at least seven on the developer's side of the table. On our side, there was an IBM real estate officer, to his right the Covington real estate partner, to his right the Covington senior associate, and to his right, lowly me.

The developer major-domo stood up and in an aggrieved tone announced their dismay that we were taking such and such a position on these contracts, as the parties had never done it that way before. I had a serious adrenaline rush. I fished in my briefcase and pulled out an agreement that had been used in a joint project a few years back and had exactly the provisions we were seeking. I handed it to the senior associate, whose eyes lit up. He excitedly passed the document to the partner, who could barely contain himself in showing it to the client. The client then quietly interrupted and pointed out that, in fact, we had done it precisely that way on the XYZ deal.

The developer honcho barely paused for breath before snidely replying that, as we all knew, the XYZ project was an extraordinary deal and that approaches taken there had never been followed again. With racing pulse I rummaged in my briefcase and pulled out yet another agreement on yet another joint project that had been negotiated in exactly the same way. I handed it to the senior associate, who nearly fell out of his chair before passing it to the partner, who was in a state of hysterical delirium as he point-

ed out the critical sections to the client. The client brandished
the contract and, in a voice that could have cut ice, suggested
that they might want to review their files, as here was yet another
precedent for doing things our way. There was stunned silence on
the developer side of the vast marble expanse and a visible defla-
tion of their entire delegation. Their principal meekly requested a
break in a voice that was barely audible; they then fled the room
en masse. The client and partner almost hugged me as we rejoiced
in the rout.

As I began to get a measure of comfort in private practice, I
found that my dealings with the tough hombres of the CIA's Operations Directorate served me well. I was accustomed to smart,
aggressive, determined clients who knew what they wanted and
were damned if some punk lawyer was going to stand in their
way. I had learned to stand my ground and shift the focus from
the wishful to the achievable. Private sector clients were more dollar than mission driven, which actually made it easier to secure a
good result.

My Agency background also proved helpful in working with
the firm's partners. They sensed I'd been tested, which seemed to
make them less inclined to yank my chain just for the sake of doing so. One notable exception was a senior partner who was notorious for calling associates and even junior partners to his office and then having them sit there while he took phone call after
phone call. On several such occasions I would start to get up from
my chair after cooling my heels for a half hour or more; he would
imperiously motion me to stay seated. I learned to take work with
me any time I was summoned by him. One morning I was in his
office discussing a deal when he took a call on his speakerphone.
A sprightly woman's voice came on the line and announced that
she was calling to confirm his appointment for an enema on
Thursday morning. I bit my lip until his secretary, who happened

to be standing in the doorway, burst out laughing, at which point I couldn't hold it in any longer. He turned to us and whispered, "It's hard getting old." He never took another call in my presence.

I had enormous admiration, however, for the older partners at Covington. They were men of parts. They had led rich, full lives, moving between the private and public sectors. Heading agencies and chairing commissions, they combined a prosperous legal practice with service to their country and community. They epitomized what a Washington lawyer should be: both a skilled professional and a committed citizen.

I aspired to be like these men, but grew troubled by the profile of partners a generation below them. These younger partners were terrific lawyers—sharp, savvy, and deft in their handling of clients—but they seemed consumed by their practice. They often billed well over 2,000 hours a year, which to the layperson might look like a work schedule of only forty hours per week for fifty weeks but in fact meant the attorney was spending far longer at the office because of departmental meetings, personnel issues, and other administrative matters that could not be billed. I sensed that many of them had come to DC out of law school because of a passion for public policy, but for most of them this had come to mean attending the occasional political fundraiser or hosting a dinner party that might include an administration official or a journalist. They were in the nation's capital, but not truly of it.

It was clear to me that this was not the fault of the law firm. Covington & Burling is an extraordinary firm with a commitment to public service perhaps unrivaled in the nation. One of the firm's leading lights in its early days had been Secretary of State Dean Acheson, for whom a firm conference room filled with Acheson photographs is named. They regularly hire lawyers like me who had served in government and had no private practice experience. They were one of the few firms anywhere that allows associates to count time spent on pro bono matters toward the billable hour expectation (although the pro bono work tends toward more progressive causes such as death penalty appeals and legal services clinics, which irked the few conservatives at the firm). They have a diverse client base, ranging from the National Football League (Paul Tagliabue was a long-time Covington partner who became the NFL commissioner shortly after I joined the firm) to a host of state governments. The feel of the place was often more like a university with a brainy faculty than a profit-driven law firm.

As I came to understand the DC legal market better, I saw that it wasn't really the fault of these younger partners. The reality was that DC was a much more competitive place to be a law firm partner than when most of the senior partners had started practice. A myriad of large, well-funded, aggressive firms from outside the area had set up Washington offices and were actively poaching accounts that had traditionally belonged to the old-line DC firms like Covington and Arnold & Porter. The explosion of private sector "Beltway Bandits," particularly in the suburbs of Northern Virginia, made corporate legal work a more critical element of law firm practice than it had been in Washington a decade or two earlier, and New York- or Chicago-based firms had stronger corporate groups than DC firms did. Partners in their thirties, forties, and fifties had little choice but to grind it out if they were going to hold their own against the competitors snarling at their door.

But that didn't make it any more attractive for a young associate like me. I had come to Washington for the thrill and intrigue of working for the CIA. That was now in the past. I was eager to résumé my involvement in Republican politics now that I was free of the Hatch Act. However, I had little time for politics and saw little chance for meaningful involvement in Washington even when I did.

Acting and then writing had conferred a certain luster on my life in DC, but that was fading. I was correct in my assessment that private practice left no time for performing, and I had begun to despair about my play ever seeing the light of day. I knew I lacked patience as a writer. Most playwrights labor for a decade or more before seeing any of their work produced. Many live for the experience of writing itself; an actual production is secondary. I am not that sort of person. Theater to me is performance, and a play that is not performed is the proverbial sound of one hand clapping. I was not prepared to let my play go, though, because I was not yet ready to give up the image of myself as a theater person.

The watershed event came when Covington offered me the chance to go to Japan for eighteen months. They had formed an association with a Japanese law firm and developed the relationship by posting a series of Covington lawyers in the Japanese firm's office in Tokyo. It was a fantastic opportunity that would have cemented my partnership prospects. I would travel, learn a new language (and with Japanese investment then at its height in the US, it was viewed as a very good language to learn), and rub shoulders with a host of investment bankers, consultants, and other great contacts. It was a chance to indulge the love of foreign adventure that had taken me to London and Langley.

But it was not what I wanted to do. I wanted to become part of a community, to be a player in local politics, to be a mover and shaker on the business and civic scene, to lead the sort of multifaceted life that I so admired in the older generation of Covington partners. Later in life I might choose to return to DC, but it would likely be through a high-level executive appointment that was the fruit of years of political cultivation. And I was hungry to see my play produced. I knew I could go to Japan for a year and a half and then leave Covington, but that would be grossly unfair to the firm that had trained me so well and given me a chance as a young lawyer coming out of the CIA skilled only in wiretaps and counternarcotics. They clearly expected whoever took the Japanese rotation to remain with the firm and help build that foreign relationship.

I also wanted to start a family. I had met Amy Bassett on a blind date during my CIA days. She was then working in computers at the IRS, so we joked that we were the ultimate Big Brother couple. We fit. She was gentle where I was aggressive, spatial where I was verbal, and intuitive where I was analytical. Amy had grown up in Baltimore and then in the DC suburbs. Her father had been an architect who'd gone on to a distinguished career in urban planning. She had studied design at college, but after a few frustrating years as a slave at a large architectural firm, had gone back to school to get a master's degree in information technology. She'd moved into my snug condo as I started at Covington in the fall of '88, and I had proposed (at the landmark Occidental Restaurant in the Willard Hotel) just before Christmas that year.

We were married outdoors in front of a modest crowd of ninety-five in September of '89 at the wonderfully named Turning Point Inn, in the country south of Frederick, Maryland. She was a lightly practicing Episcopalian and I was a non-practicing Jew, so we decided to have a justice of the peace officiate. We wrote our own ceremony, including a reading by me from Kierkegaard's *Either/Or.* A handbell choir played beautifully, although they decided to bring along a trumpet player who was ghastly. We rode off in a motorcycle sidecar on our way to a honeymoon in Sweden and Finland, chosen by Amy (with minimal input from me) because of her love of Scandinavian design. I did, however, get to select the soundtrack for our reception, including our song: Al Green's *Let's Stay Together.*

By the time the opportunity in Japan was presented, we were eager to have children. Amy was a few years older than I, so there seemed little reason to wait. Bringing up baby in a cramped apartment in Tokyo was not enticing to me, although Amy was more game to try it than I was. I passed on the chance, to the astonishment of my Covington friends. I told them it was because I needed more of a chance to develop my corporate and real estate skill set, but I think they knew that was a smokescreen. Another lawyer at the firm leapt at the chance and was heartily congratulated on his good fortune.

I started scouring a map of the United States. Amy and I had each rejected the other's first choices (my hometown of Chicago, which was not neutral territory for her, and her college town of Richmond, which was too Southern for me). I wanted a city that was smaller than DC, which would make it easier to get plugged into the community, but large enough to offer the amenities of a major metropolitan area. I wanted an economy that seemed to be on its way up, where an enterprising young lawyer could build a practice. I wanted a state where Republicans were not an endangered species and where conservatives and moderates could co-exist. I considered myself fiercely conservative on fiscal issues and more moderate on social issues and didn't want to be subject to a barrage of political litmus tests. I wanted a culture that was open to outsiders, where your family didn't have to go back generations in order to be taken seriously and make an impact. We both loved urban living, but as products of public school systems didn't want to feel forced to send our kids to private schools in the city.

I also wanted a city that had a critical mass of small theater companies. Even though I felt my play would be appealing to the more traditional audiences of major regional theaters, it was a long shot that such a company would take a chance on an unproven script by an unknown playwright. My best chance, I felt, was with up-and-coming companies working in venues seating 100–150. They had enough resources to do a solid job with the script but were small enough to consider taking a risk on new work.

Portland, Oregon quickly went to the top of our list. Portland was in the top twenty-five metro areas in the country, but seemed manageable and accessible. Technology investment, particularly from Intel and other Silicon Valley companies, had been pouring into the state and had revived an economy that for decades had been heavily dependent on forest products. Oregon was represented in the Senate by two powerful Republicans, Mark Hatfield and Bob Packwood, both of whom were widely respected and viewed as open-minded, non-ideological coalition builders. I had visited Portland while in law school, and the casual atmosphere of the city contrasted nicely with the more formal, tradition-bound style of the East Coast. And Portland's middle class not only had not abandoned the city's public school system, they seemed to embrace it.

In early '90, Amy and I made an exploratory visit that confirmed our favorable impressions. I made a close study of the theater listings during our visit and discovered a number of smaller companies offering an eclectic range of productions. I only had time to attend one of these, but liked what I saw. We decided that I should send out my résumé, which brought a round of job interviews that summer. My concerns about an Iran/Contra taint seemed unfounded, as almost no one asked me about my time at the CIA. I accepted an offer from a highly regarded Portland firm, Ball Janik & Novack, that at only twenty-five lawyers was dwarfed by Covington but had an impressive number of attorneys from national law schools.

There was, however, major reverse sticker shock. The salary offered by my new firm was almost exactly half of what I was making at Covington, and our plan was that Amy (who had a good job at the IRS) would not have to work outside the home. I received a call from the loan processor working on the mortgage for our new house, who said, "Do you realize, Mr. Cole, that your household income moving from Washington to Portland will shrink by over two-thirds?" I admitted that, sadly, I was aware of that dismal fact.

I thankfully did not have to endure the exit tongue-lashing from the Covington partners that I had received from my CIA boss. Their response, as I made the rounds, was plain befuddlement—why would anyone want to leave one of the finest firms in the country and one of the great centers of legal activity for a humble provincial practice in a remote state best known for large evergreens? I was tempted to trot out my best Polonius rendition of "Though this be madness, yet there is method in it," but I contented myself with a smile, a shrug, and an elliptical comment about family and community.

# A NEW MAN IN TOWN

I arrived in Oregon, thirty years of age, with the wind in my sails. I had rolled the dice a little in my twenties and the gamble had paid off. Instead of taking the beaten path of a safe, high-dollar law firm job out of law school, I had skated on the thin ice of the CIA and thrived. I'd enjoyed top-flight assignments and foreign travel. I had borne low-level witness to one of the great government scandals of the century and had survived, seemingly untainted. The CIA gambit had actually improved my hiring prospects, as I'd gone on to land a job at one of the nation's finest law firms—a firm that had passed on me as a law student. I had taken my career seriously but had not abandoned my passion for theater, where I had managed to trade an actor's greasepaint for a playwright's pen. And I got the girl, the lovely woman beside me in our road-weary old Saab as we pulled up to our first home, a 1920s Cape Cod in a charming neighborhood on Portland's east side.

We had barely moved in when we learned that Amy was pregnant. This news made the grind of the bar review class easier to bear. The fact that I had passed the California bar out of Stanford, been admitted to the DC bar, and practiced law for five years didn't cut any ice in Oregon, which required me to take its full exam. Ball Janik had agreed to let me finish the bar and settle into our home before beginning work.

Then, three months into her pregnancy and two days before the bar exam, Amy miscarried. She'd had one miscarriage before, but that had been just days after we'd found out she was pregnant, before we'd really had a chance to take in the news. This time we had already started mapping out changes to the house to prepare for our new arrival, and the miscarriage hit us hard. The bar exam seemed a trivial exercise after the hell we'd been through the forty-eight hours before. What had been planned as a weekend of post-exam celebrating on the coast turned into hours of consoling each other as we trudged down the beach.

This trimmed my sails more than I knew. I'd grown accustomed to catching the breaks and found myself ill prepared for this sort of blow, which seemed totally beyond my control—I responded by redoubling my efforts in areas I could do something about: building my legal career and becoming a player in Republican politics and the community. One of Ball Janik's major clients was a fast-growing forest products company called Crown Pacific. Shortly after I arrived, Crown had signed a letter of intent to buy a company in Central Oregon that owned one of the finest remaining stands of Ponderosa pine in the country. With my corporate and real estate background, I was a good match for the project and drew the assignment. It was a wonderful introduction to an industry so vital to Oregon and so alien to someone reared far from the magnificent forests of the Northwest. A fascinating twist to the deal was the seller's ownership of the little company town of Gilchrist, Oregon, which our client had no interest in buying. We had to devise ways of separating the town from the mill that had been its lifeblood for decades, including the roads, utility systems, and town governance.

Additionally, I threw my name into the political arena. Tom Campbell, now in Congress, had given me a letter of introduction to the state Republican Party. He was kind enough to embellish my modest contributions in the way that only a congressman can. The state party chair, an investor and entrepreneur named Craig Berkman, and his executive director seemed impressed with my credentials and introduced me to a Portland-based group of Republican activists. In short order I was rubbing shoulders with state legislators, lobbyists, campaign operatives, pollsters, rumor-mongers, and gossips—the motley crew that lubricates the machinery of local politics.

I soon learned that Republicans in Portland were not exactly a thundering herd. The divide that exists in many states between liberal urban areas and conservative rural sections was even more pronounced in Oregon. The state's population is concentrated in the Willamette Valley, with heavy Democratic majorities in Portland—easily the largest city in the state—and Eugene—home of the University of Oregon and sort of a down-market version of Berkeley. For over a decade Portland had been a magnet for progressive refugees from around the country, in particular environmental stalwarts keen on preserving the awesome beauty of the state's forests. The odds of a Republican holding office in the city of Portland or in Multnomah County, in which most of Portland sits, were about as high as the state repealing its contrarian bans on sales tax and self-serve gasoline.

Republicans held the upper hand in the vast rural expanse east of the Cascade Mountains, but the area was lightly populated. The Republican senators Mark Hatfield and Bob Packwood had entered public life before the great tilt leftward in the Willamette Valley and were able to hold on to their offices through a shrewd balancing act and the accumulation of political clout—Hatfield in the Appropriations Committee and Packwood in the Finance Committee. By the time I arrived, all statewide offices other than the U.S. Senate seats were held by Democrats, who also controlled a majority of the five-member congressional delegation.

The declining fortunes of Republicans at the state level had emboldened religious conservatives, who claimed that the party's failings were due to a drift away from core social values. Shortly before I arrived, these conservatives had run a third party candidate in the governor's race in '90 that destroyed the prospects of the distinguished moderate Republican nominee, Attorney General Dave Frohnmayer (brother of then NEA Chairman John Frohnmayer). The social conservatives had also declared war on the state party leadership and had targeted the chairman Craig Berkman for removal.

Out of these sagging electoral fortunes and internecine warfare, however, came opportunity. The fiscal conservative/social moderate wing of the party was desperate for new foot soldiers who brought energy and passion to the arena. I was sympathetic to this branch of the party, but considered myself a classic "Big Tent" Republican. I had had little religious upbringing, but felt comfortable working with people of strong faith. I identified myself as pro-choice, but considered this to be an issue of personal conscience and conviction, not a point of candidate disqualification. I told everyone I met that I was prepared to knock on doors, lick stamps, work call banks, and in any other way subordinate my Stanford Law-enhanced ego to the greater good of electing Republicans—of whatever stripe.

It was oddly thrilling being in a community so foreign to me. We knew literally no one when we arrived and had no family there. The ways and means of Portland were a great mystery, and I eagerly sought data—as well as rumor and innuendo—to get a better grasp of my surroundings. It was a complex jigsaw of competing interests, values, and personalities, and I had brief moments of triumph as little pieces came into focus.

Of course, I wanted to be a piece of the puzzle myself. I had rejected the money and prestige of Covington to be a player in a real community. I approached Craig Berkman—a close-mouthed self-made man given to an assortment of impeccably tailored suits with eye-catching handkerchiefs on some occasions and gaudy open-necked shirts with gold chains on others—and asked for his help in getting involved in civic groups. He handed me over to his significant other Karen Hinsdale, a gracious woman whose wine industry connections and philanthropic spirit seemed to put her on intimate terms with the entire town. Karen was then on the board of the foundation for Portland State University, the only public university in the metro area, and asked whether the foundation might be of interest to me. As both my parents had been educators and I had rarely seen a top-rank city without a well-funded university, I said that I would, but I thought I had no chance of being admitted to the board. I was a mid-level law firm associate with no family connections whose modest salary and student loan burden did not permit major contributions. I pictured the glittering foundation boards of Northwestern or the University of Chicago and assumed that PSU's foundation, while perhaps a notch below those great heights, would be out of my reach.

Karen smiled indulgently at my ignorance of Portland, asked for my bio, arranged a meeting with the foundation president, and in short order had me attending my first board meeting. This is not a city that stands on ceremony, she said. Portlanders prize their Oregon Trail lineage, but don't disqualify newcomers from civic life and do value talent as well as treasure. Portland State University, she explained, started as a teacher's college and had only recently become a full-fledged university. It struggled as a commuter school in the shadow of the state's two major universities, the University of Oregon and Oregon State University, whose rabid alumni competed for slots on their foundation boards. PSU's board had attracted a few big players in town, but it needed new blood who had no prejudices regarding its status. Karen also introduced me to Waverly Children's Home, a venerable institution in Portland that had started as a home for foundlings in the late nineteenth century and had developed into a multifaceted children's services agency. I soon joined Karen on the Waverly board as well.

While in Washington I had attended a few events sponsored by the local Williams College alumni association and was curious to see the strength of the Oregon association. I soon learned why Portland events listed in the college alumni publication always referred to Portland, Maine. Some young turks had built up the local association a few years back, but their interest and energy level had waned, leaving the organization in a state of benign neglect. I joined up with two other younger alums who wanted to revive the group and made plans to expand our membership and schedule more events.

One of my fellow Williams enthusiasts, Bruce Davis, decided to run for the state legislature in a suburban Portland district, which gave me the chance for my first grassroots political campaign. This was total war on a scale that was easy to grasp, and I loved it. Bruce's opponent in the Republican primary was a lawyer who had made a fortunate marriage to the daughter of a prominent area businessman and had run for the legislature twice before, giving him a substantial advantage in name recognition. He had managed to make a lot of enemies during his prior campaigns, however, and was viewed by lobbyists as a loose cannon. Bruce had done a nice job of courting the lobby as a bright, enterprising alternative (he had an MBA from Yale and had worked on Wall Street), had built up a significant fundraising edge, and had landed several key endorsements.

Amy and I went door to door, stamped mailers, and cheered on the weary candidate. Bruce let me sit in on strategy sessions with his campaign manager; my lack of hands-on political experience did not stop me from expressing my opinion. The major question in the closing weeks of the campaign was whether to go negative on our opponent. Bruce had run an upbeat campaign, focusing on his credentials and local support. While our opponent had high negatives, Bruce thought our resources were best used to keep pushing the positive. It also looked as if the opponent was short on money and would be hard-pressed to go on the offensive himself.

We miscalculated—badly. The opponent threw a ton of family money into the campaign in the last week and put out a scathing hit piece on Bruce. We had no funds left to respond and no time to do so anyway. The momentum shifted, and Bruce was finished.

It was a bitter lesson, but great schooling. I thrived on the intensity of the campaign, the incredible concentration of energy and resources on a single day's voting, the interplay of low-hitting hostilities and high-minded rhetoric. More than anything, I savored being a player—a combatant in the fray—not just a faceless name on the host committee of another predictable DC fundraiser.

There were also major statewide campaigns that '92 election year, including the re-election bids of George Bush and Bob Packwood. I had made solid inroads into the local Republican scene, but I hadn't paid enough dues to merit a leadership position on those campaigns. This didn't bother me, as I enjoyed the intimate scale of Bruce's legislative race and figured I'd have more chances in the next election cycle.

And frankly, I had found it hard to shake the ambivalence toward President Bush that dated back to his '80 bid for the White House. I had respect for him personally as a decent, honorable man who had compiled a fine record of public service and had shown great resolve in the Gulf War, but politically he seemed to have lost his way. He couldn't decide whether he was the Eastern Establishment, good-government moderate of his forebears or the Texas populist conservative of his later-in-life oilman persona. He sensed that social conservatives distrusted him because of his prep school/Yale/silver spoon heritage, which only made it more difficult for him to reconcile these divergent strains in his background. Rather than blazing his own trail, he waffled, which led to Patrick Buchanan's brutal assault from the right in the '92 primaries. I admired Buchanan as a withering commentator, but his candidacy took an awful toll on the President. Bush, of course, helped to dig his own grave by giving Buchanan a prime-time speaking slot at the Convention in Houston, which shamed the party with its anti-gay vitriol.

Despite, or perhaps because of, my relentless networking in the community and politics, I found it hard to get out and promote my play. The steady stream of rejection letters had taken its toll, and my confidence in the script had faltered. The rebels were still stuck somewhere between full-fledged characters and idealized types, and I decided to impose a moratorium on marketing and see if I couldn't flesh them out more fully. Somewhere between the crunch of billable hours and the escalating rounds of board and committee meetings, I tried to squeeze in time for revisions.

However, I could feel my theater identity slipping away. There had always been an element of opposition in my turning to theater: I'm not just a Stanford law student, I'm an actor. I'm not just an associate at a prestigious law firm, I'm a writer. But with the move to Portland, I felt less compelled to hold on to this maverick streak, as I had already set a bold course in leaving the comfort and status of Covington for my new role as a small city player.

And Amy was pregnant once again. She was already some five months along, and all signs were positive. Soon I would be adding fatherhood to my lengthy list of responsibilities; it seemed like there would be little time for playwriting or promoting. I was disappointed in myself, because I had come west with such resolve to pursue *Bodyhold*, but as hard as I was pushing in so many other areas I couldn't beat myself up too badly.

Then Amy miscarried again. We had decided to do amniocentesis because of her age and concerns about Down's Syndrome. Within days of the procedure, the baby's development stopped, and the doctors told us that the fetus would have to be removed from the womb. I felt a crushing, aching emptiness as I drove my wife to the hospital for this final indignity. Raising a family had been central to our conception of ourselves and our marriage. We had looked forward to playing out the traditional roles of parents of a prior generation: Amy as the devoted, stay-at-home mom and I as the man-in-the-dark-suit provider. These icons were now in pieces. After this third successive miscarriage, it looked as if we would never become parents.

We dug deep. We said the right things about remaining committed to one another come what may, and I think most of the time we meant them. But both of us faced the awful realization that the pretty family pictures we had painted in our heads when swearing to love, honor, and cherish were not the images likely to accompany us into middle age.

To counter the numbness I fell back on familiar comforts: the box scores, the bridge column, the morning run, the *South Seas* short stories of Somerset Maugham. To my surprise, I found I needed my play. Perhaps it was another form of opposition: I'm not just another childless professional, I'm a produced playwright. But I suspect it was something more, my grieving psyche seeking refuge in those idyllic rhythms of longhand creation by the banks of the Nile. I plunged into a reshaping of the rebels and soon had a script that I thought might be ready for the Portland market.

But month after disheartening month, I found that the Portland market did not appear ready for me. The Oregon style of rejection differed from DC, where artistic directors would not hesitate to tell you they had no time for or interest in your project (or simply would not respond at all). Portland theater types were more responsive, but decidedly more oblique: *there is some very promising writing here, maybe we could arrange a reading sometime in the future, you know we have a new play festival in the summer so by all means submit it then.* I would try to grab hold of these slender threads, only to find in each case that they spooled away.

I sought to modulate my pitch to suit the different cadence of the Northwest. I had discovered this difference in the office as well, where the intensity forged in competitive environments at Williams, Stanford, and Covington played well with the Ball Janik partners but less so with those beneath me in the firm pecking order. I gradually learned that quiet suggestions and subtle nudges were more likely to win friends and influence people in the Northwest than the full frontal assault I had practiced on the Eastern seaboard.

After these tantalizing leads for *Bodyhold* came to naught, I decided I had to join forces with a director to have any hope of being produced. I had learned through my networking that readings, not the cold call equivalent of sending an unsolicited script, were more likely to generate interest in a play. A reading presents a play in a mode much closer to performance than black typescript on a white page and shows that a director and some actors thought enough of the script to prepare it for an audience. But I had never directed, nor had any aspirations to, and I knew almost no actors in town.

One evening I took in a production of Christopher Fry's *The Lady's Not for Burning* at the second stage (called, a little naughtily, the "Blue Room") of the Portland Civic Theatre. I had heard of Fry's brilliant play, but had never had the chance to see it live. I was dazzled by the playwright's verbal facility—every bit the equal of the Shaw and Coward wordplay that had first turned my head in London a decade ago. I was impressed at how tightly the director had exercised control over his actors, who could have gone well over the top if left to their own devices, while allowing Fry's wondrous verse to shine. I flattered myself by thinking that a director who had the command of language to pull off this show could do a very nice job indeed with my play.

I made my way to the tattered and dreary lobby of the theater after the show, ready to display my newfound Portland-style capacity for gentle suasion. But as soon as I found the director, a soft-spoken giant of a man with a wispy beard and longish hair that suggested abiding youthful fancies, I reverted to my usual oral battery. I gushed on about the similarities between Fry's play and my own as the director—who had introduced himself as Robert Holden—stood there, cornered, a polite grin frozen on his face. Thankfully Mr. Holden had insufficient playwright avoidance skills to make a quick escape and was too kind not to share his address and phone number with me.

I dispatched the latest copy of the script to him and waited. And waited. I knew I had come on too strong in our first meeting, so like a high school swain angling for a date, I tried to play it as cool as I could. There were plenty of other potential directors in Portland, of course, but something had clicked at *The Lady's Not For Burning* that told me this was the guy. After several months, however, I had reached the limits of my cool. I called. He graciously acknowledged receiving the script, but no, he had not yet had time to read it. Would I call back in a few weeks? I did and was put off again and again.

This was intolerable. In DC I had put up with such treatment because I understood myself to be a nobody, just one of the horde of high-priced, big firm associates. But dammit, in Portland I was becoming a somebody. I was on the partnership track at a prestigious downtown firm logging big-time hours on acquisition after acquisition for our major client Crown Pacific. At Portland State I was introducing some of the alumni development practices that worked so well for Williams College in order to boost the university's anemic annual giving rate. At Waverly I was hard at work coming up with auction packages for their big yearly fundraiser. Our new team had breathed life into the moribund Williams alumni association. And I was a definite up-and-comer in local Republican circles.

Bob Holden was blissfully unaware of my lustrous résumé. My credentials and connections meant nothing to him. But he finally called to tell me that my script did. In a quiet, almost diffident voice, he said that he'd been struck with the fluency of my language and the bold twists of the plot. He, too, had struggled a little with the anchoring of the rebels, but he thought the project had promise and would be pleased to take whatever next step I had in mind.

We met several times at one another's homes and spent as much time learning about each other as we did discussing the script. Our backgrounds were radically different. His natural father had disappeared from view when he was young, and his mother, a brilliant but erratic commercial artist, had raised Bob and his two sisters alone. She moved the family incessantly, sometimes as often as five times a year. As Bob put it, whenever his mother ran out of ways to rearrange the furniture, she decided it was time to move on. Bob had attended over twenty-five grade schools and three high schools, all in and around the Portland metro area. He had managed to overcome these formidable obstacles to win a scholarship to Reed College—an outstanding liberal arts school in Portland—but had to drop out when the college lost the funding for his program. He had enrolled as a theater major at a local community college, where he'd met his wife. When their first of three sons arrived, he dropped out of school just short of his degree to get a job as a truck driver at the window and door manufacturer where his stepfather worked. After several years on the road, he was promoted and ended up running the entire trucking division for the company, with responsibility for some thirty drivers.

But theater was his passion, and he devoted his evenings and weekends to acting and later directing. He had started theater companies and seen others go down in flames. He had been in smash hits that extended for months and flops that drew audiences in the single digits. He had shared the stage with just about anyone who was anyone in Portland theater, including Lindsay Wagner (who went on to become the Bionic Woman). He had seen many friends leave town for Los Angeles or New York, and seen most of them come back again, disheartened. He had an inexhaustible store of war stories and a treasure trove of green room gossip.

He was also an incorrigible liberal verging on socialist. He had been to San Francisco in the halcyon days of the Summer of Love and had the tie-dyed shirts to prove it. He had been a Teamster in his early truck driving days, and though he now found himself on the other side of the collective bargaining table as a member of management, it was clear where his sympathies lay. He couldn't remember the last time he had voted Republican, and he remembered just about everything. It was good that we did not come to blows over politics, as Bob carried well over 300 pounds on a frame that was slightly over six feet.

Despite this odd coupling, we found a rhythm and decided to push the script in the direction of a staged reading, where *Body-hold* might finally attract the interest of a local company. Bob suggested the interim step of holding a few informal readings at my home with actors, but with no audience present. This would give me an opportunity to hear for the first time how trained voices gave life to my internal dialogue.

On the appointed Saturday morning, the actors arrived in our charmingly bourgeois living room, which featured original stenciling by Amy and antique furniture of undistinguished provenance but pleasing walnut and mahogany appearance. Uncertain as to the protocol for such events, we had laid out a tea and coffee service that would have done any Junior League hostess proud. I began the festivities with a modest welcoming speech that I thought was appreciative without being servile.

No one appeared to roll his eyes, but it may just have been that I could not see through the bloodshot. It was clear that these were strange surroundings and an unfamiliar hour to these slightly scruffy creatures of the night and the quicker we got on from me to my script, the better. Bob took charge, gave a few pointed directions, and off they went.

God, what a rush. The cast was uneven, and their command of the material halting, but that morning they made my work tangible—work that after five years of non-presentation had seemed consigned to the ether. The repartee among the Pudgethorpe family members positively sang at times, and the actors laughed out loud at places I had hoped an audience would. Our living room was transformed from a conventional middle-class repository of our finer things to a chamber bewitched, bursting with wit and élan. And I, for perhaps the first time ever, felt like a real artist, not simply a slumming lawyer poser.

There was no shortage of constructive criticism from the departing cast members as they gulped down their third cup of coffee and took their leave. There were plenty of misfires noted on my ever-present yellow legal pad. But both Bob and I came away with the sense that we had something worth our time and attention.

I massaged the script in parts, broke it up and gave it a thorough hammering in others. We reconvened the core group of actors for a second reading, with the inevitable last-minute dropouts and substitutions. This second session was less exultant for me than the first but also more fruitful, as my ear was better attuned to the modulations of the actors, who in turn were more in sync with the script.

Bob and I decided after the second round of script revision that we were ready for a public reading. Bob had worked on and off for years with a hazard-prone but indestructible Portland theater impresario named Guy Peter Oakes, who ran a shoestring company called Paula Productions (allegedly named after a long departed girlfriend). Guy had been dogged for years by rumors of sexual indiscretions with those beneath the age of legal consent and had been in and out of a number of dingy, nondescript performance spaces. But he was a true-blue champion of new work and always open to making room for readings in his schedule. I knew I could go out and rent a more upscale venue, but I was concerned that would just make me look like some rich lawyer trying to buy notice for his little play (and on my over two-thirds reduced household income, I little felt like a rich lawyer in any event). I could have tried to suck up to the artistic directors of one of the more prestigious companies in town to see whether they would agree to host the reading, but I'd been trying to get a seat near the popular girls in the classroom of Portland theater for two years and thought that my luck was unlikely to change. Paula Productions it was.

Casting the staged reading was chaotic. It had been relatively easy for Bob to prevail on old theater buddies for the odd Saturday session at my home, but a staged reading called for some degree of preparation. Readings are often scheduled on Monday evenings, as all theaters are dark then and actors have no performance conflicts, but we hoped to make a bigger splash than we thought could be achieved on a Monday. Actors are not generally compensated for readings—at least in markets the size of Portland—and usually do them because they think it might land them a hot part, they're looking for exposure, or they're friends with the writer, director, or someone in the cast. None of these reasons will get in the way of a good paying gig, however, as we found to our chagrin. We lost body after body as better opportunities came along. We had a wonderful Pudgethorpe, though, an actual Englishman who was a senior executive at Hewlett Packard by day and the closest thing the Northwest had to Alec Guinness by night.

As the audience filed in for the first of two readings scheduled on successive weekend evenings, I shuddered at how mismatched the Paula Productions seats were and how the lights looked more like a tacky, luau-themed beach party than a true theater setting. But my parents had flown in from Chicago, and I had imposed on a few bemused Republican friends, so I flashed a hearty grin and made them welcome. Tasteful invitations had gone out to artistic directors and producers all over town. While I didn't recognize any of them in the modest crowd, I hoped that was because the circle of my acquaintance in Portland had simply not extended far enough.

But damn, we gave them a show. Pudgethorpe was charming and self-possessed. Wilkinson was frightfully earnest. One of the maids—a bluesy black woman with a booming voice that I later learned made her one of the leading vocalists in town—brought a sass and a brass to the scenes with the Pudgethorpe women that I'd never imagined. The audience gave a resounding ovation. My mother was in tears. I couldn't wait for the next night.

I should have. The chemistry had somehow altered. Lines that had been proven winners the evening before fell fatally flat. The rhythm of the cast, so steady and composed the first night, flailed and lurched. It was the same script, in the same venue, with the same actors, but it was as if the beautifully wrapped gift that had been handed to me the first performance had been repackaged in an ill-fitting box with ripped second-hand tissue paper. And again, there was no sign of theater world VIPs.

Bob, the sage veteran, told me that the second evening's performance had actually been much stronger in places and that some cheap mugging had resulted in laughs the first night that were not worth holding on to. He declared himself well pleased and pronounced the script very close to performance level.

I returned to my familiar posture by the phone. I gave it a few weeks to let word of mouth about the readings take the ambling, coffee-stained path of Portland buzz. Then months. I summoned the courage to call a few of the leading lights and ask whether they had heard about the reading. No one had, although some agreed to take another look at the script. It was as if all our fevered preparations had never taken place.

# OVERT HOSTILITIES

The contrast between my nocturnal bohemian labors and my daytime conventional exploits was stark. I was becoming a caricature of the young man in a hurry, but I was doing exactly what I had set out to do and was determined to keep right on doing it. I had ridden the Crown Pacific wave to an IPO, targeted for late '94, on which I would be a key player. I had also started to develop a niche practice working with developers who were converting old warehouses into mixed-use condominium projects in a former industrial district chicly dubbed the "Pearl District." I was up for partner soon, and things looked very promising.

My efforts to boost annual giving at PSU had led to an officer position on the board. I learned there was a natural progression to these appointments, and I might even be considered for the presidency of the foundation in a few years. Waverly and Williams had taken something of a back seat to PSU because of my new officer role, but I was still hard at work on both.

Just as I had hoped, I was swept into some higher profile campaigns in the '94 primary election cycle. One of my friends had decided to run for Congress in Oregon's First District, a seat that the Republicans had lost in the wake of Watergate and had been trying to recapture for twenty years. The key to success in the district was winning the western Portland suburbs, which featured educated, prosperous soccer-mom families with an independent streak. Republicans had consistently rejected centrist, pro-choice candidates in contested primaries and nominated social conservatives who scared off these crucial swing voters.

My friend Cleve Larson seemed the perfect moderate candidate and was inordinately lucky to boot. He had won a multi-million dollar prize in the Oregon lottery some years before, which— added to his other assets of a beautiful wife, athletic build, and glib tongue—seemed to make him a potent candidate. He drew as his main opponent a dour lawyer turned photocopier salesman named Bill Witt who sported a perpetual, Nixonesque five o'clock shadow. Witt, a religious conservative, had briefly muscled into the '92 primary and then disappeared amidst rumors of a business-related scandal in Washington state.

I had learned from the Bruce Davis campaign not to let negative opportunities pass us by, so I volunteered to see what, if anything, there was to this scandal. I had learned a little about the Freedom of Information Act (FOIA) in my CIA days and knew that each state had an equivalent statute. I filed the Washington version of an FOIA request and to my astonishment was sent a file of over 1,500 pages. I hunkered down over numerous affidavits and interviews given by former employees of Witt's company, all of which demonstrated that his firm, Wittco Systems, had systematically sold or leased used photocopiers as "new" and "slightly used" photocopiers that were in fact ancient. They had used the age-old used car salesman trick of rolling back the odometer (called the totalizer in the copier trade). To compound their sins, Wittco Systems had sold the hapless customers lucrative maintenance contracts that minted money for the company once the machines began their inevitable breakdown. Even worse, they had targeted unsuspecting nonprofit organizations, in many cases churches.

After receiving numerous complaints, the Washington Attorney General's office had launched an investigation of Wittco Systems that resulted in a consent decree against the company and a hefty civil penalty. As is typical in these cases, the company had admitted no wrongdoing, but the voluminous file painted a damning picture and strongly suggested that Witt—the President and CEO of this modest-sized private firm—was well aware of what had gone on.

Even to a jaded Chicagoan weaned on a steady diet of Daley machine corruption, this was bad stuff—particularly in Oregon, a state celebrated for its squeaky-clean, good-government image. I genuinely believed that a man with this sort of tainted business background had no business running for major office. I set about what I thought would be the easy task of enlisting the aid of the media to inform the electorate. While Cleve approved each step I took, I wanted to do this work myself, as I thought that if the finger were pointed by my candidate it would be easier to dismiss as negative campaigning. I prepared a well-packaged presentation with an executive summary and tabs for the key affidavits and interviews and made appointments with Portland's major newspaper, the *Oregonian*, and the leading independent weekly, *Willamette Week*. Republicans tended to savage the *Oregonian* as a lazy, aimless publication whose monopoly position gave it little incentive to challenge the liberal-tinged status quo of the metro area, but I was new at this game and couldn't believe they would pass on such a compelling story.

They did. The political reporter with whom I met, Jeff Mapes, asked if I were connected with any of the other Republican primary campaigns. When I said that I was, a smug, we-know-your-type look came over his face. I urged him to let the facts of Washington state's file speak for themselves, but never heard from him again and saw nothing in the paper. *Willamette Week*, who made few bones about its progressive editorial ideology, was admirably candid. They might take a look at the story if Witt won the primary, but they had little interest in a contested Republican primary. I took this to mean that they would not be heartbroken if a flawed nominee came out of the Republican primary, but the effect—no coverage—was the same either way.

I tried the news departments of the major television network affiliates, but this wasn't sufficiently bite-sized for them. My only taker was Lars Larson, the reporter and producer of the lone investigative reporting show in town, *Northwest Reports*. I met with Lars (no relation to my candidate Cleve) over breakfast, and he was the first media person to express any of the moral outrage I felt about Witt's candidacy. He agreed to take it on.

I had already been in contact with some of the former Wittco employees who had given statements to the Washington Attorney General's office and got back in touch to let them know that *Northwest Reports* might want to interview them. In a matter of hours after making these follow-up contacts, I received a call from someone identifying himself as Bill Witt's lawyer, threatening to sue me for libel, defamation, slander, and a few other ominous causes of action if I continued this vile character assassination. I was shaken by the call, the first of its kind I had ever received, but managed indignantly to answer, "Truth is a defense," and slam down the phone.

Witt put similar heat on Channel 12, the local station that aired *Northwest Reports*. They capitulated, allowing Witt and his wife to give a nauseating version of Nixon's "Checkers" speech as a rebuttal at the end of the segment (though Witt refused to be interviewed on camera by Lars Larson). This diluted the impact of the piece and gave the Witts the last word. Cleve and I knew that *Northwest Reports* was hardly a household name around Portland, but hoped that the story's appearance on television would embolden others, in particular the *Oregonian*, to pick up the gauntlet.

It did, but with a result diametrically opposed to the one we had sought. One of the *Oregonian's* columnists, a curmudgeonly sportswriter turned political gadfly named Steve Duin, decided to do a piece on negative campaigning and selected Cleve and me as Exhibit A. Duin lambasted us as "kneecappers" and portrayed Witt as the party wronged. It was absurdly off-base, but the damage was done. The only negatives that stuck were to Cleve's campaign, although as it turned out it hardly mattered. Another centrist had joined the race, splitting the moderate vote and handing the nomination to Witt, who managed to lose the general election, despite '94 turning out to be a tsunami-like high-water mark for Republicans. Cleve and I commiserated, but I did not unlearn my earlier lesson about the value of negative campaigning. In the future, however, I would know not to rely on the media to do my dirty work for me.

My other campaign involvement in the '94 cycle was more high-minded. Craig Berkman, the now former state party chair who had taken me under his wing after I arrived in Portland, had decided to make a run for governor. He recruited me to join a policy squad that would develop a far-reaching and innovative platform. I researched a proposal to privatize elements of the state's highway maintenance operations, following a model that had realized great savings in British Columbia. I also explored whether a Connecticut program that invested a small portion of the state's public employee pension fund in local emerging companies might be feasible in Oregon. This was classic reformist, good government Republicanism, particularly the highway maintenance program that went after a bloated bureaucracy. I earnestly ventured hither and yon—legal pad in hand—interviewing experts and making our case.

My efforts were to be combined with the work of a dozen others who were laboring on all parts of the policy spectrum and then presented to the media in a series of position papers with weighty names like "Oregon's Economic Future." What actually happened was the burying of this genteel endeavor in an orgy of mud-slinging over a publication called the *T&A Times*. Our opponent in the primary, a former congressman named Denny Smith, had made his money as the publisher of a group of newspapers, one of which was an esteemed guide to the region's sex clubs. Berkman considered this sleazy rag to be fair game considering Smith's pandering to religious conservatives, but the result was an avalanche of criticism directed at Berkman for negative campaigning. Berkman's positive agenda sank beneath the mud, and he was soundly trounced by Smith in the primary.

Three contested Republican primaries, three losing candidates. I was hardly proving to be a juggernaut in the trenches, but at least I had been battle-tested. I had also learned how to have a little fun in politics courtesy of an Oregon tradition called Dorchester. This annual political conference/variety show/weekend booze bash on Oregon's northern coast was started by Bob Packwood and then taken over by moderate stalwarts intent on dominance at the grassroots. The hallmark of the conference is the debating of a handful of resolutions by the 500 or so registered delegates—each of whom is assigned to one of over thirty tables in a single bunting-festooned hall. Aged Social Security recipients sit cheek by jowl with oily state legislators and peach-fuzzed high schoolers during the often feisty debates, which are prefaced by issue advocates laying out pro and con arguments on each resolution and concluded by an up-or-down vote. In between the debates are flowery speeches by invited dignitaries, which have included the likes of Ronald Reagan, George Bush, and Bob Dole. On Saturday night after a cheesy pasta dinner there is a "tent show" featuring sketches and songs that range from the sublimely hilarious to the shockingly awful. And all along there is the throbbing pulse of solicitation, whether of campaign volunteers or motel room flings. It is all that is best and worst in politics.

My introduction to Dorchester had come via a board member friend, who asked whether I would be willing to serve as an issue advocate. I moronically agreed without bothering to ask what the topic was. I soon learned that I would be taking the religious conservative side of Measure 9, a gay-bashing initiative that any right-thinking person I knew, Republican or Democrat, adamantly opposed. My "friend" hastened to assure me that issue advocates were introduced with the caveat that the views they presented were not necessarily their own, but I found that cold comfort when my rhetorical gifts won me votes in the single digits of hundreds cast on the resolution. Apparently this was some sort of hazing ritual, as shortly thereafter I was asked to join the Dorchester board—giving me license to unleash all my pent-up thespian energy in manic tent show skits.

This was my only theater-related outlet. *Bodyhold* continued to languish. I would have an occasional conversation along familiar lines, some summer new play festival or local playwriting competition, but it was all I could do to feign enthusiasm. Every once in a while I would run into somebody who had been at or in the reading at Paula Productions and get a nice ego boost as they praised the work. But I had no more tricks in my bag and no other obvious options for bringing the play to the attention of the world at large. I was pretty much prepared to consign the script to oblivion and stick to lawyering, politicking, and all purpose ladder-climbing.

And, thank God, fathering. We had found a new reproductive specialist who diagnosed scarring of the uterine wall as the reason for Amy's miscarriages. He performed a procedure to remove the scar tissue, and Amy had become pregnant again almost immediately. This one had been trouble-free. Our son Graham had arrived in the summer of '93. We rejoiced not just in the triumph over misfortune, but in at long last attaining the hoped for roles of nurturer and hunter/gatherer.

I made partner at Ball Janik, effective at the beginning of '95. This was of course tremendous news, but it served to concentrate my mind vividly on the fate of *Bodyhold*. Many associates view partnership as a terminal event, an ascension to some sort of mahogany-paneled heaven where all of the pinstriped paradise dwellers float on essentially the same plane. I knew better. Up until that time I had been judged primarily on the work I had done for others' clients. I knew that Ball Janik, like many law firms, re-cut the pie each year and that the size of my slice would depend largely on revenues from clients that I myself had generated. I knew that there could be huge disparities between the compensation of one partner and another. I was not terrified at the prospect, as my eager beavering around town had been making me just the sort of contacts that could translate into clients. But it was a new and pitiless game that would leave less time for theater than was now possible in my already frenetic schedule.

# ON BROADWAY

I suddenly, strangely sensed the same desperate urgency about the play that I'd felt prior to joining Covington. I had to act now, or this project would never come to pass. I had never viewed writing *Bodyhold* as an academic exercise, and I knew I would always consider a never-produced play to be a crushing failure. I didn't want to end up as some lined and doddering old lawyer who pulled out a yellowing script from time to time to show his grandchildren.

Bob Holden and I had fumed in our cups about the gutlessness of the local artistic directors, damning them all to hell and threatening to produce the play ourselves. I don't think we ever took ourselves seriously, though. I had been on the fringes of producing—from watching Marc Fajer pull together those brave plays at Stanford to mounting the public reading at Paula Productions—and the producer's job had seemed a massive and thankless undertaking.

I saw little choice, however. The only other alternative was to approach a local company and offer to write them a big check to underwrite the production, and that seemed tacky and artless. I sat down with Bob and started—in my best corporate lawyer manner—a long checklist on a legal pad.

The biggest challenge would be finding a venue. Portland suffered from an acute shortage of theater spaces, and those on the market were already in heavy use. I found no decent prospects for anything affordable that was available for more than a scattered week or two. We didn't know exactly how long we would run the show, but we figured that if we were going to go through all the trouble of putting on a full-length production we didn't want to close it down after a week.

I hit on the notion of using a hotel. It occurred to me that hotels had conference rooms that were in active use by day but were often empty at night and on weekends. I started making the rounds of the downtown Portland establishments: the Heathman, the Governor, the Hilton, the Riverplace. It was a peculiar rush trolling the corridors of these familiar settings in my lawyer's double-breasted suit in search not of a meeting place but of a home for my play. The truly desirable rooms in the hotels were the banquet facilities, with their high ceilings and unobstructed sightlines, but these were in constant use for evening events and were priced accordingly. Anything in our price range always seemed to have a catch: an access door whose position in the room would not work for actor entrances and exits, a column right in the middle of the space, or a location right across from the kitchen that would make for great catering but too much clattering.

I finally made my way to the Benson, one of the city's grand old hotels, best known for hosting visiting Presidents and for its magnificent paneled lobby. Ball Janik usually held its holiday party in the hotel's stunning Crystal Ballroom, but I knew that would be out of our league. To my surprise, I found in the lower level of the hotel a suite of four connected meeting rooms for some reason called the Parliament Rooms (though they would have been suitable for only the lowliest of backbenchers). They were separated by retractable partitions rather than actual walls; the whole space (roughly seventy-five feet in length by twenty-five feet in width) could be opened up into one large area. Because every room could be set up as its own individual meeting space, there was a separate door to the adjoining corridor serving each room, which created all sorts of entrance and exit possibilities. The ceiling height was cramped at eight feet, but Bob thought this was workable.

We plotted and schemed. Bob devised the ingenious space plan of presenting the action mostly in Parliament Room 3, with the audience seated on either side in Rooms 2 and 4. Parliament Room 1 would be the only room with its partition left intact and would be used as the green room for actors and equipment storage. The audience would enter from the common corridor to the west of the suite through the door of Room 4, and the door of Room 3 would be the primary entrance/exit for the actors. It was improvised and improbable, but it would work.

Now we had to persuade the hotel. Thankfully, one of Ball Janik's clients was part of the ownership group at the Benson, and he agreed to put in a good word. It also turned out that my mentor Karen Hinsdale, through her years in the wine industry, knew the head of the hotel's catering operation and offered to set up a meeting. It all seemed amazingly fortuitous, but it struck me that these were just the types of connections I thought a smaller city would afford when I decided to leave DC for the western provinces.

The catering chief was a huge fan of theater and said he would love to see a play produced in the hotel. I told him of our plans (as yet nowhere close to realized) to bring in a number of groups, who may well need the services of their catering department.

The Benson would, of course, enjoy all our concession business, which could be brisk because the hotel would allow patrons to bring drinks—however stiff—into the show.

We worked out a deal for a six-week run of four performances per week for a total of $2,000. The hotel would consider reducing their charge depending on the amount of catering business we created. They would provide seating platforms and chairs that their staff would set up and take down. I had originally hoped to open in late '94, prior to the deluge of partnership, but November and December were two of the hotel's busiest catering months so we agreed to push our opening back until early '95. They also had sound and lighting equipment, but it was clear we would need to arrange for some outside rentals.

We had a theater, makeshift though it was. Now we needed some actors—ten, to be exact. Bob was far less concerned on this score. He had acted and directed in Portland for over thirty years and said he was continually amazed at the level of acting for a city of its size. I refrained from commenting that he had never lived anywhere else and so had little basis for comparison, but I, too, had been impressed by the caliber of much of the work I'd seen around town. My question was whether quality actors would be prepared to work outside the familiar contours of an established company in an improvised venue on what might appear to be some lawyer's vanity project.The first returns were not encouraging. We contacted the Englishman who had played Pudgethorpe at the Paula Productions reading. He was perfectly charming, but passed on the opportunity without giving much of an explanation. This hurt, as he knew the script and seemed to imply he didn't have much confidence in it. He was a recognized name in the local theater world and would have nicely anchored our cast.

We decided to hold open auditions requiring a single prepared monologue. We ran a notice for several weeks in the "Call Board" section of the *Oregonian*, a free casting call and audition posting that appeared each Tuesday. It was nice to be in the paper as something other than a "kneecapper." For the auditions we used a no-frills photography studio on the edge of downtown owned by a fellow Dorchester Conference board member. We did no pre-screening of our auditioners, which meant we attracted a range of talent that would have put *American Idol*™ to shame. We had pimply teenagers being squired by obvious stage mothers, superannuated pensioners barely able to wheeze their way through a monologue, macho men in leather who seemed to be doing this on a dare from their girlfriends, and lots and lots of pretty women in their twenties and thirties. The most memorable of these was a blonde who began her audition by vomiting what appeared to be a coagulation of Milk Duds onto the floor of the studio. She proceeded without missing a beat into her audition piece, which she concluded by smoothly sweeping up the Milk Dud residue—with a soft apology for the mess—and sashayed out the door. If the purpose of an audition were to be remembered, she succeeded beyond measure.

We were ready to cast the daughter, Nancy, and the maids many times over, and we had some decent candidates for Rita, the assistant Wilkinson, and the younger rebels. It was the older men—Pudgethorpe and the two older rebels—who left us wringing our hands. Bob said that many actors in this age bracket were accustomed to being called for parts rather than suffering the indignity of open audition cattle calls. He pledged to start working the phones. I fretted.

As the corporate lawyer on the production team, the business end of things was my responsibility. I had no intention of pulling any money out of the show—even if the colossally improbable should occur and we were to end up in the black—so setting up a nonprofit seemed the sensible way to proceed. That would enable good-hearted friends and family members to achieve tax deductibility if they chose to contribute to the show. Filing for nonprofit status required a company, however, and a company required a name, which Bob and I had given no thought to. After weeks of deliberation, he claimed to have emerged from the shower one morning with the clever moniker CoHo Productions, a play on both our surnames (Cole and Holden). The Coho salmon is an icon in the Northwest, which prompted concern that we might be confused with a fish market, but he was persistent and had been good enough to put my name first. I could come up with nothing better. CoHo Productions it was.

We took our nonprofit mission seriously. Because of my involvement at Portland State, we decided to hold a special benefit preview performance that would help endow an English Department scholarship. Additionally, Bob lived in the Portland suburb of Gresham, home to many families of limited means who did not have the resources to attend professional theater. We set out to raise enough money to bring a class of Gresham High School students to the show, which we would then follow with a classroom discussion of the play.

We decided that if we were fortunate enough to make money, everyone involved in the production would receive a share of the net proceeds on top of the modest amount budgeted for each actor or technical specialist. I decreed that Bob would have a triple share because of his longtime commitment to the project, and Bob and I felt that the stage manager in a ten-actor production was deserving of a double share. I found it was easy to hand out shares when there seemed no prospect of their having any value.

Bob managed to land some veteran Portland warhorses to play the older rebels. He also came across a couple who he thought could handle Rupert and Rita Pudgethorpe. There were, however, ominous clouds hanging over this would-be Mr. Pudgethorpe, who had once been a prominent Portland actor and had then—for reasons unclear—fallen on hard times. His significant other had not acted in years, although Bob said she had been quite good in her prime. They did not appear to be in danger of eclipsing Spencer Tracy and Katharine Hepburn, but we were short on both options and time.

Now that we had a cast, we needed a place to rehearse. I prevailed on a Ball Janik client who had a vacant ground floor retail space in a downtown office building. The space featured lovely storefront windows, which meant that our rehearsals were on display for the patrons of the bus stop located directly in front of the building. This led to some unfortunate confusion, particularly in those scenes where the actors brandish guns and swords. We finally had to post a sign in the window that stated this was just a theater rehearsal and asked people not to call 911.

I was astounded at how infectious this "Gee, kids, let's put on a show" spirit proved to be. I had approached my parents and a handful of good friends about each donating $100 to CoHo. This would reserve them seats for an opening night "gala" (designer gowns were in short supply and Joan Rivers was nowhere to be seen) and land them on the do-gooders list in our program. Each of these supporters had suggested contacting several others, and before we opened some sixty people had contributed at the $100 level. Ball Janik agreed to buy the house for an evening (although I was petrified at the prospect of my partners seeing the play), as did a Republican group, and we organized a night out at the theater for the local Williams alumni association. The one notable exception to our record of fundraising success came in the public domain. We applied for a grant from the Regional Arts & Culture Council, the area government arts funding source, but had a miserable experience. We found that they catered to the more established companies and would not give a grassroots start-up like us the time of day.

I knew that a stable of contributors and presold groups were a nice boost, but they could not compensate for a lousy show. Rehearsals were maddeningly erratic. Mr. Pudgethorpe was rising nicely above his troubled past, but his significant other was a nightmare: moody, unresponsive to direction, and completely lacking in confidence. Three weeks prior to opening Bob was ready to let her go. We thought we could replace her, but had no idea whether Mr. Pudgethorpe would follow her out the door as a matter of household solidarity. Bob tried one last heart-to-heart with her, with miraculous results. Almost overnight she blossomed and within a week it was as if she had been born to play the part. I asked Bob whether he had threatened bodily harm or demanded sexual favors in his last-ditch session with her, but he declined to elaborate on the tricks of the directorial trade.

With the cast finally hitting on all cylinders, we waited for the set to appear. Our requirements were modest, as the audience was seated on two sides of the action, leaving only the two end walls to be designed. As the plot shifted back and forth between the Pudgethorpe home and the rebel den, Bob hit on the resourceful notion of a reversible panel system with the suggestion of an elegant drawing room on one side and a crude outbuilding on the other. Our set designer, an amiable recent theater graduate with an uncomfortably short design pedigree, kept putting off the date for delivery of the final panel system. With only forty-eight hours before the opening, he finally pulled up at the Benson in a borrowed pick-up truck. His work product was not only not what we had discussed, it was laughably inept. A prosperous expatriate family would not have wiped their posteriors in the room of his design, let alone have used it as a drawing room.

My wife, toting our then twenty-month-old son and pregnant with a second child due that fall, rode to the rescue, deploying her interior design training to redesign the set. She replaced the execrable painting job with stylish wallpaper, hammered on tasteful mouldings, and added a few other elegant touches. The key furniture pieces were plundered from our own living room. It took until the afternoon of our opening, but we finally had a set worthy of the name.

The casting headaches, the rehearsal agonies, the last-minute technical disasters—these are the oldest of theater clichés, and I had seen them all in my inglorious career as an actor. I was not so arrogant as to think that I would be entirely spared the wrath of the theater gods, but I thought I might avoid a few of the usual pitfalls. I don't think we missed one.

But the flipside of those clichés is that somehow, in some way, the show vaults over these insurmountable obstacles and is ineffably sprinkled with the fairy dust of theater. The kinetic charge that had surged through my pen in the moody coffeehouses of Prague and the Nile-side watering holes of Aswan crackled through the unprepossessing confines of the Parliament Rooms and transformed them into a charmed chamber of the arts. Ovations resounded, critics praised, partners gushed, drinks flowed. The hotel made so much off of catering that they waived our fee. *Willamette Week* made us a "Pick of the Week." We even survived a police raid. A passing hotel patron heard a gunshot and, not bothering to read the notices posted on the door, dashed off to call the cops. Many of our cast and crew made more on *Bodyhold* than they had ever earned in theater. I kicked in my share to the common pot, as I'd realized returns far beyond what I'd ever imagined. The play was nominated for a Drammy (Portland's version of the Tony Awards) for Best Original Play; although we didn't win, the cast turned out in force for the awards ceremony to provide me with my first-ever entourage. It finally occurred to us that the address of the Benson was 309 SW Broadway: damned if we hadn't opened on Broadway!

Throughout the entire six weeks of rapturous delirium, I plied my lawyer's trade by day (mostly digging out from the rubble of Crown Pacific's IPO in December of '94), then headed to the theater for every performance to work the box office (it struck me as unpardonable extravagance to actually hire someone to run credit cards and take tickets.) I don't know that I will ever recapture the snap in my step as I closed down my practice for the day and swaggered the half mile of downtown high rise-lined pavement to my hit show. It was the sweetest of double lives. My wife indulged me as I made more than my share of after-show drinking sessions with the cast and crew.

And still I felt that the actors inhabited a world apart from mine. I was not prepared to renounce the trappings of my comfortable professional life: the healthy income, the partner's office, the ministrations of my secretary, the sleek suits. This was to be my last hurrah in the realm of the bohemian. There were no other plays in me bursting to get out. Even if there were, the demands I'd placed upon myself as husband, father, partner, civic pillar, and politico left little opportunity for artful expression.

Admiring audience members would come up to Bob and me after each performance and ask what was next for CoHo Productions. When we gave our pat reply that the company had been formed to produce just this one show, we'd be met with this incredulous stare as if to say: "What sort of performer has no encore?"

# INNER CIRCLE

Despite the acclaim for *Bodyhold*, Oregon was more captivated by a taut drama starring its junior Republican senator, Bob Packwood. It turned out that, just prior to his '92 reelection bid, the *Washington Post* had been sniffing at his door regarding reports of sexual harassment. Packwood and his chief of staff, Elaine Franklin, had managed to stave off any reporting until after his narrow victory, but then the floodgates opened. More than twenty-five women accused Packwood of unsolicited fondling, groping, kissing, and sexual misconduct over a period of several decades. Packwood—who had once been the darling of the women's movement because of his progressive views and hiring and promotion of women in his Senate office—became the target of demonstrations and resignation demands by the National Organization of Women (and Oregon's greatest contribution to late-night talk show palaver since Tonya Harding and cronies went after Nancy Kerrigan during the '94 Winter Olympics).

Oregon political circles are small, and I knew Bob Packwood reasonably well. He was the godfather of Dorchester, which now faced a ticklish problem because of his connection with the conference. The Dorchester board heard that prominent speakers were shying away from addressing Dorchester because of concerns over Packwood's political radioactivity. We entered into delicate negotiations with the Senator's staff to preserve a role for him at the conference without ruining our prospects for a marquee keynote speaker.

There was no question that Packwood's political enemies in Oregon piled on when they smelled blood. But there was also little doubt that the Senator contributed to his own demise by choosing to attack his accusers. America loves repentant titans, and had he admitted to inappropriate sexual behavior due to a problem with alcohol, he might well have been able to ride out the scandal. His refusal to show contrition finally led his own colleagues to turn on him, and he resigned in the fall of '95 after the Senate Ethics Committee voted for his expulsion.

Packwood's resignation and the resulting special election in January '96 touched off a chaotic scramble among Oregon politicians. Hatfield and Packwood had enjoyed a stranglehold on the state's Senate seats since the sixties; a vacancy presented an opportunity of massive dimensions. It had been widely rumored that Hatfield would not run for reelection in the fall of '96, so there had already been some jockeying for position, but the special election forced prospective contenders to show their hands.

My man was Gordon Smith. I had come to know Gordon through one of my best friends, Oregon's Republican boy wonder Dan Lavey. Dan was one of those preternaturally astute, twenty going on fifty wunderkinds that one meets more frequently in politics than in probably any other field. He was managing campaigns in high school and college at an age when most guys are thinking only of kegs and bra straps. He knew the basic political dynamics of every one of Oregon's thirty-six counties. He had an impish grin, a premature potbelly, and a precocious penchant for mixed drinks.

As a staffer for the Republican leadership in the Oregon Senate in the early nineties, Dan had recruited a wealthy young businessman named Gordon Smith from the rural town of Pendleton to run for the State Senate. Gordon was a natural. He'd been born to the political game: Gordon's father had been a high-ranking agriculture official in the Eisenhower Administration before turning lobbyist, and he had raised Gordon and his many siblings in the Washington, DC suburbs. Gordon was related through his mother to the legendary Udall family of Arizona, which had placed Morris, Stewart, and others in the national political spotlight. Gordon had trained as a lawyer but then returned to Oregon to revive the family's frozen food company, which had fallen on hard times. He had looks, brains, money, a lovely wife, and a nice story about restoring the fortunes of his father's small business.

Gordon quickly rose to become the President of the Oregon Senate. He secured his rural base but wisely chose to take leadership positions on issues, such as the light rail, that would bring him to the attention of Portland. His sage political decisions were no accident. My friend Dan (after a brief stint in the investment business) decided to return to his natural domain and hitched his wagon to Gordon's star as the Senate President's chief of staff.

While Gordon could have used the extra time and preparation permitted by a race in the next cycle, he was head and shoulders above any other Republican candidate and breezed to victory in the primary. His opponent in the special election was a Democratic congressman named Ron Wyden, who was widely regarded in Republican circles as the idiot savant of Oregon politics. Though rarely articulate, Wyden possessed an uncanny knack for landing on the right side of an issue and an unerring ability to get in front of a television camera. He had started his political career as an activist for the elderly and developed a loyal base that turned out to vote.

Wyden was no pushover, and Gordon—for all his natural gifts—had some serious political liabilities. He was from east of the Cascade Mountains in a state where most of the population resided on the west side in the Willamette Valley and viewed eastern Oregonians as uneducated bumpkins. He was pro-life in one of the most pro-choice states in the union. He was an active Mormon in a state with one of the lowest churchgoing rates in the country and where Mormonism was still viewed as vaguely cultish and bizarre. Mormons had ventured west from Utah and made great inroads in the neighboring state of Idaho but were not yet a force to be reckoned with in Oregon.

I still considered myself pro-choice, and my only interaction with Mormons had been a high school choral teacher who used to go on a bit apocalyptically about the year's supply of canned foods he kept in his basement, but I'd been very impressed with Gordon. The special election seemed a great chance to both help my friend and get in on the ground floor of a U.S. Senate campaign. I signed on for Gordon's finance committee and soon came up with the novel idea of screening the old Frank Capra classic, *Mr. Smith Goes to Washington*, for a campaign event. This appealed to my producer instincts and also promised to be more fun than the usual fundraising routine of stale hors d'oeuvres in tired hotel suites. We rented the old Aladdin Theater in Southeast Portland (which I learned after we'd signed the contract had once been notorious for showing the X-rated Linda Lovelace classic *Deep Throat*) and recruited a good host committee. The event did nicely, and as the organizer-in-chief I had the privilege of introducing Gordon, whose angular earnestness recalled the Jimmy Stewart of that era.

Dan and I had been comedy sketch partners for several years at the Dorchester Tent Show. Dan recruited me to write some jokes for Gordon's appearance at an annual event called Hacks and Flacks, which featured area politicians and media types squaring off in a roast format for the benefit of the Portland Public School Foundation. This was a non-partisan event, but it was the darling of the Portland liberal establishment and was not a friendly crowd for Republicans. I was no professional joke writer, but I knew that the most effective humor for a politician managed to poke fun at his electoral liabilities. I figured it was time to come up with my first ever Mormon jokes. "It was not easy growing up Mormon in the sixties," I had Gordon say. "The rest of you had your heroes—Bob Dylan, John Lennon, Jimi Hendrix. All we could manage was…Donny Osmond." And: "I wish I had done my mission after John Belushi and Dan Aykroyd came along. Nowadays if you wear a white shirt and a dark suit and say you're on a mission from God, they think you're a Blues Brother."

This material didn't have Mel Brooks or Carl Reiner quaking in his boots, but it wasn't bad for a Senate race in Oregon. Gordon loved the jokes, which got a decent reception at the event. Oddly, the experience gave me the first sensation I'd had in a long time of being a clever Jew among Gentiles. Oregon didn't have much of a Jewish population to speak of, and almost all the Jews I came across were Democrats (including our opponent Ron Wyden). It was clearly unusual to be a Jew in Oregon Republican circles, but to date most of my political work—opposition research, position papers, grassroots door-knocking—didn't implicate religious stereotypes. But writing jokes for a photogenic Christian candidate made me feel a little like Morrie Amsterdam on the old *Dick Van Dyke Show*, and while I enjoyed the attention, I didn't much care for the role.

Gordon and Dan devised a campaign right out of the national Republican playbook, focusing on Gordon's background as a successful businessman and pledging to run government like a business. This contrasted nicely with the lackluster private sector credentials of Wyden but ran into trouble when environmental groups aired a series of independent ads—mostly in the Portland area—which showed gritty footage of pollution at Gordon's frozen food plant. Wyden belatedly denounced these outside expenditures but did nothing to stop the ads, which took an awful toll despite their exaggerations of Gordon's environmental record. Gordon threw some two million of his own money into the campaign to try to undo the damage, but it was too late. Oregonians had no trouble electing politicians with modest private sector backgrounds (Hatfield, Packwood, and former governor and Portland mayor Neil Goldschmidt were obvious examples), and given a choice between a dorky career pol and a businessman with a seemingly dirty environmental record, they chose Wyden by a very narrow margin. This was a landmark election because of Oregon's decision to conduct balloting entirely by mail, which appeared to help Democrats by boosting the participation of voters who may not have always made it to the polls.

This loss stung. My previous defeats had come in primaries where I backed the underdog, so my expectations hadn't been particularly high. Many pundits had picked Gordon to win the special election, however, and our polling showed him ahead going into the final weeks of the campaign. I was starting to wonder whether a moderate Republican could ever get out of a contested primary in Oregon, and whether a Republican of any stripe not named Hatfield or Packwood could win statewide.

Shortly after the special election, Mark Hatfield confirmed that he would not seek reelection. This announcement left an exhausted, emotionally spent, and financially drained Gordon Smith almost no time to decide whether to jump back into the fray. If he remained serious about a political career, there really was no choice. He was the Republican Party's obvious standard bearer, he had widespread name recognition as a result of the special election, and he had a team of financial supporters and grassroots volunteers primed and ready for another battle. If he waited, his next chance wouldn't come until '98, when Wyden (who was serving out the balance of Packwood's term) and Democratic Governor John Kitzhaber would be in cycle but would have all the advantages of incumbency. This was an open seat that the still popular Senator Hatfield would help to protect for the Republicans.

Gordon made the only sensible choice: to run again. Somebody had to take the fall for the special election failure, however, and that turned out to be my buddy Dan. He was demoted from his position as campaign manager to a still vital but less prestigious role as chief strategist. It hurt to see my friend take the first serious hit of his political career, particularly with party graybeards crowing about the uppity boy wonder's fall from grace, but he knew he was in a nasty business. He always called politics "the only game for adults."

My loyal service during the special election and the fact that I'd been with Gordon from the beginning paid dividends as the second Smith campaign took shape. I was invited to serve as part of a small inner circle of advisors that would function as Gordon's "kitchen cabinet." I would continue to work on fundraising (including another incarnation of *Mr. Smith Goes to Washington*) but would also be called on for strategic advice. My chief contribution in this regard was urging Gordon to stress his independence. There was no mileage in a candidate advertising himself as a Republican partisan in this Democratic-leaning state. Mark Hatfield and Bob Packwood had prospered politically for years by their willingness to buck the party from time to time. My recommendation resulted in "independent" being added to the campaign's tag line, along with "effective" and "ready." It was a minor triumph, but I could actually see the impact I'd made as the lawn signs and bumper stickers came off the press.

All the breaks that had gone against us in the special election turned around. We drew an untested opponent: a high-tech maven named Tom Bruggere. He had never held office, which made it easy for Gordon to assume Wyden's mantle of seasoned public servant, leaving Bruggere to inherit Gordon's "millionaire businessman" albatross. Outside groups had been able to wage a massive effort against Gordon in the special election because it was the only such race in the nation at that time and was seen as a precursor to the '96 election season. This campaign was part of the regular cycle, so independent expenditures had to be rationed around the country. Bob Packwood would have been the kiss of death had he campaigned for Gordon in the special election, but Mark Hatfield's willingness to come to Gordon's aid gave us a welcome boost. Gordon's almost drunken sailor flinging of his own money in the first campaign had actually undermined our fundraising efforts, as many would-be contributors asked why they should give if this guy had so much money of his own to burn. This time around Gordon made it plain that he was tapped out, and his previous expenditures essentially served as a challenge grant to spur party donors. And this election was conducted at the traditional ballot box, not by mail.

Gordon and Dan also inserted a deep bomb in their previous off-tackle oriented playbook. While Gordon had gone a long way to moderating his image as an Eastern Oregon right-wing religious nut, his stand on abortion was still a major bar to attracting moderate Republicans, independents, and right-leaning Democrats. This time, Gordon cut a television commercial—clad in an unthreatening sweater—where he looked right into the camera and said (in as many words) that he respected the law of the land regarding abortion, that for him it was an issue of private conscience and not a public crusade, and that he understood this was a very difficult issue on which good and decent people could differ. It was a brilliant strategic move that served to neutralize a damaging issue.

Gordon beat Bruggere handily. He became the first person in the country's history to lose and win a U.S. Senate election in the same state in the same year. It had taken me almost seven years and many painful lessons, but I was now a player in a winning politician's inner circle, and I didn't feel as if I'd had to prostitute myself to get there. I think I respected Gordon Smith more at the end of this campaign than when I had first met him, which is a rare reaction to a politician. I admired the strength of character he had demonstrated in jumping into the second campaign after a brutal first race. He had learned to smooth his rough edges and project a more appealing image, but I saw no sign that he had compromised his basic principles or altered his fundamental character. He stood for the type of Republicanism I championed: an inclusive, enlightened, cosmopolitan party that did not rely on litmus tests or ideological dogma. He was a conservative who was not afraid to take stands on moral issues but did not insist on shoving his own private morality down everyone else's throat. He was a worthy successor to Mark Hatfield and exactly the sort of Republican politician I'd hoped I would find when Amy and I set out for Oregon.

# CO-PRODUCER

During the campaign, Bob Holden and I brainstormed about what role CoHo Productions might be able to play in the Portland theater community. We had not dissolved the company after *Bodyhold*, so there was still a framework in place if we decided we wanted to continue in theater. What really fired our imaginations was a vision of CoHo as a co-producer that would invite local theater artists—directors, actors, technicians, playwrights—to submit proposals for productions they were passionate about. CoHo would focus on the business infrastructure of producing—finding and equipping a venue, raising funds, marketing and promoting the show—which would free our co-producers to concentrate on the artistic and technical elements that were their real expertise. Bob told me story after story of shows he had been involved in where a great script and gifted actors could not save a production that foundered because of inadequate funding, poor publicity, and other business-side deficiencies. I had seen it myself in that arctic production of Mamet's *The Water Engine* in DC, among others. I also had vivid memories of the futile courtship process I had gone through in both Portland and DC trying to attract interest in my script.

I didn't share this notion with Bob for fear that it would scare him, but I really saw this model as a Republican approach to producing theater by (my apologies for the blatant cliché...) helping artists to help themselves. We were saying to the Portland theater community: "Show us that you can develop high quality projects, including a sound budget and a solid team, and we'll find the funding and the venue to make your dream a reality." Rather than treating theater artists as hired hands, we would make them our partners, including a share of the upside if the production did well.

Bob was enthusiastic but concerned about how much new ground we would be breaking. In his experience, theater companies were usually started by actors and directors looking for opportunities to work together on stage. They brought an artistic passion and collegial commitment to their work that supported them through the unavoidable hardships. Could a company that was a production vehicle rather than a collective artistic enterprise sustain itself show after show?

Bob's concern was more than just theoretical. His interest in theater was as an actor and director; he wasn't interested in merely raising money to help other people put on their shows. I told him that he and I and anyone else who joined us in CoHo would be artistically engaged because we would select the proposals to be produced. I was sure that we would see proposals from playwrights who had struck out with the traditional companies; if Bob liked a script and he and the writer developed a rapport, he would have the opportunity to direct.

I felt that our co-production model might actually have a better chance of surviving long-term than a more conventional approach. What I had seen in most theater companies was heavy reliance on a charismatic artistic director who chose the productions and directed many of them. No person, no matter how talented, can shoulder that sort of burden indefinitely, and many such companies collapse when the founder succumbs to the inevitable burnout. Our co-production approach would bring fresh artistic energy from outside of CoHo to each show and not depend on the invincibility of a single person.

We could have debated the merits of our model indefinitely, but felt that there was no substitute for trying a collaboration on a pilot basis. We put a notice for co-production proposals in the Call Board section of the *Oregonian* and waited to see the response. We were not overwhelmed. *Bodyhold* had done well for an upstart independent production, but it had hardly made CoHo Productions a household name. We needed only one good submission, however, and mercifully we got one—*Blood Relations*, a taut play about the notorious axe murderer Lizzie Borden written by the noted Canadian playwright Sharon Pollock. We were impressed with the credentials of our co-producers, a prominent local actress and with a director recently arrived from New York. As shameless promoters looking at opening around Halloween of '96, we liked the bloody Lizzie Borden angle.

Bob and I decided to change venues. We'd had a wonderful experience at the Benson, but $2,000 was the best they could offer for rent and we thought it unlikely that we could replicate the group sales (and resulting catering charges) we'd achieved for *Bodyhold*, many of which were tied to my being the playwright. I went back on the prowl, this time focusing my search on Northwest Portland, a densely populated, up-and-coming area near downtown with many acclaimed restaurants. On one of my scouting expeditions (with my three-year-old son in tow), I passed a lovely brick church, the Parish of St. Mark's, with the ethereal sounds of organ music wafting out the imposing doors. We wandered in and struck up a conversation with the resident organist, who was excited by the opportunity to host a theater production. My mouth watered at the prospect of producing a play in the church—a stunning Romanesque design—but it seemed more practical to mount the show in the adjoining parish hall. The organist secured the approval of the church's governing body, who offered use of the hall for free provided parishioners could attend our performances without charge.

Free was an excellent rate, but it was a tall order to prepare the space for performance (although it had been used as a theater long ago). We had to build over a dozen staging platforms and configure them in such a way that most could be pulled up if the parish needed the use of the entire hall. The church had no stage lighting or sound equipment, all of which had to be rented from outside vendors. We also had to bring in Bob's portable camper toilet for use in the actors' dressing room: the parish hall's only restroom was located on the other side of the stage and was not accessible from the dressing room.

Our greatest challenge, however, was to lay out the ground rules for this newfangled contraption called a co-production. It sounded great on paper, but we had to figure out as we went who was responsible for each element of the production. Our co-producers were ready and willing, but like most theater artists they were accustomed to working as the wage slaves of a theater company that was in charge of everything. A cardinal principle for us was that CoHo would not interfere in artistic decisions. It was up to our co-producers to cast the show and direct the actors as they saw fit. They could also exercise discretion when it came to selecting set, light, sound, and costume designers, as well as technical crew. We stipulated only that these artistic and technical choices be made within the context of an approved budget. We agreed that if revenues from the production exceeded budgeted costs, CoHo and our co-producers would split the upside. Bob and I were nervous about it, but we knew that working with impoverished theater people would require us to cover any losses, although we were hopeful that with no venue costs we would be able to make budget.

We had anticipated that CoHo would take charge of the box office, including individual and group ticket sales. We had rented a voicemail box for *Bodyhold* to use as a reservation line and renewed this rental for the new show. There was no way that we could afford to have a real person answering ticket calls; the only warm body in the box office process for Bodyhold had been mine, regularly checking the reservation line and selling tickets at the door. CoHo (meaning me) also would send out press releases for the local calendar listings and theater critics, as well as recruit a graphic designer to produce a poster and postcard-type mailer. Fortunately, the director had come across a wonderful old photo of Lizzie Borden that was in the public domain, which minimized our design costs. CoHo would also be responsible for the layout of the program.

This was fine as far as it went. Where we ended up courting disaster was the actual construction of the set. We understood that CoHo would need to do the basic equipping of the venue, including building the platforms that would serve as the stage. We had assumed that our co-producers would literally take the platform we had developed and design and build the show-specific set. We assumed too much. Neither of our co-producers had a technical background, and they kept their focus on what they knew best: rehearsing the cast. Because of Bob's experience as an actor and director, he served as the primary liaison on the theater side of the production (while I focused on the business end) and grew increasingly agitated as the opening date drew near and no set had materialized. Finally he forced the issue in one of those shrill, emotion-laden pre-opening confrontations that was proving to be a regular ritual on the technical side of a show. The result was a series of near all-night sessions with Bob and our assistant stage manager from *Bodyhold*, with limited assistance from me, hammering out a passable final set.

Thankfully our confidence in the artistic skills of our co-producers was rewarded. They put up a solid show that earned decent—though not spectacular—reviews. We helped boost our box office by scheduling late night shows on Halloween weekend featuring a local actor with a voice like Orson Welles reading Poe's *The Telltale Heart* and *The Cask of Amontillado* (we hit up a neighborhood wine shop to donate bottles of Amontillado sherry as door prizes). We ended up modestly in the black, thanks in part to the generosity of a developer client of mine who was doing a condominium conversion a few block from the theater and agreed to a $2,500 sponsorship of the production. The St. Mark's parishioners raved about the play and voiced pride in their role as patrons of the arts.

Another sponsor also helped us continue our educational outreach efforts by flying down the playwright Sharon Pollock from Canada and having her teach classes for local high school and college students who came to see the show. We found that while the experience of attending the play was powerful, the reinforcement of going into the classroom to discuss the show afterward was invaluable. The students loved the direct exposure to the person who had written the words they had heard delivered on stage.

The experience was both exhausting and traumatic, and certainly not as fulfilling for us personally as *Bodyhold*, but we came away from *Blood Relations* convinced that co-production was a viable approach. I had a long debriefing with our co-producers, who shared our enthusiasm but stressed that we needed to draw up a clear delineation of responsibilities the next time around. The director felt so empowered by the co-production opportunity that she decided to form her own theater company.

I loved having the theater back in my life. I missed not having some artistic skin in the game as a writer or actor, but it was hugely satisfying to have our own company and a mission of helping others realize their theater dreams. I experienced a little thrill each time I checked the messages on the reservation voicemail from my law firm office.

# ITINERANT PLAYER

We thought CoHo had found a home at St. Mark's. We were concerned that certain plays might be off limits in a church setting, but the congregation seemed open-minded. The organist was a huge fan of our company and appeared anxious to cement an alliance. We loved the neighborhood, which had no local theater other than a children's company.

Then suddenly, St. Mark's priest was fired, apparently for having his hand in the till. Unfortunately, he had been crucial in mediating between warring factions within the congregation, which had split from the U.S. Episcopalian Church to join the Anglican Church based in England (these schismatic distinctions were a little lost on a Jew like me, but were obviously of huge consequence to the parishioners). The end result was that the parish had weightier matters to grapple with than accommodating a resident theater company. After an agonizing wait that took us well into '97, our friend the organist advised us to move on.

We had already selected our next project from a noticeably stronger pool of co-production submissions, which meant I was once again scouting for a venue. We had chosen Christopher Kyle's *The Monogamist*, a hip and witty exploration of marriage and monogamy that cried out for a cool urban setting. My condominium practice in Portland's Pearl District had truly exploded. Empty nesters and upwardly mobile first-time buyers were flocking into the district, with upscale retailers following in hot pursuit, joining the art galleries that had already been in the area for some time. One of the clients I worked with had hit a home run converting an old hardware company building and was doing another project right across the street that featured residential units over ground floor retail. Several of the retail spaces had not yet been leased, and I asked on bended knee whether he would be willing to make one of them available for our show. He not only agreed, but offered to be a sponsor and hold a reception for building residents and prospective buyers in one of the model units. Producing theater in the neighborhood was a perfect fit with the artsy, trendy image that was the centerpiece of the district's marketing campaign.

Mounting a show in the Pearl District also presented an opportunity to sell ads to local merchants. We'd had a fair amount of ad success with restaurants for *Blood Relations*, but now we branched out to retailers of all stripes. I went door to door on Saturdays—sometimes shamelessly carting along my son and newborn daughter with me as marketing props—selling ads that ranged from $40 for a business card size to $150 for a full page. We also included free tickets with each ad so that the advertiser could get a sense of the quality of our work up close. I was astounded at how supportive the merchant community in the Pearl District proved to be: both because we were a good cause and good for business.

The empty retail space we used for *The Monogamist* was just a concrete shell, and it made St. Mark's look like Carnegie Hall. The actors performed on the floor of the space, and we rigged up the platforms left over from *Blood Relations* to serve as several rows of tiered seating for a capacity of around ninety. Our co-producer was a retired theater professor, and he was able to scare up chairs from his department for our audience, as well as a number of set pieces and props. The concrete walls made for terrible acoustics, so we had to scrounge for any material we could drape on the walls to dampen the sound. The fire marshal scared the hell out of us by paying a surprise visit to the space the week before we were to open. He didn't shut us down but left us with a long list of remedial items that we barely completed before opening.

Amy and I decided to throw an opening night pre-theater party at our house and bring the whole assemblage over to the show after dinner. This had become something of a CoHo tradition, as opening weekend—with no reviews out yet—is the toughest for recruiting an audience. As CoHo had no permanent home, we had no subscribers. We rounded up over fifty friends, many of them colleagues at Ball Janik or fellow travelers in Republican circles. I talked up the play but did not mention that there would be nudity; I had no idea that our retired don of a director had decided to take some undisclosed liberties with the script! I thought several of our Gordon Smith supporters—middle-aged and Mormon— were going to meet their makers right then and there when one of the young male actors appeared in his full frontal birthday suit. The shock over his appearance was fortunately overshadowed by admiration on the part of the men in the audience for the charms of the female lead, who the director decided to expose to one and all from the waist up. While I was taken aback by the director's license, I couldn't say that his direction was out of line in the overall context of the script. We did, however, modestly modify our policy of non-interference on the artistic side of a co-production to at least require prior notice if the director decided to bare what was not bared in the text.

A curious political sideline of *The Monogamist* came out of our co-producer's connection to Portland's Lewis & Clark College. He recruited a number of alums to work with him on the production, as well as the Theater Department's scene shop foreman to serve as our technical director. The Monica Lewinsky scandal was then in full media-feeding frenzy. It turned out that Ms. Lewinsky had graduated from Lewis & Clark. While a student there, she reportedly had an affair with an older married man who was an unemployed theater technician. In a misguided attempt to help her lover, who was locked in a custody battle, Monica arranged for him to interview with the foreman (introducing the lover as her cousin), then apparently forged the foreman's signature on a letter written on college stationery referring to the lover's employment at the college. The letter proved to be undeliverable because of indecipherable handwriting and was returned through the mail to the foreman, a mild-mannered fellow with no background in political chicanery. In between his ministrations to the set of a play ironically spotlighting monogamy, he agonized over whether to go public with this obscure footnote to history. Visions of hitting the talk show circuit and a lucrative book contract danced in his head. I referred him to a colleague at Ball Janik, who helped put him in touch with the staff of the independent counsel, Ken Starr. Alas, Starr's office did nothing with the information and the foreman returned to obscurity.

This sorry interlude was about as close as I came to political involvement in the '98 electoral cycle. The Republicans ran no-hoper sacrificial lambs against Senator Wyden and Governor Kitzhaber. I did flirt for a weekend with launching a quixotic candidacy against Wyden myself, which would have involved my taking a leave of absence from the firm and barnstorming around the state. I attempted to rationalize this delusion by pointing to the invaluable hands-on experience I would gain and the name recognition I would achieve, but Dan Lavey persuaded me that "cannon fodder" was not an appealing first line on any candidate's political résumé.

My first political mentor, Craig Berkman, traveled in the upper echelons of national GOP circles and, at his elbow, I enjoyed a few chances to breathe that rarefied air. Craig invited me to join him at a meeting of the Republican Leadership Council, a group of wealthy, mostly pro-choice moderates who were committed to spending big dollars to support like-minded candidates, even in contested primaries against religious conservatives. I had the chance to hear aspiring presidential candidate John McCain and rising stars like Governors Christine Todd Whitman of New Jersey and John Rowland of Connecticut, but what was most striking was the number of Jewish Republicans represented at the event. I had come across precious few Jews in Oregon Republican politics, and it was a novelty to see this largely New York- and New Jersey-based contingent so engaged in GOP infighting. I found it ironic that the Eastern Establishment wing of the party—for decades the bastion of WASPy blue bloods like Dewey and Taft—now featured so many Jews among its stalwarts. I was impressed with the breadth of the agenda of these kindred spirits and the depth of their resources. If I were ever to jump into the elective fray myself, I thought, this was a group to bear in mind.

Craig also introduced me to a character named Heinz Prechter. Prechter had emigrated from Germany as a penniless young man and had become a pioneer of the automobile sunroof in Detroit, as well as a major fundraiser for the Bush family. He was a fabulous storyteller, one of his best being about building a sunroof for Lyndon Johnson and riding along in the President's enormous

Cadillac as LBJ stood and fired a shotgun out the roof at passing varmints on his ranch. He regaled us with accounts of Henry Ford II and Prechter's mentor, the Jewish automotive industrialist Max Fisher, effectively locking their suppliers in a room and strong-arming contributions for Republican candidates. It was curious to hear this man with a heavy German accent, who sadly has since committed suicide, proclaiming Fisher's conviction that the GOP was the natural party of the Jews.

I dabbled a little in the '98 First Congressional District race, the scene of my earlier "kneecapping" exploits, but I did not live in the district and was fighting too many other fires to make it a priority. While Amy had married me knowing of my penchant for burning the candle at both ends, I was pushing the limits of both her patience and my stamina. I usually saw my two young children just before their bedtime at the end of grueling days marked by long hours in the office, meetings for Portland State and Waverly, and calls to CoHo co-producers, patrons, and advertisers.

I had not set out to become involved in the Portland community just to generate clients, but a number of the contacts I had made led to new business. Bruce Davis—my Williams friend and first adopted candidate—had asked me to represent him and his family in several matters. He then formed a group that purchased a NASDAQ-listed restaurant company, giving me my first publicly-traded client. Craig Berkman asked me to become outside general counsel to several companies he was involved in and then appointed me to represent a small investment fund he had formed. Almost overnight this exploded into a series of venture capital funds that committed most of its $75 million to the booming high tech sector, giving me an up-close view of the tech mania that convulsed the country in the mid-to-late nineties. I no longer spent most of my day working on Crown Pacific matters, as my own clients took up the lion's share of my time.

As my billings increased, so did my stature in the firm. I was made a member of the management committee and asked to chair the firm's business group. It had taken me almost five years at Ball Janik to reach my last Covington & Burling pay grade, but there was no question in my mind that I'd made the right decision in leaving DC. I was not an underling holding someone else's bag but a player in my own right, albeit in a less exalted circle.

I had also risen through the ranks at Portland State's Foundation, ultimately becoming president for a year. Almost the day I took office, civil war broke out between Portland State University and its sister school, Oregon State University, over the allocation of engineering-related resources. There were engineering programs at both schools, which the OSU brass argued the state could ill afford. They pressed to consolidate the engineering curriculum at the OSU campus in rural Corvallis. While couched in the passive, institutional language of academic-speak, this was tantamount to a hostile takeover. PSU retorted that it made more sense to concentrate engineering resources in Portland, the state's major metropolitan area and home to most of Oregon's high tech companies, and that the two schools served different student populations, with PSU focusing on older, employed commuter students and OSU focusing on an on-campus student body just out of high school. Because the university could not devote its own funds to waging a public battle, the foundation decided to spearhead an aggressive campaign trumpeting PSU's accomplishments. It was a bruising battle, but finally OSU was forced to back off.

During my tenure as president, the university also landed its first million-dollar pledge. The donor (in a world that was growing ever smaller for me) was the CEO of my law firm's client Crown Pacific—and a rabid PSU alum. While PSU's development and athletic staffs were responsible for cultivating this donor, I had recruited one of his top lieutenants to the foundation board, which certainly didn't hurt.

My specialty for Waverly had become pulling together big-ticket auction packages for an *Evening With Lady Luck*, the agency's annual fundraiser featuring silent and oral auctions followed by the flinging of funny money at gaming tables. I shamelessly offered up CoHo theater tickets combined with dinners at advertiser restaurants and overnight accommodations at the Benson and other nearby hotels. My most inspired auction item came out of the '96 special election. One of the local TV stations had sprung a pop quiz on Ron Wyden, calling on him to locate Bosnia (then a world hotspot) on the globe. He stuttered, hemmed, and hawed, but could not come up with the right answer. Gordon and Dan Lavey jumped on this, producing a TV spot featuring young children identifying Bosnia on a small plastic globe. Gordon had kept the globe they used for the ad as a campaign memento, and I asked whether he would be prepared to donate it for the Waverly auction. My thought was to add to the value of the piece by having both Gordon and Wyden, who was then the honorary chairman of Waverly's board, autograph the globe. Gordon readily agreed to both the donation and the autograph, but Wyden's staff turned me down. They were kind enough to offer us several Senate coffee mugs instead. And this from the man who had won the damned election!

The *Portland Business Journal* recognized my frenetic networking by naming me to its "40 Under 40" list, ostensibly the forty top area leaders under the age of forty. I was grateful for the award, although I recognized there was an element of Babbittry in my quest to become a pillar of Portland. Obviously my multi-dimensional business, political, and civic commitment furthered my own interests, but I truly felt a connection to my adopted community and was able to help the cash-strapped students at PSU and the troubled children served by Waverly. I was not the high-priced faceless DC lawyer drone I'd feared I would become, but an activist engaged at both the boardroom and grassroots levels to make my city a better place.

In the midst of this relentless self-promotion, the theater was an oasis of purity. While at times I questioned my motives in chasing all these other badges of community glory, I hadn't founded CoHo to build my law practice or my standing with local titans and powerbrokers. On the contrary, I produced theater to prove there was more to me than bourgeois boosterism. There was no shortage of ego involved—the first two letters of CoHo, after all, came from my name—but here the ego was directed at fostering the bond between artist and audience, not at boosting my partnership compensation or my power behind the political thrones of Oregon.

# ON THE MAP

The space where we had performed *The Monogamist* was leased even before we closed the run of the show, so we had to find yet another location for our next production, an historical drama about Henry VIII's elder daughter, Mary. Several years before, I had met the writer, Sam Gregory, as I was promoting *Bodyhold* in front of a chic Northwest Portland restaurant while shamelessly shouldering my infant son in his babypack. Sam took one of the proffered handbills and matter of factly introduced himself as a playwright, the first person ever to present himself to me as such. He was a huge man, well over six feet and pushing 300 pounds, with an Oscar Wilde-whirled thatch of blonde hair. He said he was from Southern Oregon, yet spoke in an affected English accent with a strangely sing-songy intonation and an officiously measured cadence. He was an odd duck, but I found him intriguing and arranged a meeting after the show closed.

Over dinner he told me that, while he was not yet thirty, he had already written close to forty plays. He wrote every day, usually for an hour in the late afternoon or evening. He had studied theater at Southern Oregon University in Ashland (home of the celebrated Oregon Shakespeare Festival), and after brief stints in Los Angeles and Pittsburgh, returned home to Oregon where he barely supported his writing with ill-paying temporary jobs. None of his plays had ever been produced, although one script had made it through several workshops at Portland Repertory Theatre, then one of the leading companies in town.

After a few more get-acquainted sessions, he shared his script, *Mary Tudor*, with me. As a confirmed Anglophile, I had expected to enjoy the play, but I was blown away. The elegance of the language captured the richness of Tudor England, yet rendered the period accessible to a modern audience. The powerful characterizations of towering historical figures, such as Henry VIII and Anne Boleyn, were striking for a playwright of any age but amazing for an unproduced writer still in his twenties. I thought it would be an excellent prospect for CoHo, but felt that we needed to develop a local constituency for the play before setting out on the risky course of producing original work set in the sixteenth century.

I approached an historical society affiliated with Portland State University called Friends of History and asked if they might consider co-sponsoring a staged reading of the play with CoHo. In the ever-smaller world of Portland, the president of Friends of History happened to be the wife of Cleve Larson, my fellow "kneecapper" from the '94 congressional campaign. She thought Sam's script was amazing and readily signed on to the reading.

Even though it had not landed him a production, Sam had managed to do with Mary Tudor something I had not even attempted with *Bodyhold*: to build a fan base in the local acting community. He had developed a loyal core of high-caliber actors who had participated in workshops and readings of the play over a period of several years. Most of them were appalled when Portland Repertory Theatre would not put Mary Tudor in its season, and they jumped at the chance to perform in a reading that might finally lead to a production. The reading was a great success, and Bob Holden said he would love to direct the play if Sam concurred.

Our play selection process, as well as the internal functioning of our company, had become more formalized. CoHo's board had expanded to a group of six to eight members, including both theater and businesspeople. A traditional theater company consists of an artistic director who selects the plays and the directors and then relies on a board of well-connected movers and shakers who raise money in support of the artistic director's vision, but do not take part in the artistic life of the company. Our model, like our co-production approach to the theater community, was more collaborative. We aimed to motivate our board by allowing them to join in the review of co-production proposals and the selection of our season, so that the board essentially functioned as a collective artistic director. The trade-off was that each board member was expected to take responsibility for at least one portfolio in the operation of our company: box office, program layout, high school and college outreach, or any of the other critical elements of putting on a play. As co-founders, Bob and I took on more duties than the other board members, but it was the board as a whole that produced our season, without the assistance of any paid staff. As a result, we recruited new board members based more on their energy, enthusiasm, and commitment than on the depth of their pockets. Board members were expected to contribute their services to the company, although we did pay one board member who had taken over management of the box office and worked almost every performance.

Our expectation from the outset was that each production would pay for itself. Because of the difficult experience with the local grants authority on *Bodyhold*, we assumed that we might never receive any grants and budgeted accordingly. We tried to limit our budgets for each show to approximately $10,000, which included all artistic and technical personnel, marketing, venue costs, and royalties. Of course this meant that we were only able to pay a relative pittance to our actors and technicians, but our scale was competitive with other small Portland theater companies and was all we could manage. What distinguished us from many other companies in town was our willingness to share the wealth by paying a bonus if a production did well.

Our main advantage was that we had no overhead, as we had no permanent home and no payroll. However, our only cushion was any profit from our previous productions, one-half of which we shared with our co-producers. Fortunately, the client who had introduced us to the Benson had become a fan of our work and had decided to make generous annual gifts to CoHo, which we supplemented with a limited annual giving campaign aimed at those who had originally supported *Bodyhold*.

Another big boost was our program advertising revenue, which I pursued with a vengeance. By *Mary Tudor*, we had already built a base of some thirty-five local advertisers, who were generating revenues for CoHo of $2,500–$3,000 per production. This was small potatoes for a major arts company, but was significant in relation to our overall production budget. I'm sure Ball Janik associates who passed by my office during the lunch hour and heard me beseeching Pearl District restaurateurs and gallery owners over the phone must have wondered if this was the way to bring in new clients.

Because we were hopping from venue to venue, we had a hard time laying out a true season, but our modest goal was to do one play in the fall and another in the spring. We tried to finalize our selections by May so that we would have the summer to prepare for the first production in the fall, but it rarely worked out that way. We would place a submission notice in the *Oregonian* Call Board section starting in the last month or two of the year, then try to start reviewing proposals by March. We had developed submission guidelines that identified the key elements of a proposal, most critically the quality of the script and the strength of the co-production team, but also the co-producer's ability to work within a budget and willingness to participate in community outreach. We made it clear that we had no ideological axe to grind and would consider any type of project if it met our quality standards and had some chance of finding a market. Each proposal would initially be reviewed by at least one board member and preferably two, after which we would go through a grueling series of board meetings to narrow the field. When we were finally down to a handful of projects, each board member would read the submissions of all finalists, whom the board would also interview in person. The final selection process was always intense, although we managed to maintain our collegiality and almost always chose by consensus, with Bob and I extended the status of first among equals.

The board's selection of *Mary Tudor* was enthusiastic, but we once again ran into venue challenges. I had approached another condominium developer and client who was willing to offer us an unleased retail space without charge in a new mixed-use project. It was ironic that as the lawyer for this project I had written condominium documents that limited noise emanating from retail spaces. The developer decided that, even with the bellowing of Henry VIII, we wouldn't be too much of an imposition on the condo residents.

One of the toughest aspects of working in these concrete shells was the lack of privacy for the actors. We created a dressing room by hanging curtains that cordoned off the performance space, but the absence of real walls meant that the actors had to be quiet as proverbial church mice during shows. This hadn't proven too burdensome during *The Monogamist* because the actors could escape outside to the springtime weather and the mood of the often comic show was upbeat. *Mary Tudor*, by contrast, was produced in the dead of winter and pushed the actors to their emotional limits. The cast was at daggers drawn through much of the run, a charged atmosphere that was not helped by our inevitable technical struggles—this time with the elaborate Tudor-era costumes.

Our other major challenge turned out to be the presence of only one bathroom, which might have been fine for a sunglass emporium—which the space ultimately became—but did not prove so for us. The play was a major hit, and we found our intermissions stretching to almost thirty minutes as our patrons queued up to use the facilities. Our problem was compounded one night when our technical director slipped trying to make some lighting adjustments above the bathroom and fell through the ceiling, fortunately not injuring himself seriously but putting the bathroom out of commission. We pleaded with the art college across the street to let us use their restrooms but were rebuffed until we went up the ladder to the college president, who recognized that art sadly does not override bodily functions and granted relief to our patrons.

Despite these obstacles, *Mary Tudor* was a huge commercial and critical success for CoHo in early '99, as well as for Sam Gregory, who had received both a guaranteed payment and a percentage of any profit. Even though we had decided to increase our customary production budget so that we could hire an actress who was a member of Actors' Equity, the stage actors' union, we ended up substantially in the black. I poked fun at Bob over his decision to cast the Equity actress, as he usually insisted in socialist fashion on paying all actors the same amount regardless of the size of their role. As a free market Republican, I viewed this practice as absurd considering the varying demands of each role and the differing experience and reputation each actor brought to a show. I delighted in Bob's squirming as I asked him to explain how he reconciled paying one actress four times more than anyone else in the cast just because she happened to be a member of a union.

*Mary Tudor* put CoHo on Portland's artistic map. The production won three Drammy Awards: for direction, new work, and ensemble acting. The Drammy Awards ceremony was held at our old haunt, the Benson Hotel, which made an already satisfying evening even more meaningful. We had demonstrated that a theater company could take a chance on an unproven local playwright and reap major rewards.

CoHo won another Drammy in '99 for our spring production, Patrick Marber's *Dealer's Choice*, a black comedy from England about the staff of a restaurant that stay after closing for a weekly poker game. Our *Mary Tudor* venue, true to form, had been leased before we closed the show, so we were once again in nomadic mode. I came across an abandoned building on the outskirts of the Pearl District that was slated for redevelopment by a local nonprofit. One of my Williams classmates worked for the nonprofit and helped to arrange a favorable short-term lease. It was a splendid old brick warehouse with massive beams and soaring ceilings. Unfortunately, it had no heat or running water. I imposed on several of my homebuilder clients, one of whom installed a temporary heating system and another who covered the cost of two portable toilets. Coincidentally, one of the waiters in *Dealer's Choice* (named Mugsy) dreams of opening his own restaurant in a converted public restroom, so we posted signs on the Honeybuckets™ (the trade name for the port-o-potties) celebrating Mugsy's vision.

The only space in the warehouse where ancient interior columns would not obstruct audience views was on the second floor, which brought several visits from our old friend the fire marshal. The fact that the building had been empty for years and had wiring that seemed to date from Edison's day did not help our cause. We found we could not operate our concession coffeemaker because it would overload the circuits and knock out our theatrical lights. We also had to cart the weighty seating platforms that had gone with us from venue to venue up the rickety steps of the warehouse, which led to serious backaches among our board members. In the midst of this angst, we discovered that the warehouse was home to a squadron of pigeons, who delighted in dive-bombing the set and leaving little mementos of their visits on the white tablecloths of our restaurant set.

But for all that, it was a magnificent place to put on theater. Our co-producer, a talented director named Jeff Meyers, deftly harnessed the atmosphere and character of the old warehouse to create an intimacy with the audience that made Marber's script sing. Patron after patron—rather than complaining about the building's drawbacks—gushed about how the venue made the evening all the more memorable. Even one of my rock-ribbed Republican groups had a great time slumming through a bohemian evening that included the show and dinner at the Low Brow Lounge a few blocks away. The cast, which did not enjoy the benefit of the makeshift heating system in their "dressing room" (a cavernous storage area opening off of the performance space), bravely triumphed over one of the coldest springs in recent memory and an appalling ignorance of poker.

Despite the success of *Dealer's Choice*, there was no way that we were going to put ourselves through the chapped lips, numb fingers, and runny noses of a fall production in that space. It had been all we could do to manage through a late spring performance slot, and we would not be able to offer winning Mugsy jokes on the port-o-potties the next time around. We didn't have the funds to invest in further upgrades of the building, which in any event was scheduled for a complete renovation sometime in the next year or two.

So for the sixth time in as many CoHo productions, I walked the streets of Portland looking for another venue. We were starting to develop a following—and growing advertising base—in the Pearl District, so that's where I focused my search. I both thrilled in and dreaded these scouting expeditions. It was exhilarating to push the limits of my imagination and picture how a particular space that had not been designed with live performance even remotely in mind might function as a theater. But the grim knowledge—now born of long experience—of the seating, lighting, sound, utility, fire code, dressing room, restroom, and myriad other obstacles we would have to overcome was often overwhelming.

Thankfully, the technical demands of our next production, a one-man show called *St. Nicholas* by the Irish playwright Conor McPherson, were modest. The play, which has nothing to do with Santa Claus, is a whopping yarn spun by a sodden, malicious Dublin theater critic who ends up pimping for a cadre of London vampires. All we really needed was a chair and enough space to let the narrator/critic amble about a bit. One of our art gallery advertisers had designed his premises to accommodate the occasional reading or musical performance, and at his invitation we took the measure of his space. We found it could hold only fifty or so patrons, a little more than half of our usual capacity, and we would have to make do with gallery-style track lighting rather than real theater lights, but the proprietor was prepared to offer the space for free and the prospect of working in heated quarters with running water was enticing after our warehouse ordeal. Because our budget for this single-actor show was much lower than our usual multi-actor productions, we decided the smaller venue would pencil out financially.

The performance was brilliant and won us another Drammy Award. It was our third successive award-winning production, a track record that nicely validated our co-production model. Each season our submissions had grown in both quantity and quality. Our itinerant existence put great strains on our board, but we had developed a strong core of loyalists who were committed to the company and rolled with the logistical punches. The weight of being CoHo's chief fundraiser, marketer, venue scout, PR flak, advertising solicitor, group sales pitchman, contract negotiator, high school outreach liaison, program copy editor, opening night party host, and buck-stops-here troubleshooter was taking a toll on me personally, but the sluicing sense of renewal each time I sat in the audience for one of our shows was addictive and cathartic.

# To the Right of Stage Left

I rarely discussed politics around the theater. I barely had time to navigate through the perilous shoals of producing shows, let alone try to take on the Democrats, socialists, and anarchists who form the great and wonderful mass of theater people. But every once in a while over a post-show beer I would be confronted with "how can you produce theater and be a Republican?" and could not contain myself. I would explain that Republican skepticism of government was profoundly compatible with working in the arts. Artists for millennia had questioned authority and resisted government efforts to twist art into propaganda. Reliance on government funding was both uncertain and hazardous to artistic freedom. Government subsidies—whatever the sector—tended to create a dependent class who compromised their independence and adjusted their course to the prevailing political winds. Artists would be foolish to think they were any different in this regard than tobacco farmers or steel producers.

I would make it clear that I was not opposed to government funding of the arts. Artists and arts organizations were at least as deserving of governmental assistance as the legion of other worthy (and unworthy) causes supported by public money, and government funding as part of a healthy and balanced diet of support should not undermine artistic integrity. But the many strains of operating an arts organization make it easy to slip into the mind set of "what type of project will get us a government grant?" rather than "how can people in our own community help us to produce the sort of art we're really interested in doing?" Many artists understandably shy away from grassroots outreach, which involves an element of flesh-pressing and rounds-making better suited to politicians. But it is this (dare I say it?) Republican-style decentralization of funding and cultivation of local resources that make for healthy, grounded arts companies in the long term.

The usual rejoinder (as we proceeded to at least a second beer) would be that it was easy for me—a corporate lawyer and civic Energizer Bunny™—to talk about developing a local funding base, as I was much better placed to pull in donations from corporations and fat cats than your average starving artist. I would concede the truth of this but say that it missed the point. The challenge is how, whatever their inherent strengths or weaknesses, can arts organizations find ways to connect with the communities around them? I had been exposed to a lot of theater artists and organizations over the past decade, and many of them were so inwardly focused that community involvement seemed almost an afterthought. Of course it is essential to establish a compelling artistic mission, without which a company has nothing. But it is equally essential to deploy the might of that mission to attract adherents.

My favorite illustration was CoHo's program advertising. By this time our advertiser base had exceeded forty area merchants, and we were bringing in over $3,000 per production in advertiser revenue, mostly from $50–$100 ads. For many of our shows this was twenty-five to thirty percent of our overall budget. We were able to make the case to these advertisers—most of them small, locally-owned businesses—that we were a valuable community resource that could also boost their business. We were successful making this pitch not because I was a high-priced lawyer who served on a lot of civic boards, but by burning shoe leather on weekends going door to door, getting to know these folks and making them aware of our presence. There was no reason why other companies could not replicate our success if they were willing to make the time to connect with the restaurants, coffee shops, and other merchants in their neighborhoods.

I would point out that CoHo Productions had produced six plays—most critically acclaimed and all at least modestly profitable—with no government funding and no foundation grants. Most of the revenue base for these productions came from box office sales and advertising. Of course we were able to compile this track record because of our absence of overhead, but overhead (a permanent venue and staff in the case of a theater company) is not an entitlement and comes only after an arts organization pays heavy dues. We were able to manage without staff because we allowed our board members to be involved in the artistic life of our company and gave them a motivation to pitch in.

As my fellow beer guzzler was usually someone in the CoHo cast or crew, they would join in singing the praises of our company, but would then get to the crux of the matter. How could I as a Republican associate with all those right-wing religious nuts who hated homosexuals and other deviant nonconformists and viewed anything edgier than *Oklahoma* as seditious? My first response would be that I was a Gordon Smith Republican and that the Republicans I spent time with were like him: smart, sophisticated, open-minded, and religious without being dogmatic. They supported my passion for theater and came to CoHo plays: nudity, profanity, and all. Many of them were pro-life, but that did not make them wild-eyed fanatics torching abortion clinics.

I would also say that I was not a religious person myself but I had come to admire the role that religion played in the lives of the social conservatives I knew. They did not just pay lip service to the ideal of commitment to family, but practiced it intensely in their homes, schools, and children's activities. I considered myself to be fiscally conservative and socially tolerant, but I both understood and sympathized with religious conservatives' view that public policy should have a moral dimension. It should not be considered right-wing lunacy to express alarm, for example, over the disintegration of the traditional family, over soaring rates of divorce and single parent households. For many of the conservatives I knew, these were genuine, principled concerns, not codewords for attacks on gays and lesbians and other alternative lifestyles.

I would acknowledge both that social conservatives had seized control of the Republican Party apparatus in Oregon and elsewhere (because of their willingness to turn out for the evening meetings that are the stuff of grassroots party politics). I also would acknowledge that many of the party's congressional leaders were certainly not in the Gordon Smith mold. The Southern Dixiecrats who had turned me off to the Democratic Party had been succeeded by Republicans in many cases. Strom Thurmond and Jesse Helms seemed every bit as paleolithic to me as John Stennis and Herman Talmadge had a generation before. But I would remind my dubious theater friends that at a national level the Republican nominees for President over the past dozen years, Bob Dole and George H.W. Bush, had not been hard-core religious ideologues at all.

And that was a trend I thought would continue. My friends in the Gordon Smith camp were beginning to gear up for the 2000 presidential election, and it was clear that Gordon was going to back Governor George W. Bush of Texas. I had paid my dues on campaigns for the state legislature, Congress, and governor. I had gone door-to-door, licked stamps, done opposition research, written candidate commentary, and raised money. I felt ready to jump into a presidential race, the next logical move in the hierarchical game of politics.

Governor Bush seemed like the logical candidate. His parents and Andover/Yale educational background inspired confidence that he understood the roots of the Republican Party. His record in Texas cast him in the model of a good government reformer, which to me was the essence of being a Republican. He had a reputation for working across party lines, which was appealing in the bitterly partisan atmosphere prevailing in the post-Lewinsky era. He had tackled issues that were not staples of the conventional Republican agenda—like education reform—and reportedly achieved great success. Although his credentials were much less impressive than his father's, he had solid executive experience as a governor, which had been the springboard to the presidency for so many recent candidates.

But most critically, Bush seemed comfortable in his own skin. He did not have the mortal fear of conservatives that had led his father to pander to the right, because he was a conservative himself. He struck me as a man who would be prepared to stand up to religious activists on certain issues and blaze his own trail, both because they had a high level of confidence in him and he in himself. The fact that an independent-minded Republican like Gordon Smith was such an early and enthusiastic supporter only confirmed this impression.

The timing seemed ideal for me to take a leadership role on the campaign in Oregon. Ball Janik had an enlightened sabbatical program that was mandatory for all partners. Every five years, a partner was required to take off four months—at full pay—from practicing law. The partner could do anything he or she wanted during those four months, as long as it was done away from the firm. Most traveled, although some took on other professional challenges like working on a newspaper editorial page. The idea behind the program was that the short-term loss of revenue for the firm would be more than made up by the long-term benefits of avoiding burn-out and stagnation. As I had made partner in '95, my first sabbatical was scheduled for 2000, which dovetailed perfectly with the campaign. My board stints with Portland State and Waverly had come to an end after two three-year terms, and I had pretty much phased out my involvement with the local Williams association. I had agreed to serve on one other civic board, a recently-formed foundation to support the county library, but my community involvement outside of CoHo was not as grueling as it had been a few years back.

My stature as a fundraiser had risen since the '96 special election. I co-hosted a major event for Gordon in '99 (dubbed "The Last Fundraiser of the Century") and raised as much as anyone on the host committee. The event was staffed by Lori Hardwick, the stunning significant other of my buddy Dan Lavey. Lori was a fearsome political fundraiser notorious for her intensity, which was a bit surprising in the daughter of a grocer from rural Burns, Oregon. I called up one prospective donor for this event whom Lori had put on my contact list and nearly had my ear chewed off. He screamed into the phone that he had told Lori he was scheduled to have cancer surgery the day of the event and couldn't possibly attend. Her response was classic: "It doesn't mean he can't send a check." Lori had recently joined the board of CoHo Productions; I was glad to have her brand of moxie on my side.

Dan, Lori, and Molly Bordonaro, a hard-charging dynamo who had run for the First Congressional seat in her late twenties and was well connected in the Bush camp, spoke with me about serving as Finance Chair for a program to be known as "Oregon Victory 2000." The Republican National Committee was intent on setting up aggressive Victory efforts in targeted states across the country. Oregon was not usually viewed as a battleground state for Republicans, but the prospect of a renegade third party candidacy by Ralph Nader put our state in play. Victory programs are operated under the auspices of the state party and directed at "get out the vote" efforts such as mailings and phone banks. Victory initiatives are supposed to promote the party as a whole rather than specific candidates, but obviously the nominee at the top of the ticket stood to get the most exposure. Contribution limits to Victory efforts are more generous than those for individual candidates, so the RNC's plan was to encourage donors to give both to the presidential nominee and to Victory and then allow Victory to handle much of the basic blocking and tackling of the campaign.

There was one major stumbling block for this grand plan: the Oregon Republican Party. Since the ouster of Craig Berkman in the early nineties by religious conservatives, the state party had disintegrated as a fundraising force. Most major donors in the state did not share the social conservatism of the state party leaders and turned their focus to particular candidates rather than party-building efforts. The right-wing shock troops that enforced orthodoxy at the grassroots had enthusiasm and conviction in spades but not many deep pockets. The upshot was that the state party could barely fund a skeletal staff, let alone serve as the fundraising engine for a sophisticated, national-class Victory program.

We in the Gordon Smith camp had the donor list to raise the necessary funds, but we were not prepared to just hand over the checkbook to the state party ideologues and watch them blow it all on their pet projects. We needed the state party, however, because without them there could be no Victory program. And they needed us, as we were the geese prepared to lay the proverbial golden eggs. Dan, Lori, and Molly conducted delicate negotiations with the state party brass and pieced together a tenuous check-and-balance system that gave the Smith loyalists considerable sway over how the Victory money was spent but also built up the infrastructure of the state party. It was a marriage of convenience, but it demonstrated how eight years out of the White House and loathing of the Clinton regime was leading conservative and moderate elements in the Republican Party to unite under the prospect of a George Bush candidacy.

My motives in signing on to a leadership spot on the Victory program were not entirely altruistic. After almost ten years, I was beginning to feel the limitations of a smaller, more provincial city. I still found Portland's natural beauty, stunning downtown, and gracious informality appealing, but tAs we worked on building our Victory fundraising team, I started plotting my ascension to the upper echelons of government.he initial wonder as to its inner workings had given way to a sense of the eternal recurrence of the same (one of my favorite lines from Nietzsche), a familiar recycling of the same cast of characters at charity fundraisers, board meetings, and the like. I was increasingly irritated by Portlanders' smug certainty that they lived in a world-class city, an assessment prompted more by a thin veneer of cosmopolitanism and a reputation for livability than by actual achievement in business, education, or the arts. Portland had but a handful of major national corporate headquarters, and several of these had deserted the area as a result of acquisition or relocation. The high-tech sector that was supposed to assume the mantle of economic leadership from the forest products industry was proving to have less depth than advertised. I had seen first-hand how little capital was available locally for start-up or emerging companies. As much as I loved Portland State University, it simply didn't have the resources to power economic and cultural development in the region. Many prominent arts organizations were floundering and—with a few notable exceptions—little national-caliber work seemed to be taking place in town.

My practice had grown substantially, but so had my workload. Amy's resentment of the firm had noticeably increased, as my long hours at the office left her to raise our two young children largely on her own.

We began discussing a possible return to DC if Bush won the election and I landed a senior position in the administration. We thought taking a break from Portland would do us good, renewing our excitement about the place when we returned. Our thinking was to spend a few years in Washington—where the kids could grow closer to Amy's mother and brothers who still lived in the area—then come back with a new outlook and also a new job. I would get out of the grind of private practice and look for a position as general counsel with a corporation, which would still be demanding but not as draining in terms of hours and client development. I might even consider a run for office myself down the road, possibly for Congress. I would remain active in CoHo even while in Washington, but would turn over my day-to-day responsibilities to others on the board who appeared ready to step up.

The job that fired my interest the most was a little-known post in the State Department called the Assistant Secretary for International Narcotics Matters, which was the point position for negotiating narcotics-related treaties and providing international counternarcotics assistance. I had been impressed with the woman who held this position during my days fighting the drug war at the CIA, and I thought my background in the field might be enough to get me the job.

# BRAINSTORM

Then one evening in early 2000 as I sat listening to a concert by the wonderful Portland Baroque Orchestra, my political machinations were interrupted by a piercing thought. The well-tempered order of Baroque music suits my mental processes, clearing the flotsam and jetsam that clog my synapses (for at least twenty minutes). In recent months, I had been reading gushing reports in the popular press about advances in digital video, as well as how the explosion of Internet use and the proliferation of narrowly targeted cable channels would create opportunities for new forms of entertainment content. As a producer of off-Broadway theater, I knew that great entertainment was being created in small theaters all over the world on shoestring budgets. Why not harness the power of digital video to shoot the best of these productions professionally and inexpensively, then sell them to consumers of alternative entertainment over the Internet and to the new wave of narrowcasters?

I drove home after the concert and sat pondering the possibilities in the rarely used living room where we had hosted the first reading of *Bodyhold* almost seven years before. I knew there was no way to capture the immediacy of live performance on video, no matter how sophisticated the technology. I had watched a number of theater productions on public television that seemed muffled and flat. But just because a viewer could not experience all the dimensions of live theater in his living room did not preclude theater on video from being entertaining and rewarding, particularly when compared to so much of the mind-numbing dreck in the video marketplace. It would be a niche product to be sure, but I sensed there was an audience out there for the brain nourishment still being produced in the theater.

I wondered about the impact of such a product on live theater. If this were successful, would it drive away audiences who would just wait for productions to come out on video? My gut told me that theater on video would have the opposite effect. Just as recorded music drives fans to concerts by the musicians, I thought that theater on video would feed demand for touring live performances of the recorded shows. In many cases, we would be shooting shows that would not have made it out of their home cities, so the threat posed by national video distribution seemed negligible. We would be creating a market that did not presently exist. It was not as if theater in America were a booming enterprise in any event. Declining attendance had been sapping the vitality of the industry for years. Far from delivering a mortal wound, producing theater on video could deploy emerging technology to rejuvenate a flagging but integral performing art.

How would the artists themselves respond? As there was so little money in live theater, everyone I knew who acted on stage did so because they loved the work and the opportunity to connect with an audience. If shooting productions on video did not compromise the artistic integrity of the play and could introduce the material to a wider segment of the population—while enabling theater artists to realize a financial return on their labors of love—I felt certain that artists would react positively and agree to make the necessary rights available. Of course there would be purists who said that theater should be done live or not at all, but that was their privilege.

I felt both electrified and petrified. This could be a staggering opportunity to launch a new venture that drew together my passion for theater with my professional expertise in start-up businesses. I had been watching enviously for years as clients parleyed their experience and enthusiasm into dynamic new companies while I drafted important but lifeless documents. Part of the thrill of CoHo was being a principal in the enterprise, rather than just a highly compensated accessory. Everyone in this era of ostensibly limitless horizons seemed to have their own deal, and theater on video appeared perfectly suited to be mine.

But I had just laid out a sensible five-year plan that looked quite achievable. Bush—despite the insurgent campaign of John McCain—was a sure bet to capture the Republican nomination. Al Gore was not in the same league as Bill Clinton as a campaigner or strategist, and Nader's outspoken candidacy had the potential to hurt Gore in a number of key states. Thanks to my longstanding ties to Gordon Smith, I was in on the ground floor of the Bush campaign and well positioned for an upper-tier job in the administration if victory were ours.

However rational and linear my designs on DC might have been, I could not shake this notion of theater on video. I mentally constructed and discarded a dozen business models. I considered camera placements and the editing of footage shot from multiple performances. I wondered whether interactive technology could enable the viewer to shift perspective in the midst of watching the performance. I assessed the differing demands of producing a live show and recording that show. I devised website features that would help to build that fashionable buzzword, an *online community*.

Most crucially, I agonized over what sorts of productions to target. I interviewed the managing director of Portland's largest theater company to see whether it would be feasible to shoot plays produced by leading regional theaters such as the Goodman in Chicago or Arena Stage in Washington. He couldn't have been more discouraging. He said that Actors' Equity, the stage actors' union that was a major force in regional theater, loathed the videotaping of live performances and sought to bar the recording of plays featuring union members other than for archival purposes.

I was too inveterate an optimist to accept his gloomy pronunciations at face value, but his counsel led me to start with what I knew: plays produced in smaller venues. I had seen first hand for years how fertile this ground could be, because in these so-called "off-off Broadway" or "fringe" venues, theater artists were prepared to buck convention and take chances. I pictured smart, hip, Internet-savvy consumers—concentrated in their twenties and thirties but by no means limited to that demographic—who were looking for daring, original, and provocative content that they were not getting from Hollywood or the major broadcasters. I was confident that by scouring smaller theaters around the country (and beyond), this new venture could find productions that would fill that niche perfectly. Committed pro-management Republican though I was, I had worked with the actors' union on *Mary Tudor* and *St. Nicholas*, as well as on Ibsen's *Doll's House*, which CoHo was preparing to produce in the spring of 2000, and was by no means averse to striking a video deal with Equity. It seemed more prudent, however, to start with fringe productions and then work up the theatrical food chain as we gained recognition and, hopefully, resources.

I had confidence in myself as a producer and start-up authority, but I was well aware of my artistic limitations. Sure, I had done some acting and written a play, but I had never directed or even dreamed of doing so. I was above the national average when it came to knowledge of theater companies and playwrights, but I was no authority on the fringe scene. I needed a creative ally who could scout new material, identify hot prospects, help me build relationships with artists, and then direct the resulting video productions.

Thankfully, CoHo's co-production approach had introduced me to a number of able directors and allowed me to evaluate their production skills up close. The best candidate from this talent pool was Jeff Meyers, our co-producer on Patrick Marber's *Dealer's Choice*. Jeff had battled through the adversity of directing in a venue with no heat or running water to produce an award-winning play. He had co-founded his own theater company, Portland's Theatre Vertigo, so he spoke the language. He was also a published writer who was actively involved in slam poetry, including organizing the national slam when it had been held in Portland. He struck me as a junkie of popular culture, fed on a steady diet of alternative weeklies and other heterodox publications. I laid out my plans to him over a few Northwest micro-brews. While he reserved judgment, he looked ready to jump from the medical laboratory work that had been his daytime job the past dozen years.

As I hatched my video scheme in the spring of 2000, I continued to develop the Oregon Victory fundraising strategy with Dan, Lori, and Molly. There had been some sticky moments with the ideologues of the state party, but the hoped-for unity under the Bush banner had largely come to pass. Oregon's status as a battleground state meant we would see the candidates in person more than in years past, but we knew we could not depend on high-profile visitors to meet our goals. There would have to be a steady drumbeat of sophisticated solicitation—much it over the telephone—of donors who would expect to be speaking to a player in the campaign, not some phone bank functionary reading from a prepared script. Others would play their part, but I would be expected to hit the phone lines more than any other principal in the Victory effort.

Much of this was to occur during my sabbatical, which was slated to begin in July so we could take advantage of the kids' summer vacation. Amy and I had decided to take the family for a month to the Eastern Shore of Maryland, a favorite haunt from our days in DC. I planned to take several hours out of the day's family activities to place calls back to major donors in Oregon. Amy and I would then spend a few cherished weeks in England alone while the kids tested the patience of their grandparents. We would wind up the sabbatical in Portland for the final fall push leading up to the November election.

This was a major commitment of time from someone who sorely needed to re-connect with his wife and children and re-charge batteries drawn down from almost a decade of relentless civic networking and practice building. Amy and the kids had grown accustomed to my being a peripheral player in the family, and the sabbatical offered a shining opportunity to reverse dangerous trends and undo bad habits.

Before we began our travels, Governor Bush made a visit to Portland that provided some needed stoking of my motivational fires. I participated in a meeting he held at the Benson Hotel with a number of major players in forest products who were alarmed at the collapse of the industry in the Northwest and prepared to spend big dollars to see the Democrats they held responsible turned out of office. There was no smoke filling the Benson's Crystal Ballroom (well above the humble Parliament Rooms where we produced *Bodyhold*), but the smell of money was very much in the air. Bush said what you would have expected him to say to these timber titans, but he did so with class, poise, self-deprecating humor, and appealing informality. He came across as a man who would set no standards for scintillating oratory, but who was well-grounded and more inclined to pragmatism than ideology. I came away from the session impressed, appreciative, and ready to dial for dollars.

# RESTLESS SABBATH

The curious contrast between my activism in theater and Republican politics was magnified during this period of intense activity on both fronts, but the two spheres were meshing nicely. Sure, I was proposing to promote the bohemian world of fringe theater; however, I would do so not through government hand-outs but by good old private-sector entrepreneurship. If I went forward, I would raise funds from investors to shoot these productions on video, then hopefully recoup our investment from online sales and other distribution channels. The new venture would utilize the profit motive to unlock a chest of undiscovered treasure buried on smaller stages around the globe.

My ardor for pursuing theater on video overran almost everything else in my life at that point, but as the breadwinner for my wife and two young children I could not just rely on gut instinct as to its prospects. I decided to devote a portion of my sabbatical to commissioning a market assessment and developing a business plan outline that I would run past trusted friends and advisors. Only after that intensive evaluation process would I decide whether to put both the practice of law and my DC aspirations aside and leap into the treacherous waters of a start-up.

I worried about diluting the family aspect of my sabbatical even further, but CoHo provided an unexpected bonding opportunity. The cast of our spring show, *Doll's House*, included the three children of Nora and Torvald Helmer, the floundering couple who are the centerpiece of Ibsen's examination of marriage and women's independence. A husband and wife acting team had been cast in the show, and their daughter was the perfect choice to play one of the children (and save them some major babysitting bills). The director was having difficulty finding two other suitable kids, however, and as opening night drew near, I reluctantly agreed to discuss the roles with our children Graham and Alaina, then six and four. They knew all about daddy's theater company, having accompanied me on numerous program-advertising expeditions, and were intrigued at getting in on the action themselves. When I mentioned that it was a paying gig and would give them extra spending money, the deal was sealed.

Ibsen had been good enough to write the children only into the first act of the play, so they were free to go after intermission. The schedule was still grueling, however, with eight o'clock performances on Thursday, Friday, and Saturday evenings and a Sunday matinee at two. Amy joined me at the theater for almost every performance, serving as primary stage parent while I acted as CoHo house manager and concessionaire. The kids delighted in working the lobby at intermission in their adorable nineteenth century outfits, with baskets of caramels and chocolates for sale. We atoned for this shameless exploitation of our offspring by paying them a modest commission on their confectionery proceeds. With the four of us and the husband/wife/daughter acting team fully mobilized, we managed to turn one of the most anti-nuclear family plays in the history of Western civilization into a real family affair.

CoHo produced *Doll's House* in our seventh venue in as many productions. The art gallery where we had put on *St. Nicholas* had proven barely sufficient for a one-man show, and there was no way it would accommodate the overflowing Victorian-era sets and costumes of Ibsen. I had met the president of a children's media company named Flying Rhinoceros through local Republican politics. They had built a new corporate headquarters (complete with an airplane-mounted rhino hanging from the side of the facade) just north of the Pearl District that included an auditorium-type space where they planned to put on multimedia programs for area students. They did not anticipate using the auditorium during the evenings or on weekends, so it looked as if CoHo might have found its first serious prospect for a permanent home since St. Mark's.

The Flying Rhinoceros space had numerous drawbacks, including a complete absence of backstage areas, no theater lighting, and indifferent acoustics; but the ample supply of heat and running water was an improvement on recent venues, the location was outstanding, and our hosts graciously assessed no charge. We were now masters of fashioning unpromising spaces into functional theater venues, so these hurdles were not insurmountable. But our rented theater lights blew the building breakers on several occasions, and one Saturday evening we found that the company had changed the locks and forgotten to give us new keys—leaving us and a sizable audience stranded outside until we could raise an employee to come from home and open the doors.

As it developed, the spring of 2000 was the high water mark for the high-tech/Internet/multimedia tsunami. Investors did not know this yet, however, and they sank more money into promis-

ing companies like Flying Rhinoceros, which then went on a hiring binge, leading the company to conclude that it didn't have
room for a theater company. We could scarcely be bitter, as Flying Rhinoceros had been extremely accommodating, but it was
hard to muster up enthusiasm to go in search of yet another venue when we thought we had finally found a home. *Doll's House*
did not meet our attendance expectations, and we had no doubt
this was due in part to our constant changes of venue. A few of
our biggest fans took perverse pleasure in tracking our move-
ments around Northwest Portland, but most audience members
expressed befuddlement at our migration.

So once again I added venue scouting to a daunting to-do list,
which this time included winding up my practice in preparation
for the sabbatical, conducting telephone shakedowns of Republican donors, and trying to order my chaotic whirl of thoughts
about theater video. I found a vacant storefront that had sat empty for a year as the owner attempted to redevelop the space. It was
filthy and depressing, but available. I entered into negotiations
with the landlord, hoping something better would come along.

I had pictured an idyllic sabbatical full of unhurried strolls
with my wife and lazy August afternoons playing with the kids.
What I brought on myself during our month-long stay on Maryland's Eastern Shore was a regimen almost as taxing as my partner's grind in Portland. After making breakfast for the kids and
seeing them off to a nearby summer camp, I would spend most of
the morning crafting the business plan outline for my unnamed
theater video company, consulting with the marketing expert I
had chosen to prepare the market assessment, and speaking with
anyone I could think of who could help me get a handle on the
entertainment industry. Amy and I would enjoy a quick lunch,
then from noon to three I was on the phone to Oregon donors.
The powers that be in DC had scheduled Dick Cheney for a major

fundraiser at the home of one of my clients, so the pressure was on to turn out the faithful and fill the Victory coffers. I did manage to spend a few hours with the kids after they got out of camp in the late afternoon, but the intensity of the prior six or seven hours didn't make me the most companionable dad.

One of the Republican honchos who made it on my call list was Bob Packwood. Since his fall from grace, Packwood had become a successful Washington lobbyist, drawing on his former chairmanship of the Senate Finance Committee to attract clients in need of tax-related relief. He had married his former chief of staff, Elaine Franklin, and split his time between DC and Portland. I asked him about his life in Washington, and he mentioned that he was playing a lot of bridge. Bridge had been one of my favorite vices from high school through the CIA, which had a mean bridge club dominated by hard-boiled senior citizens. He pounced when I said I used to play a little, as he had no partner in Portland (Elaine preferring politics to cards). We went on to become a partnership and acquitted ourselves reasonably well in several local competitions. There was no rancor toward Bob in any of these tournaments, where bidding and making a tough slam seemed to trump any prior misdeeds.

As my enthusiasm for the theater video project waxed, my political motivation inevitably waned. I was a seasoned fundraiser, but I'd previously worked in short bursts, not dialing for dollars day after day for hours on end. I had also attempted to weigh in on arts policy with the Bush policy team, but my offers to help develop an arts platform went nowhere. The Republican Convention held in Philadelphia provided a needed lift for my flagging spirits. I drove up from Maryland for the final day of the festivities, and the Oregon delegation arranged to get me on to the floor. Campaign-hardened operative that I was, I assumed that all the hoopla and pageantry was manufactured for the television audience and would make little impression on me. Instead, I found myself genuinely taken with the incongruity of the whole spectacle: immaculately tailored Beltway sharks rubbing shoulders with little old ladies in ridiculous hats and yeomen from Nebraska sporting button-festooned vests. Of course I knew that the entire ritual was elaborately scripted, but the grassroots vitality that bubbled up from the various delegations was still contagious. Our efforts at party unity in Oregon had gone swimmingly, and I had pleasant chats with the head of the local Christian Coalition and the son of the state party chair. As the sensory-overload cascade of red, white, and blue balloons burst across the hall at the end of the evening, I headed back to the Eastern Shore, fortified for another round of Bush boosting.

Later that summer Amy and I deposited the kids with their grandparents and escaped to the United Kingdom. This supposed respite, too, was overshadowed by the theater video enterprise, which I had tentatively christened StageDirect. We were in London, the center of theater in the English-speaking world, and I might soon be a fringe theater video producer in need of material. I hit shows in fringe venues all over the city, from the back room of a pub in Camden Town to a drafty, cramped basement whose address still managed to confer West End prestige. I felt a little like the recent college graduate of some twenty years before who had combed the London theater listings armed with his student ID— although my selections then (Shaw, Coward, et al) were more upmarket than my current slant. It was August, so the pickings were slim, but I came across some promising productions and great interest from the theater types to whom I pitched my concept.

The consultant I had tapped for the market assessment was encouraging. She found no one else carving a similar niche, other than one company whose focus was on big-ticket Broadway shows. She saw a nice convergence of trends, with new avenues for delivering content intersecting with an emerging class of video consumers hungry for more than formulaic pap. She struggled to quantify the resources that would be needed to sell the product, but she saw a market well worth pursuing.

This assessment was reinforced by a book I had picked up for sabbatical reading called *Bobos in Paradise* by the columnist and commentator David Brooks. Brooks's central thesis was that the long-standing polarization of bourgeois and bohemian segments of American society (the two "bos" that made a "bobo") had given way to an intermingling of mainstream and counterculture. His far-reaching cultural analysis ranged from the mushrooming of coffeehouses like Starbucks and purveyors of weathered country furniture like Restoration Hardware in suburban enclaves to the shifting values reflected in the *New York Times* wedding announcements, which in a generation went from proud recitations of Establishment ancestry to proud descriptions of culturally adventurous careers.

I didn't embrace the whole of his critique, but Brooks crystallized for me a pattern in society that mirrored my own individual development. I had no desire to reject the bourgeois values of educational advancement, professional achievement, marriage, and parenthood that had informed my first forty years, but I did not view my treading of the conventional path as a vow of cultural or intellectual poverty. Time and again, I had insisted on preserving a vital bohemian element in my life. I took comfort in Brooks's view that these were no longer mutually exclusive paths but overlapping spheres, both of which prized cultural innovation.

And I was hopeful that a Bush presidency would help to further these trends. I knew that Bush was no bohemian, but his record of bipartisan tolerance in Texas and his message of compassionate conservatism suggested that he was not intent on waging cultural warfare. The fact that moderate insiders like Gordon

Smith lined up early for Bush could have just been bandwagon opportunism, but I took it as a sign that Bush was not a captive of social conservatives. I understood that choosing to become a theater video entrepreneur would mean shelving my plans for a senior position in a Bush administration, but I had no sense—as I labored on the StageDirect business plan and on fundraising for the Republican nominee—that I was operating at cross purposes.

I returned from England determined to proceed with Stage-Direct if I could raise the necessary funds. I contemplated an initial round of equity investment in the range of $750,000 followed by a $1.2 million second round, after which I did not anticipate needing any additional outside funding. These were modest capital needs by the frothy standards of the tech boom, but I did not see the company as a serious IPO prospect that would have to scale up so as to catch Wall Street's attention. I projected a staff of only four, including myself, with a team of independent contractor videographers, sound technicians, and editors whom we would bring on board as and when needed.

My plan was to develop a library of video productions that would be sold in VHS and DVD form over our website, achieve first-mover status in the marketplace, and establish an online community of alternative content enthusiasts who would return to our website not simply to check out trailers for new StageDirect videos but also to access interactive features that reinforced our basic message: small-stage theater offers some of the best entertainment anywhere. Chief among these features was the Virtual Audition Room, which would enable actors to post a brief video audition online that could be viewed by casting directors and talent scouts as well as the casual Web surfer looking for a quick video jolt. We also planned a parallel feature for writers. In addition, we would post a series of short solo performance pieces that could be downloaded for free. At that time, it was not cost effective to present movie-length videos via download or streaming from our website, but we planned to keep abreast of technological developments and offer our customers that option when it became feasible.

Based on research that Jeff Meyers and I had done, we thought we could produce a feature-length (80–120 minute) theater video for $25,000–$35,000, including upfront payments to writers, actors, directors, and camera and sound crew, as well as equipment rental and post-production costs. We would also offer the creators of these shows a royalty in the range of five percent of the gross revenues generated by their productions. Needless to say, production budgets at this level compared very favorably with the cost of a feature film. If we could achieve this sort of cost control in production and post-production, we would not have to sell huge quantities of product in order to become profitable. I projected that we would lose money in our first two years of operation, then turn the corner and become profitable in the third year. My exit strategy was to sell StageDirect after we achieved profitability to an entertainment and media conglomerate with the marketing and distribution resources that a start-up could never hope to achieve on its own.

After completing my business plan, I sat down with Craig Berkman, whose family of venture capital funds then had some $75 million under management. I did not look forward to the conversation. Regardless of his take on StageDirect, it signified a major change in our longstanding professional relationship, but I felt it would be insulting to him and foolish for me to not run the business plan past him. I urged him to evaluate the investment as he would any other potential portfolio company and told him that I would not be offended if he decided to pass, as I understood StageDirect was unlike any other company in which his funds had invested. I also told him that I knew any outside investor would expect me as the founder to commit my own money to the company; I said I was prepared to invest $125,000–$150,000 in the first round and possibly join in the second round as well. He took the plan and promised to get back to me shortly.

In the meantime, the Bush-Gore race was taking on an intensity not seen in a presidential campaign in Oregon in a very long time. Our polling was showing that Nader stood to score at least five percent of the vote in the state, which could throw Oregon into the Bush column. The national Bush people were committing more resources to the state and expecting us to come up with additional funds as well. Bush himself came to town for a major campaign rally at Portland's Memorial Coliseum, the former home of the NBA Trailblazers. I had met the Governor as part of a queue-up/grip-and-grin photo opportunity during his earlier visit, but this time I was one of a handful of Victory leaders and Oregon Republican VIPs who greeted the candidate as he emerged from his limo and then appeared with him on stage—much to the delight of my kids who were standing with Amy amongst the throng of loyalist well-wishers. Bush did a magnificent job, whipping the crowd to a frenzied pitch and telling them—without rhetorical flourish—that Oregon could determine the outcome of a national election. This was the sort of high-stakes political engagement I had been dreaming about for years, and it looked as if we were going to pull off a one-for-the-ages victory.

# TWO LEAPS

My political exultation was more than offset by CoHo's hor-
rendous experience on our fall production, a world premiere
called *The Folio* about the first publication of Shakespeare's plays.
We had not been able to locate a better venue than the sorry storefront I had found before my sabbatical, and it proved even more
dismal than expected. We learned that the utilities had been shut
off for a year, and it turned out to be no mean feat to have them
turned back on again. Even after power and gas were restored and
the heat was cranked up, the performance space was barely tolera-
ble, and the backstage area was frigid. We had rented an industri-
al-strength cleaning machine to deal with the year's worth of ac-
cumulated dirt and debris, but repeated sorties did not repel the
invading particulates, which just seemed to settle in different corners of the building. One of the actresses quit during the run because the cold and dust played havoc with her lungs. We brought
in a replacement who tried to pick up the part on a few days' re-

hearsal, but it was just too much for her to handle. We ended up doing several performances with our intrepid stage manager, in costume, reading the departed actress's part with script in hand. It was deeply embarrassing.

*The Folio* was the proverbial straw that broke the camel's back of CoHo Productions' itinerant existence. Bob Holden and I both declared that it was either time to find a permanent home or take up another hobby. As my plans for StageDirect took shape, I saw that the new venture might present an opportunity for CoHo as well. StageDirect would need office space and would benefit from access to a theater where it could shoot its productions. The two companies might be able to share a venue that neither could manage alone.

I had been scouring the streets of Northwest Portland on and off for the past several years and had not found anything in our price range that was a strong candidate for theater conversion. I felt hoisted on my own petard, as the success of my Ball Janik clients' redevelopment of the Pearl District had jacked up property values and rents beyond anything we could handle, even with a CoHo-StageDirect cohabitation.

Then I happened upon an empty building that had been home to a bookbindery. It was just a half block off of NW 23rd Avenue, a flourishing shopping corridor about a mile from the Pearl District that featured major national retailers and fine restaurants. The landlord had divided the 8,000 square foot building in half, which was tight for what we had in mind but adequate. The interior was essentially a concrete shell, which gave us design flexibility, and the ceiling height was a magnificent eighteen feet with no sightline-impeding columns. Electrical panels were everywhere, so there appeared to be plenty of power for our theater lighting. The landlord was seeking $3,000 a month, which was too much for CoHo alone but was manageable if StageDirect used a portion of the space for its offices and we could enlist another resident theater company. We were confident we could bring in another troupe because of the perpetual scarcity of decent venues in Portland, so going forward hinged on the funding of StageDirect.

I had been on tenterhooks as Craig Berkman reviewed the StageDirect business plan. After an excruciating wait of several weeks he came back and said he was very impressed with the plan and was prepared to fund most of the first round (other than the amount I had committed to invest) and would likely be a major participant in the second. He was in the midst of raising a new venture fund, which would be the source of capital for the Stage-Direct investment. He anticipated closing on this new fund by the end of 2000 and being in a position to complete the StageDirect investment in January of '01.

This joyous news touched off a jolting chain reaction of life changes. I told my partners at Ball Janik of my plans to leave the practice of law and launch this new venture. My hand was actually forced a few days before I had intended to announce the news, as the firm's senior partner called me to say there was gossip all around the office that I had agreed to join the corporate group of another law firm in Portland. I marveled at the mislabeled grist of this ever-smaller town's rumor mill and found myself in the odd position of assuring my partner that I was not betraying him for a competitor but for the far more jealous mistress of theater.

I suspect most office toilers believe (and at times fantasize) that word of their departure will leave their colleagues gaping in astonishment, but I know I stunned the Ball Janik partnership. I was viewed as one of the most driven partners the firm had ever produced, and the notion that I would walk away from a thriving practice for some flaky, arts-based start-up defied credulity. The firm had graciously humored my theater avocation by photocopying CoHo's low-tech programs, buying blocks of tickets, and running program ads, but I think they viewed theater as a harmless if mildly eccentric hobby of mine that certainly wouldn't interfere with the serious business of generating clients and billing hours. I offered to cut short my sabbatical and return to work, but to their credit they replied that the sabbatical had been earned by dint of prior service and that I should feel free to take it all. I came back to the office a little early anyway and negotiated a phased withdrawal, under which I would leave the partnership at year end and then remain for three to six months on a contract basis as we recruited a replacement corporate partner and transitioned my clientele.

Having set my own career ship adrift, I turned to securing a safe harbor for CoHo. A nonprofit theater company was not high on the landlord's list of dream tenants, but the space had been empty for a long time and we finally cajoled him into an initial three-year deal with two additional three-year option terms, as well as a decent tenant improvement allowance (and no personal guaranty from me). We had engaged an architect to begin planning the new theater on a budget of $100,000. Frankly, I had no idea how much CoHo would be able to raise to build out the venue and was daunted by the prospect of finding contributors at this level, as no donor had ever given us more than $10,000. The alternatives to not rolling the dice on a new theater, however, were closing down the company or continuing the harrowing life of an itinerant, neither of which was palatable to our board. We shut our eyes and signed the lease.

I also sold the '67 fire-engine red Mercury Cougar I had owned for the past five years. The grease monkey who had it before me had installed a double exhaust, much to the thrill of my kids (who called it the "voom-voom" car) and the chagrin of my neighbors. It got nine miles per gallon on a good day. I figured I could only manage one mid-life crisis at a time.

# ROLL CAMERAS

I was scarcely in need of more stimulation, but the denouement of the 2000 presidential election provided it anyway. The Victory program in Oregon unleashed a well-financed hail of get-out-the-vote body punches in the closing weeks that had the Democratic effort on the ropes. Nader was still tracking at some seven percent of the vote, which hurt Gore badly. The Gore-Lieberman campaign was forced to devote resources to Oregon that they desperately needed to deploy elsewhere. The handicapping of the race across the country by my professional, political friends showed a narrow but odds-on Bush victory.

The mood was guarded but cheerful as I sat down to an election-day lunch with the Oregon Republican brass at Jake's Famous Crawfish, the heart of the McCormick & Schmick restaurant empire run by longtime GOP fundraiser Bill McCormick. My service as Victory Finance Chair had earned me a seat at the table with Gordon Smith, Mark Hatfield, Molly Bordonaro, Dan Lavey,

Lori Hardwick, and a few other select party stalwarts. I was at once fiercely engaged in the battle—having fought so hard for almost a year—and curiously distanced from it, as my decision to proceed with StageDirect meant that the outcome of the election would have little effect on my personal fortunes.

Most of this same group reassembled that evening in a suburban hotel room to watch the returns. We experienced the same roller-coaster mood swings as viewers across the nation that night, but our personal investment in Bush's cause and the fact that our own state was so pivotal heightened the tension. Gordon was receiving insider reports by phone that sometimes confirmed and at other times contradicted the television pundits. We dispersed after midnight when it became clear that the outcome would remain in doubt.

The ensuing weeks of recount posturing, hanging chads, guerrilla-style litigation, Florida state court machinations, and ultimate U.S. Supreme Court resolution were surreal for any political observer, but for me they formed a bizarre backdrop to the selection of fringe plays to shoot on video. Jeff Meyers and I were determined to seek out productions that were daring, original, and intelligent, but also entertaining and marketable. Our target audience were culturally active consumers whom our marketing consultant termed *experiencers*: vital, enthusiastic, impulsive, and rebellious, they sought out variety and excitement, savoring the new and the offbeat. While in marketing buzzspeak we considered this to be more of a psychographic than a demographic, we assumed that most of our viewers would fall within the eighteen to forty-five age range.

We had nothing against Shakespeare or Neil Simon, but they didn't offer the departure from the conventional that was to be our hallmark. Also, successful video productions of *Macbeth* or *The Odd Couple* would have required a level of star power that we did not have the resources to deliver. We were looking for future stars—writers and actors with the guts and the chops to challenge the status quo. An example we often cited was Chicago's Steppenwolf Theatre Company, where a dedicated group of young theater artists (including John Malkovich, Gary Sinise, and Laurie Metcalf) operating in tiny venues had emerged from obscurity by taking chances and maintaining a fanatical devotion to quality.

Two artists that went rapidly to the top of our prospect list were David Schmader and Jeff Goode. David was a hilarious, incisive, and openly gay columnist for the Seattle weekly *The Stranger* who had developed a series of one-man shows that culminated in his tour de force *Straight*. *Straight* was a deft and wry examination of conversion therapy, the Christian-based movement to convert gays and lesbians to heterosexuality. David's story gently unfolded through his recounting of undercover visits to a doctrinaire psychiatrist, a conversion support group, and a spiritual retreat. *Straight* impaled many in David's path with its caustic wit, with the gay community on the receiving end of as many barbs as the conversionists. David had toured *Straight* all over the country, garnering favorable reviews from the *Los Angeles Times*, *San Diego Union Tribune*, *Seattle Weekly*, and others.

Our marketing consultant and I had identified gays and lesbians as a significant consumer segment for StageDirect. Gay households, in particular, were often culturally active, above average in disposable income, and open to new and unconventional modes of entertainment. Jeff and I saw *Straight* as a wonderful vehicle to reach this demographic, although we thought heterosexuals would enjoy the show as well.

I did not agonize as a Republican over whether to produce *Straight*. It was an extremely well written production that seemed ideally suited for an important target market of our little theater video company. It had earned strong reviews from gay and straight publications alike. It met StageDirect's criteria: daring, original, intelligent, entertaining, and marketable.

I admit I had my share of ambivalence about homosexuality. The scourge of AIDS had touched me personally, as I had lost several Williams friends and classmates to the disease, but I deplored the promiscuity that had contributed to the epidemic. As someone who had chosen to have a traditional nuclear family, I was concerned about the decline of the institution of marriage and wondered how best to recognize the relationships of gay and lesbian partners in the eyes of the law. But abstract discussions of gay rights required a level of objectification and depersonalization that I could not achieve and would never wish to. It's easy to fulminate about the "homosexual agenda" if there are no homosexuals who play a meaningful part in your life. Gay men and lesbian women, however, had been my collaborators, partners, and friends in theater for almost twenty years. The genius of *Straight* was its withering use of humor to debunk stereotype and myth and present the contestants in the conversion struggle for who they were—warts and all.

The second artist, Jeff Goode, was best known as the author of *The Eight: Reindeer Monologues*, a biting series of single-actor pieces in which Santa's reindeer take on rumors of scandal and corruption at the North Pole. Goode's wicked satire had played to outstanding reviews nationwide and had become a holiday cult classic. Jeff Meyers and I saw it as a great debut release for the '01 Christmas season. Unfortunately Goode—while himself willing—had sold the rights to *The Eight* to a small New England publishing house that refused to grant us authority to record the show out of concern that a video would squeeze their live performance royalties. I was convinced that making *The Eight* available on video would only expand the demand for the live show, but I couldn't persuade Goode's publisher.

Jeff Meyers mentioned that Goode had written another riotous satire that had also earned great reviews. He described *Poona the Fuckdog* as a collection of bedtime stories for grown-ups. At first I questioned whether the profanity in the title was gratuitous, but after I read the script I was hooked. *Poona* was a brilliantly written laceration of commercialism, mass media, and sexual exploitation, cleverly cloaked in fairy tale garb. Poona is a little lost fuckdog who lives in the woods and has no one to play with until her Fairy God Phallus arrives bearing a gift of a big pink box. Suddenly, Poona is very popular, particularly with a handsome prince who comes often to play in her pink box. She then embarks on a series of adventures, becoming a football star in the Kingdom of Do, where no one did, and then a washed-up has-been in thrall to the rapacious Man Who Can Sell Anything. Goode's play—which had been favorably reviewed by the *New York Times*, the *New Yorker*, the *Chicago Tribune*, and many others—skewered our culture's obsession with naughty words while so many worse things were visited upon us without complaint.

Theatre Vertigo, the Portland theater company that Jeff Meyers co-founded but subsequently left, was planning to produce *Poona* in early '01. Jeff and I decided to make it StageDirect's first video production. We thought its subversive yet cartoonish quality would make it highly desirable to the smart, nonconformist Generation X consumers that we considered a key target market. Jeff's biggest concern was that the unwieldy cast size would strain our videographic capabilities. We had hoped to start shooting shows with a limited number of performers on stage at any one time—such as *Straight* or *The Eight*—and then build up to larger productions as our technical proficiency increased. But we had the advantage of working in our own backyard with a theater company we knew well, and they were prepared to let us record as many as seven performances, allowing sufficient coverage of the many crowded scenes. Jeff also scheduled several shoots without an audience, permitting camera and microphone placements that were not feasible with an audience present.

I had been invited to the Bush inaugural, but it fell on the weekend of our first shoot. My priorities were clear at this point, so the political glitz fell by the wayside. The incongruity of foregoing a Republican inauguration to shoot *Poona the Fuckdog* on video was not lost on me.

In any case, I had already started to cinch my belt on extraneous expenses. For the time being I was still making good law-firm money, but the salary I would earn once we closed on our first round of financing was less than a quarter of what I had made as a partner. I thought it critical that our investor funds go toward producing top-quality video and marketing, not my paycheck.

I was also growing anxious about Craig Berkman's ability to close on his new venture capital fund. The collapse of the tech boom was inflicting casualties across the board, including venture capitalists with longer track records and deeper pockets than Craig's upstart family of funds. He said he remained committed to StageDirect, but almost every conversation brought word that he would have to put off the investment a while longer. One of my recruits for StageDirect had given notice at her current job; as weeks went by with no sign of funds and the end of her notice period looming, I urged her to see if she could rescind her notice. Luckily her boss valued her so highly that he was willing to keep her on. I felt helpless and humiliated. I had already resigned my partnership and was plowing money into the production of *Poona* and the negotiation of new projects in reliance on this funding.

It was clear that I needed to look elsewhere for investors if I were serious about launching this company. As painful as his inability to deliver on the promised funding was proving to be, I did not blame Craig personally. I considered us both victims of the cruelly cyclical capital markets. I updated the business plan to reflect the progress we'd made and approached the traditional sources of funding for start-up ventures: family members and old friends. I understood that, with Berkman's fund out of the picture, I would have to increase my own investment to demonstrate my confidence in our prospects. My grandmother had recently passed away and left me a legacy, which I would ordinarily have socked away for retirement or college funding for the kids. Not now. I chose instead to commit these funds to StageDirect.

I was able—through a combination of my own funds and commitments from a Williams classmate, my parents, a close friend at Ball Janik, and a local investor—to raise about sixty percent of what I had originally projected for our first round. To make the deal, I had to offer the option of acquiring additional shares at the first-round purchase price, which could prove a valuable right for the investors if the company prospered. This shortfall in funding forced me to significantly cut our marketing budget. I thought it essential that we not reduce funding for video production. The crown jewels of StageDirect would be our library of content, and I felt that we needed to build up a critical mass of quality product in order to be taken seriously.

Jeff Meyers did a magnificent job of developing new projects. He discovered a delightful one-man show in Seattle called *The Haint*, a Southern Gothic ghost story featuring a single actor playing thirteen different characters in a Tennessee town that is haunted by a restless spirit. The amazingly gifted performer, Troy Mink, shifted on the fly from character to character simply by changing posture, accent, and intonation.

Jeff had lived in Chicago before moving to Portland and had a high regard for a company there called The Neo-Futurists, who were best known for a long-running late night show called *Too Much Light Makes the Baby Go Blind*. This dauntingly innovative production featured thirty two-minute plays performed every Friday and Saturday night. Each weekend an audience member rolled a die to determine how many new two-minute plays needed to be added to the repertory for the following weekend. The company then had to write and rehearse the new pieces during the week. Over the long term, we hoped to shoot a number of the short plays for posting on our website, but in the meantime we had heard great things about a feature-length project The Neo-Futurists had created called *Jokes and Their Relation to the Unconscious*. The play, like its namesake essay by Freud, sought to kill comedy by explaining what made it funny. Far from destroying humor, *Jokes* left its audience in hysterics as it examined theories of comedy from Bergson to Milton Berle.

Jeff and a group of writers had created an acclaimed show in Portland consisting of monologues by actors playing notorious serial killers, which included Ted Bundy and "The Night Stalker" Richard Ramirez. The result was an intense examination of psychopathic denial coupled with chilling confession that they called *Mass Murder*. Far from glorifying these killers or investing them with superhuman powers (a la Hannibal Lecter in *The Silence of the Lambs*), the play treated them with unswerving honesty as the failed human beings they truly were. To his credit, Jeff was reluctant to propose his own work as a StageDirect project, but I was struck by the vivid authenticity of the monologues and their disturbing depictions of aberrant psychology.

We shot four of these productions—one in Portland, two in Seattle, and one in Chicago—before finally closing on our financing in July '01. I felt we were accomplishing exactly what we had set out to do: capture sharp, provocative, unconventional yet entertaining writing and performance at a very modest cost that averaged about $20,000 per production. We were not in a position to offer our artists much money, but we preserved the artistic integrity of their work and delivered on what we promised with regard to camera, sound, and other technical elements. While no two of our shows could be classed in the same genre, I thought that each offered solid marketing hooks that would enable us to find an audience. David Schmader had rebuffed our initial overtures to shoot *Straight*, but I was hopeful that once he saw our other work he would come on board, and Jeff had identified a number of other promising prospects.

Initial operations for StageDirect were conducted from my law office at Ball Janik while CoHo's theater project lurched slowly along. It was a curious existence, as I continued to handle transactions for longstanding clients while setting up the infrastructure for StageDirect and fielding frantic calls and e-mails from Jeff, who was learning a new field under trying circumstances. It was reassuring to be in familiar quarters among old colleagues and loyal clients, but it lent a distinct air of unreality to the proceedings. The income from my practice was welcome, but I felt it was time to end my long-running law-and-arts straddling act and throw myself fully into StageDirect and CoHo. The desire to sever old ties was accentuated by Doubting Thomas drop-bys from my former partners, who had heard about the collapse of the Berkman funding and wondered (a little smugly) whether I would ever make it out of the gate. Not to mention the caustic comments regarding the appearance of the website designer working with me at the firm, who sported various piercings and wore shorts exposing heavily tattooed shins amongst the pinstripes of my colleagues.

# IN THE HOUSE

A number of my comrades in arms on the Bush campaign were scoring plum positions in the administration. I must confess I felt a twinge each time I heard about another Republican angel getting his wings, particularly as my venture capital investment vaporized before my eyes. I consoled myself that these foregone opportunities bolstered the virtue of my cause—I was not only spreading the gospel of fringe theater and building a new performing arts venue, but also giving up the spoils of political war to do so. But these momentary surges of good feeling would often be interrupted by my office phone ringing in the disaster of the day.

The CoHo theater project seemed to be spiraling out of control. Our board had gone through countless brainstorming sessions with our architect as we tried to shoehorn a ninety-nine-seat performance space, backstage area, lighting booth, prop and set storage, lobby, box office, handicapped accessible men's and women's restrooms, and office area of at least 1,000 square feet into premises of only 4,000 square feet. We were thrilled with the design that had emerged from these skull sessions: a three-quarter round performance space with only three rows of seating that made for intimate theater. Passageways behind the wings would lend the venue a dynamic energy by enabling actors to make entrances through the audience. A mezzanine, made possible by the towering ceilings of the old book bindery, would allow performers and sets to operate on a second level. The building's industrial roll-up door would be replaced by a gleaming glass storefront opening on to an airy lobby.

But our architect, though a pleasure to work with, had badly misjudged both the cost and the timetable for the project. He had suggested that we obtain an estimate on the job from one of the larger construction firms in Portland. He expected that the smaller contractors he usually worked with would be able to beat the big firm's price by twenty-five to thirty percent and come in at or near our budgeted cost. He was seriously wrong. The larger firm came in with an estimate that was 180 percent of our original budget and the smaller builders came in well over the larger firm's bid, as their lack of familiarity with a theater and related public assembly code requirements led them to estimate cautiously. By the time we finished negotiating a contract with the larger firm, the construction cost was twice our original budget, not including theater lighting, sound, and other extras.

The tragedy in this was that we had far exceeded our expectations in fundraising. After eight productions and numerous Drammy awards, we had a good story to tell. Several major foundations in Portland stepped up with sizable grants. They were impressed with the success we'd achieved without foundation support or a permanent home. They bought into CoHo's unique co-production model and the commitment demonstrated by our all-volunteer operation. I believe they would have given us more money if we had asked for it, but unfortunately our requests were based on our original budget.

There was no public money available for the theater. We hadn't asked for money from the Regional Arts & Culture Council since our unpleasant experience on *Bodyhold*, but I made an exception because of the extraordinary demands of building a new theater. I contacted the Council staff to let them know about our plans; they advised me that they had no funds for capital projects. They acknowledged that the scarcity of decent venues was one of the greatest challenges facing the arts in Portland, but said they had allocated their limited resources to other programs.

I saw that I had little choice if we were to proceed with the theater but to hit up my friends, colleagues, and family members for donations. This squeeze couldn't have come at a worse time: I was already in frenzied fundraising mode for StageDirect after the Berkman investment fell through. Additionally, I was still reeling from the Bush campaign overdrive of the previous summer and fall. CoHo had done a general solicitation letter that had proven quite successful, but I now intensified my efforts by making one-on-one pitches and calling in chits built up over the past decade of community activism. The response was gratifying but still left a significant shortfall. The only way the contractor would go forward under these circumstances was if I stepped up and personally guaranteed the construction contract.

Amy was already suffering through the shock of an over seventy-five percent reduction in household income and the severe shaking of our piggybank for StageDirect. I dreaded going to the well again, especially as I knew her support for CoHo was tempered by the natural resentment of a wife and mother left at home while her husband slaved over his labor of love. She knew how vital the new theater was to me, though, and agreed that with all the other risks we were running, this one seemed manageable. The contractor made the decision a little easier by assenting to a ninety-day grace period after construction was completed to enable us to pull in more donors.

The financial obstacles in the path of the new theater were at times surpassed by City of Portland permit nightmares. Our architect had emerged from a preliminary meeting with a smile on his face. They love the project, he declared; we should have all our permits in a month. We'd expected a warm reception at City Hall, as this was the first new theater to be built in Portland in several years and was to be funded entirely by private sources. We understood that a theater was a place of public assembly and subject to a stringent fire and life safety code. We had no intention of cutting corners in these areas after years of fending off the fire marshal in makeshift venues, but we'd hoped that the planners would be supportive of a small all-volunteer non-profit tackling a huge capital project.

They weren't. First came a decision that would have caused a dramatic increase in our fire system budget by classifying our performance space and our lobby as two separate occupancies. We prevailed in an appeal by explaining what seemed to us self-evident: we were not a movie theater with large crowds waiting in the lobby to see the next show, but a live theater venue with an audience that was either watching the play in the performance space or sipping coffee and munching cookies in the lobby at intermission.

This was just a warm-up to the main act, which involved our parking lot. I use the term "lot" advisedly, as it consisted of two-and-a-half faintly striped spaces on tired concrete in front of our building. The planners said that our parking had to be screened with landscape buffers, ostensibly to shield neighboring properties from the eyesore of vehicles on our premises. This verged on absurdity, as the neighboring properties consisted of an overgrown gravel parking lot on one side and a commercial print shop with cars and delivery trucks constantly coming and going on the other, but we were prepared to play along if it didn't blow a hole in our budget. Then we found that the buffers had to be five feet in width and could only be situated at the end of the building on the side adjoining the gravel parking lot. The problem was that there were two premises in our building, ours and our neighbor's, and a five-foot landscape buffer would run right in front of our neighbor's roll-up door, which they used on a regular basis. The only way out of this, our architect advised, was to secure a variance, which would take weeks and require payment of a substantial fee—not a welcome expenditure with all our other cost overruns.

Thanks to the variance and other wrangles with the bureaucracy, the promised four-week permit-review period turned into four months and would have been much longer had an old friend from my Portland State days not pulled some strings at City Hall. The planners were not, in general, rude or arrogant; they just displayed epic inflexibility. I think I would have preferred a Chicago-style payoff to being killed with such kindness.

We had negotiated an agreement to share the theater with another small Portland company, the wonderfully named Stark Raving Theatre. They would open the season and have four six-week performance slots in rotation with CoHo, which would have three such slots. Stark Raving patiently put up with the construction delays and pushed off the scheduled preview for their first show of the season until the last possible Saturday. The City of Portland issued the necessary certificate of occupancy that Friday afternoon.

We were gnawing our nails regarding our own season in the midst of coping with the exploding theater budget and timetable. We had chosen Rebecca Gilman's *Spinning Into Butter* as our debut production in the new space. We thought Gilman's play, about racial attitudes on a seemingly progressive and tolerant but overwhelmingly white small college campus, would be a wonderful mirror to hold up to liberal, lilywhite Portland. Our challenge was that the recent popularity of the play in London, New York, and other major cities had resulted in its gaining restricted status, meaning that any large professional company in our area could put a hold on the rights. We waited through the summer for the rights to clear, but they didn't. We passed several internal deadlines before finally setting a drop-dead date of August 15th, a little over two months from our scheduled October opening. Just days before we would have had to abandon the project, the rights came through.

The gamble paid off splendidly. The reviews were superb, and the box office took off. We were selling out by the third week of the run, something we hadn't even accomplished with *Mary Tudor*. Our only regret was that the theater-share arrangement with Stark Raving, which favored stability over opportunity, precluded extending the run.

Both audiences and critics raved about the new theater. The Oregonian called our space "a wonderful new theater-in-the-semi-round." *Willamette Week* said that CoHo "succeeded in creating one of the finest and most versatile black boxes in the city" and that "the new CoHo Theater hits a new mark...for theatrical venues in Portland." While we lost some of our old advertisers from the Pearl District, we found new ones closer to the theater. We ended up clearing a healthy profit from the production and achieving a nice paydown on our construction debt, which was still a daunting figure despite our accelerated fundraising.

The overall project cost had ended up topping 250 percent of our original budget. The contractor did a first-rate job, but there were inevitably surprises—few of which redounded to our benefit.

Even with all the electrical panels remaining from the book bindery, we still had to put in another electrical service dedicated to the
theater lights, which required an amazing amount of juice. At least
we knew that we would be able to accommodate a full house on a
sweltering day in August and still be able to run the air condition-
ing and a galaxy of stage lights. I advanced my own funds to enable
us to pay off the contractor, then negotiated a line of credit with an
area bank that naturally insisted on my personal guaranty.

I was not exactly feeling flush. The investors in StageDirect
had allowed me to extend the first round in an effort to attract
more capital, but I had had little success. The tech/dotcom melt-
down followed by the events of September 11, 2001 had dried
up funding for all but the most sure-fire start-up ventures, which
ours assuredly was not. We had to scale down the promotional
blitz I had hoped would mark the launch of our website in early
'02. It was also taking longer than projected to complete post-production on the shows we had already recorded. Jeff had shot four
plays in succession—out of scheduling necessity, not by choice—
and faced the unenviable task of editing them back-to-back. He
was exhausted and unable to devote time to other matters, which
meant that website features such as the Virtual Audition Room
had to be postponed.

Then lightning struck. Because we had so little money available for marketing, I decided that our limited funds were best
spent on public relations. I thought that StageDirect's story of capturing great theater on small stages across the country would res-
onate well with the media, so I hired a small but hip and aggressive Portland-based PR firm, Media Cabin. I considered looking
in Los Angeles for a firm that specialized in the entertainment
business but concluded that face-to-face engagement was more
important. I was initially put off when the head of Media Cabin sent two twenty-somethings—one with a tongue piercing—to

meet with me in a formidable Ball Janik conference room. I soon came to recognize that I had to put aside my middle-aged law-firm partner snobbery and embrace our target demographic. Our strategy was to deploy media relations and targeted advertising to drive prospective viewers to our website, where they would be wowed by our trailers and plunk down their credit cards to watch great theater in the comfort of their living rooms.

Their media specialist set to work pitching our story and managed to score a feature in the *Wall Street Journal*. We had made a deal with a local company that was marketing a video-on-demand technology to mid-range hotels. They were excited about including our content in their package and elected to feature several of our productions in a pilot project they were running at a new area hotel. The *Journal* writer, a freelancer based in Portland, checked into the hotel and watched *The Haint, Mass Murder*, and *Jokes and Their Relation to the Unconscious* from the cozy confines of her hotel room. She also went up to Seattle to watch us shoot our fifth production, a powerful one-man show called *The Magnificent Welles* about the legendary Orson Welles in the wake of Citizen Kane.

The *Journal* story, published in the March 1, 2002 weekend edition, was fabulous and was followed a few months later by an Associated Press national wire service article that was picked up by the *Los Angeles Times* and a number of other large papers. In the meantime, we started a modest advertising campaign, primarily with the online version of *The Onion*—a saucy anti-newspaper that we thought hit our hip target customer spot-on—and with Playbill.com, *American Theatre* magazine, and *The Onion's* Chicago print version.

My spirits were at long last lifting. Jeff and a fuzzy-cheeked, ear-pierced Portland video editor he had recruited were working wonders with our product and staying on budget. They had an enormous amount of footage to draw from—usually four cameras all shooting four performances of each show plus the no-audience sessions—but they made smart, tasteful choices that they wove into the seamless, professional productions I'd hoped we could achieve. We were excited by *The Magnificent Welles*, where we thought the name recognition of Orson Welles would give us a lift. David Schmader had finally come around, and we were slated to shoot *Straight* at the CoHo Theater over two weeks in May. Boosted by the media coverage and the new production deals, some of the original investors (including me) and several new ones committed approximately $125,000 in additional money to the company, which gave us a much-needed cushion.

Above all else, I found it exhilarating to go to work in a theater I had been instrumental in building. After years of playing at theater while lodged in a well-appointed law office, I was fully committed and literally in the house. It felt so genuine to hurl myself into StageDirect while making a home for CoHo. The tumult of performances, rehearsals, and readings sometimes made it hard to get any work done, but it was immensely gratifying to see such activity in a space that had been an empty shell just a few months before. The community newspaper conferred an extra measure of validation by honoring me with their '02 Award of Excellence in the Performing Arts, which meant more to me than the *Business Journal* "40 Under 40" award that had crowned my years of eager-beaver networking.

CoHo was thriving. We had never previously been able to sell season tickets, because we had never known which makeshift venue would host our next production. By the end of our first season in the new theater, we had signed up over 175 subscribers, a modest but encouraging beginning. The success of *Spinning Into Butter*, which we revived for a second run over the summer, enabled us to pay down our line of credit by almost fifty percent.

Both the quantity and quality of co-production submissions had increased substantially, which augured well for the second season in our new home. We had to modify our co-production financial model, however, because of the financial burden of the theater. Though we could no longer afford to share half of any upside with our co-producers, we paid out small bonuses after the initial run and increased compensation for the summer revival of *Spinning Into Butter* in an effort to share some of the "wealth."

The community had also made us feel welcome, with the notable exception of our next-door neighbors. They vigorously enforced the no-parking signs in front of their side of the building and had several of our theater patrons towed. The neighbors were an oddly matched couple. He was middle-aged, tattooed, and almost always clad in Lycra stretch pants, which did not flatter his expanding paunch. She was much younger and buff, with a vivid hair and eye color not readily found in nature. The only evidence of a business on the premises was a small sign reading *Bolder Productions*, and our landlord had told us only that they did some sort of video production. Our enterprising website specialist looked them up online and discovered that they were big-time purveyors of sado-masochistic pornography. We found this a little hard to believe until a stage manager reported hearing the sounds of whips and chains next door during a rehearsal. Then, a red SUV proclaiming "The Demonatrix" kept appearing in their parking lot. We wondered whether our landlord was trying to establish some sort of alternative entertainment office park.

There were times when I felt like approaching our Bolder buddies for tips on selling online. StageDirect was having little success moving product from our website. Media Cabin had designed some ingenious ads that drove traffic to our site. I would sit at my computer reveling in website tracking that showed thousands of daily hits. Unfortunately, most of the visitors stayed only to watch a trailer or two. We were discovering what so many other e-commerce entrepreneurs came to learn in this sobering post-boom period: it is extremely difficult to establish a prosperous online business without a brand name nurtured on years of brick-and-mortar operations. Sure, we had been in the *Wall Street Journal* and the *Los Angeles Times*, but that scarcely made StageDirect a household name. However impressed would-be consumers might have been with our trailers, it turned out that few of them were prepared to plunk down twenty dollars to buy a product they had never heard of and featured unheralded actors and directors. I had banked on the daring and original character of our productions generating an online buzz that would be fed by favorable PR, but it simply failed to materialize, and the fact that we had fallen behind in adding community-building features like the Virtual Audition Room didn't help.

In short order I shut down our advertising campaign. It was clear that we had nowhere near enough funding to push viewers to our website in numbers that would generate meaningful sales, and I thought it critical that we conserve our remaining cash and refocus. I had considered the traditional video distribution channels—broadcast and home video—as secondary opportunities for StageDirect because of the tremendous margins a producer could realize retailing its own product. I now decided we had no choice but to make them the centerpiece of our business. We had demonstrated that we were not a one-off bit player. We already had an impressive core of four productions, with two more excellent shows (*The Magnificent Welles* and *Straight*) in the pipeline. Our national media exposure, I felt, would validate StageDirect's credibility with potential distributors.

What we sorely lacked was knowledge of the entertainment business. I was a skilled corporate lawyer and an experienced theater producer, but I knew almost nothing about broadcast or home video. Nor did any of our investors. I had tried to recruit an entertainment industry insider to our board, but my range of acquaintance was limited and our under-funded status did not make us an attractive candidate for a busy professional. I called anyone I knew who might be able to offer guidance.

A former Hollywood entertainment lawyer whose investment company had participated in several deals with clients of mine came to our rescue. He viewed several of our titles, was impressed, and sent them over to a contact of his at ICM—one of the premier agencies in the entertainment industry. To my astonishment, they expressed interest in representing us. I had seen countless movies where big-time agencies take on clients and then proceed to do absolutely nothing for them, so I opted to jump on a plane to LA and meet with the ICM agent face to face.

It was a grand day. I had lunch with the Los Angeles entertainment lawyer we had hired to prepare our actor, writer, and theater company contracts (I was not so foolish as to represent myself in this treacherous field) and a drink with Bob Holden's actor son at one of the landmark Beverly Hills hotel bars. I then wheeled through the afternoon sunshine in my subcompact rental car to ICM's sleek Wilshire Boulevard offices, where I was ushered into the agent's cramped but chic office. She came across as one of those hard-bitten/heart-of-gold types who would give our product the tough love it deserved. She said that they had identified a prime prospect—an up-and-coming cable broadcaster out of New York called Trio—but they had numerous other candidates in mind if that didn't work out. I asked all the right questions, and she gave all the right answers.

Or so I thought. For all intents and purposes, I never heard from her again. She stopped returning my calls shortly after I went back to Portland, and I learned later that the head of Trio had been shown the door and replaced by a music video maven who had little interest in theater. I suspect this was all ICM needed to put us on ice. Thankfully we hadn't signed anything with the agency, which left us free to go swimming with other sharks.

On the home video front, I made a host of inquiries resulting in referrals to two companies: Kultur and Image Entertainment. I was impressed with Kultur but concerned that their focus on fine arts such as opera, ballet, and classical music would not be a good fit with our edgier, more alternative content. They also insisted on locking us into a five to seven year deal, which made me nervous. Image Entertainment was a larger company that distributed a number of rock concert and other performance videos that seemed more compatible with our mission, and they were prepared to accept a shorter-term contract as well. After consulting with our lead investor who served with me on the StageDirect board, I decided to go with Image.

Right after we verbally committed to Image, the line to them seemed to go dead as well. I was already bitter after the cold shoulder treatment by ICM and did not take well to unreturned phone calls in what should have been our honeymoon period. Perhaps the toughest adjustment in launching StageDirect had been the recognition that I was an utter nobody in the entertainment business. For the past ten years I had dwelt in an admittedly provincial universe, but in that world I was a player who was accustomed to being treated respectfully and having his calls returned. It was galling to find at age forty-two that my status as a bigshot Ball Janik partner, pillar of the Portland community, and major Oregon political fundraiser didn't mean squat to these entertainment types. I sent a courteous but pointed e-mail complaining about their communications, after which they almost immediately pulled the deal. For a week or two I was despondent, aghast that my fragile ego might have destroyed the company's future. I came around to the view that they couldn't have been that excited about our product to have walked away with so little provocation. We were better off finding that out early on, but the experience left my stomach churning for some time.

We ended up signing a representation deal with a small firm referred by Ingram (one of the largest video distributors in the country). These reps clearly didn't have the sales and marketing muscle of Image or Kultur, but they were responsive and engaged. They were also prepared to work cooperatively with the educational distributor we had selected. From the outset, I had viewed our product as both entertainment and art, commercial and educational. I saw opportunities in marketing StageDirect to colleges, high schools, and libraries and had sent an introductory letter to university theater departments across the country as part of our initial marketing thrust. I had learned that a key to success in this marketplace was to arrange for reviews in publications like *Library Journal*, *Booklist*, and *Video Librarian* and sent screening copies of our titles to the appropriate editors. The reviews were universally favorable, which helped us to land a leading educational distributor out of Southern California. At their suggestion, we developed instructional guides for most of our titles, which would enable them to charge a premium price.

One of my most gratifying experiences came when a librarian from a rural district in Madras, Oregon contacted me to say that their library had raised enough funds to open a small film center in a converted church (there was no cinema in town) and that they wanted to show a StageDirect video as their premiere. While our core demographic was urban hipsters, I had also thought that we might have appeal for rural audiences who would never enjoy the chance to see productions like ours live. I readily agreed to their request and drove several hours out to Madras with a digital copy of *The Haint* in hand. I received a celebrity's welcome and was truly moved by the delight that this earnest small-town audience took in Troy Mink's performance.

We had flirted with the idea of theatrical release for our titles, but thought it might be asking too much of an audience to go to the cinema to watch a video of a live theater performance. However, we had aggressively pursued film festival opportunities, as these seemed like a low-cost means of gaining exposure for our product. *Poona* was accepted at the New York International Independent Film and Video Festival—the largest film festival in the world—and numerous gay and lesbian film festivals screened *Straight*. The leading art house cinema in Portland, Cinema 21, also held a three-day StageDirect film festival featuring *The Magnificent Welles, Straight*, and *Poona*. *Poona* drew the biggest crowds, although a small crew of distinctly sleazy patrons left in the middle of the screening when they discovered they were watching biting social satire, not porn.

The notion of presenting our video in hotel rooms was intriguing, but elusive. First, I learned (or, more accurately, confirmed a long-held suspicion) that an overwhelming percentage of what is shown in hotel rooms has an X rating, which left us competing with Hollywood studio releases for the limited non-porn-seeking viewership. Second, I found in the in-room hotel entertainment business what I was discovering throughout the entertainment industry: an extraordinary degree of consolidation that made it daunting for small independent producers to find a market. Two companies—LodgeNet and On Command—controlled most of the in-room hotel market. As a result of the *Wall Street Journal* article and dogged persistence verging on the obnoxious, I was able to find my way to the right people in both companies, each of whom viewed our product, praised its quality, but declined to take a chance on it.

This proved to be the pattern with most major distribution opportunities. Those who didn't dismiss our work out of hand because of the lack of star power were impressed with its high caliber and professionalism, but wouldn't risk taking it on board because of the absence of marketing muscle behind it. Our rep couldn't get us into Blockbuster or Hollywood Video, the two titans of the video rental industry. My political chum Dan Lavey had done some consulting for the head of Hollywood, which is based near Portland, but Dan's efforts to pull strings went nowhere. We met a similar fate with Borders, Barnes & Noble, and Tower, all big players in the non-rental market.

Smaller independent players loved us. Facets, whose encyclopedic film catalog is the art house bible, snapped up our product. The leading independent video rental stores in Portland and Seattle, Movie Madness and Scarecrow, brought in our titles as soon as we released them. TLA Video, one of the top distributors of gay/lesbian-targeted video, raved about *Straight* and featured it in their catalog and online. An Icelandic film company contacted us about translating our plays into various Nordic languages and producing them both live and on video throughout Scandinavia. But the volumes these and other similar lower-echelon distributors could muster were inconsequential, even by the modest standards of our projections.

I decided to go to the annual home video convention in Las Vegas to see whether the personal touch could spur greater interest. For reasons unknown, the Video Software Dealers Association event is held in the insufferable heat of August, when temperatures reach 110° and hotel shuttle bus stops feature misting machines so that guests will not keel over in a dead faint. The conventioneers were a tawdry array of gold-chained, hairy-chested sleazeballs; storm-trooping Hollywood Video retail managers in matching corporate polo shirts; and a few pony-tailed indie types who seemed adrift in a sea of crass commercialism. I learned that one genre where independents without star performers could secure distribution was "urban," which was a euphemism for hip-hopping gang-bangers gunning down one another. I made a few useful contacts at the convention and had a good skull session with our existing distribution team, but achieved nothing approaching a breakthrough.

I, who felt I had never really failed at anything before, was failing. I was out of my league, and I knew it. Our online retail strategy had proven illusory, and the fallback home video and broadcast approach was requiring a substantial marketing war chest and a level of industry connections that I did not possess and could not manufacture. It was devastating to find no market for such well-received work that met our content criteria of daring, original, intelligent, and entertaining. Our funds were draining away, and I saw little prospect for replenishing them. Even if the start-up equity markets were not at atrocious levels in the wake of the tech crash, I was not comfortable attesting to projections of profitability when we faced such enormous obstacles in distribution. I had assembled my core of four—our creative director Jeff, our website/information systems guru Randall, our administrative/bookkeeping/payables/order fulfillment/film festival jackette of all trades Liane, and yours truly—on the assumption that our sales would support continuing production of new product. Without a predictable revenue stream, it was clear that it made no sense to produce additional product and equally clear that I would have to lay off my team.

I had been straight with them all along as to our financial condition and gave them several months' notice as to the likely layoff date, but the actual lowering of the boom was still a brutal, humiliating experience. All of them had left secure jobs to help me realize my now dimming vision. They had worked harder than they had ever been called on to work in their lives and for the most part had done exactly what I had asked of them. They were friends who had all been a part of CoHo before leaping with me into the void of a start-up. The only thing that even vaguely redeemed me in my own eyes was that I took myself off the payroll on the same October Friday I let them all go.

The week after the StageDirect layoff, I co-hosted a revival of the now traditional *Mr. Smith Goes to Washington* for Gordon Smith, who was up for reelectionin the '02 cycle. I had remained on Gordon's Finance Committee since his initial run in '96 and had agreed long before to handle this fundraiser. There was a certain surreal sense to hobnobbing with Republican stalwarts in a movie theater screening a Hollywood classic as my would-be theater video empire crumbled around me.

I had already experienced a feeling of out-of-place bohemianism while attending Smith's finance committee meetings earlier that year, in part because I was out of uniform. I had stopped wearing a suit to work after leaving Ball Janik's offices and saw no reason to change for these late afternoon meetings downtown. No one demurred—partly because of Portland's informality and partly because of my track record on Gordon's behalf—but I still felt I was in the room under slightly different (though by no means false) pretenses.

Gordon won easily. He had brilliantly positioned himself in the tradition of Mark Hatfield as an independent-thinking centrist prepared to defy party orthodoxy on matters of principle. He'd had a few dust-ups with social conservatives that had only reinforced his moderate credentials without really damaging his base, which wasn't going anywhere. He continued to be my model of what a Republican leader should be and won praise on a national level for his political savvy.

Later that fall, Amy and I joined a phalanx of Oregon Republican glitterati at the wedding reception for Gordon's daughter.

The receiving line stretched well out the door of the tony Waverly Country Club and into a bitterly cold late November evening. Badly chilled, I headed to the bar for some bracing, only to find that as faithful Mormons the Smiths were not serving booze. I found myself commiserating with a DC lobbyist named Arthur Mason whom I met through Dan Lavey. Mason was Gordon's golfing buddy-in-chief and had played storied courses with the Senator all over the world.

It was a curious conversation. Mason and I both represented to one another the proverbial greener grass on the far side of the fence. Mired in StageDirect-induced self-pity, I wondered whether I would have been wiser to have stayed in DC all along, made partner at Covington & Burling, pulled down a high six-figure income, and led the good life in Bethesda or Chevy Chase. For his part, Mason romanticized the virtues of living in a city like Portland, far from the madding crowd of Washington. It all made me yearn for the stiff drink that, alas, was not to be had.

In introducing us, Dan had mentioned my passion for theater. Mason said I should get in touch with his wife. Eileen Mason was serving as the acting chair of the National Endowment for the Arts (NEA), replacing Bush's initial appointee who had died after less than a week in office. He thought she would find my background fascinating.

I sent her an introductory e-mail, but received no response and was soon caught up in other matters. StageDirect suddenly seemed to have risen from its deathbed. Our educational distributor had introduced us to a New York agent, DLT Entertainment, who was interested in representing our titles in the broadcast market. DLT had strong credentials in both television and theater. Their primary niche in television had been packaging British programs for export to the US, most notably as producers of the hit series *Three's Company* and as distributors of the classic Britcom,

*As Time Goes By.* They owned the Shaftesbury Theatre in London's West End, which was affiliated with The Theatre of Comedy, a pioneering company founded by Judi Dench and a number of other prominent British actors and writers. DLT was optimistic about our prospects in international markets such as the UK, Scandinavia, and Holland, markets in which I put more faith after watching the supposed niche narrowcasting in American cable television become a race for the lowest common denominator.

We also had finally found an entrée to public television. Our first agent, ICM, had warned us off PBS as requiring maximum effort for minimal return, but I hadn't been prepared to dismiss such a major purveyor of the arts on television. I had been advised to enlist the support of a local PBS affiliate but had been rebuffed by Oregon Public Broadcasting and WTTW in Chicago—where I had proposed a partnership to spotlight Chicago's great fringe theater scene. Surfing online one day, I noticed that one of the board members of WETA, the DC public television affiliate, was a senior partner at Covington whom I knew a little. He generously led me to the head of arts programming at PBS, who expressed interest in our work and invited us to pitch a new production to them.

I floated a few trial balloons, one of which caught their eye. It was a play about being Arab in America that had impressed Jeff during a scouting expedition to the New York International Fringe Festival, the largest fringe theater festival in the world outside of Edinburgh, Scotland. Entitled *Sajjil* (Arabic for *record*), the play was a stereotype-defying tapestry weaving together dozens of interviews with Arabs and non-Arabs alike in the manner of *The Laramie Project*. In the aftermath of September 11, and with the drums of a second Gulf War beating stronger daily, it seemed like perfect timing for a sensitive, thoughtful play that could help overcome prejudice in a way that political rhetoric could never hope to achieve. I enlisted the support of the Arab-American theater company Nibras, the creators of *Sajjil*, and pulled together a proposal according to PBS guidelines.

Our educational distributor also introduced us to the home video side of Boston-based WGBH, one of the powerhouses in American public broadcasting as producers of *Masterpiece Theatre*, *Mystery!*, *American Experience*, and *Frontline*. They had a potent home video catalog and expressed serious interest in including *The Magnificent Welles* among their offerings, perhaps as part of a solo performance three-pack with *Straight* and *The Haint*. Media Cabin helped our cause by scoring a solid, three-star review of *The Magnificent Welles* in *USA Today* and a nice sidebar in the widely-circulated *USA Weekend Magazine*, as well as a profile in *Movie-Maker* magazine and a chorus of favorable reviews for *Straight* in the gay and lesbian press.

I had pitched *The Haint* to Southern public television stations and had landed the program on the PBS station in Memphis as a Halloween feature. They loved the show, and I was hopeful that a positive response in Memphis would lead to airings around the South.

With these stirrings of life, I was not yet ready to pull the plug on StageDirect. There was so much of my identity and spirit—not to mention personal assets—bound up in the company that I could not walk away while there was still a chance of salvaging a viable business, albeit not at all like the one I had originally envisioned. Rumors of StageDirect's imminent demise had reached my former partners at Ball Janik, who made an overture through the firm's senior partner to have me return to the fold. He was as gracious and tactful as could be, but to my ears his inquiries sounded like the flapping wings of circling vultures.

I also felt I owed it to the investors in StageDirect to pursue these opportunities, even though the company was no longer in a position to pay me a salary. I committed to stay on into '03 in exchange for the right to acquire additional stock, which I was well aware might prove to be worthless. Amy and I had many searching conversations, the upshot of which was that we would refinance our mortgage in favor of a line of credit on which I could draw up to a specified maximum, but not touch any of our other savings.

CoHo was a balm for my aching psyche, over-extended though I was. I had always enjoyed the classroom discussions that were a critical part of our high school outreach program, and the chance to escape from my lonely office and mounting stack of payables to witness the spark of recognition from a first-time theatergoer who all of a sudden grasps the gist of a play was highly therapeutic. It had been one of my greatest frustrations as a theater producer that the success of *Mary Tudor* had not led to widespread recognition for the playwright Sam Gregory, who continued to labor in impoverished obscurity. The CoHo board had supported various readings of Sam's work, however, and were excited about a sparkling script, called *Child of Pleasure*, about the seventeenth century French courtesan and Epicurean Ninon de L'Enclos. We chose *Child of Pleasure* as the winter production of our second in-house season, and it performed almost as handsomely for us as his first show. I savored the contrast between the makeshift chaos of the condominium storefront where we had performed the first production and the elegant intimacy of our new theater, for which we had scored another foundation grant to upgrade our lighting and sound capabilities.

Sam, a gay man, was keener to interest the gay community in *Child of Pleasure* than he had been with *Mary Tudor*, perhaps because sexuality was more at the forefront of a play featuring a courtesan. Additionally, when StageDirect brought *Straight* to the CoHo Theater for a two-week run and video shoot, I approached *Just Out*, the Portland gay/lesbian newspaper, to be our media sponsor. The editor had seen the show during an earlier tour and readily agreed. I was charting virgin territory as I marketed *Straight* and then *Child of Pleasure* to groups ranging from the Portland Lesbian Choir to the Rosetown Ramblers, a gay and lesbian square dance group, but it was just another of the many niche marketing campaigns I had mounted for CoHo aimed at a target demographic.

I also took some small pride in arranging a commission for Sam, who had mentioned in passing that he took a keen interest in Winston Churchill. I belonged to a local Churchill appreciation group called the Chartwell Society, which gathered at the most old-boy of the downtown clubs in Portland for an annual all-male black-tie dinner that featured roast beef, Stilton cheese, port, cigars, and grandiloquent toasts of the great man. Several of my Republican cohorts were on the Chartwell board, and I approached them about commissioning Sam to write a Churchill-based play. They enthusiastically agreed, and Sam developed a two-man piece based on the legend that several of Churchill's wartime speeches were read on the radio by an actor for security reasons. Sam directed a reading of one of the play's scenes at the annual dinner, and it was at once gratifying and incongruous to see this huge, Oscar Wilde-coiffed, penurious gay man present his work before the well-fed, tuxedo-clad, hail fellow Chartwell worthies.

Reminders of my former orbit brought home how drastically my political and cultural neighborhood had changed. I had been accustomed to operating in liberal circles in my CoHo producer capacity, but that had always been offset in my law firm years by my daytime chums and fellow travelers. Now I could go for weeks without seeing a friendly Republican face. Most of the time my heresy was dismissed with playful banter by my arts friends and collaborators, who respected my commitment to the theater and were prepared to forgive my partisan failings. Every once in a while, though, things could get a little testy.

CoHo had agreed to open our theater for three nights of readings of a new play called *The Afghan Women* by William Mastrosimone, best known as the author of *Extremities*. The readings were to benefit a foundation established by Mastrosimone and others to aid Afghan orphans, and we were pleased to offer our venue without charge for such a deserving cause.

But then the organizer of the readings asked if Physicians for Social Responsibility and Amnesty International could set up tables and distribute literature in our lobby in conjunction with the readings. The rest of our board had no objection to this, but I spoke out. CoHo had selected plays advancing any manner of creeds based on the merit of the script and the caliber of our co-producer. But I saw a significant difference between producing a work of art from which an audience could infer certain political messages, and offering the facilities of a non-profit arts company to organizations with no arts-related mission and an explicit social or political agenda. I felt that allowing such groups—however worthy—to use our lobby without charge would constitute an implicit endorsement of their advocacy efforts, which in my view was none of our business as theater producers. I asked my fellow board members how they would feel if the reading of a conservative-themed play were accompanied by the National Rifle Association and Right to Life prosletyzing in our lobby. There was some gnashing of teeth, but ultimately my view prevailed. The readings were terrific, and the lobby was left not for political advocacy but for the buzzing of amazed audience members.

I was no more abashed in professing principled conservative positions at CoHo board meetings than I was in inviting my Republican friends to attend *Straight* at our theater or to view the video of *Poona the Fuckdog*. There was a time when I probably espoused rightist views just to get a rise out of my mother or took a part in a play just because it seemed cool to be a law student or CIA attorney or law firm partner who was also into theater. But I was long past that. Being a theater person and being a Republican were integral parts of who I was. Perhaps these strange bedfellows should not have cohabited in a single person, but they did. I had made huge commitments of everything I had to offer—energy, time, money, will—to these disparate callings because they both exerted a hold on me I could neither explain nor escape.

# CONGRESSMAN

By early '03, arts entrepreneurship had taken an awful toll on my marriage. My wife had endured almost three years of never-ending flux, declining income, and vanishing savings. My hours were every bit as long as in my law firm days, but with none of the accompanying perks. As a partner I was usually able to shut off the mental machinery of work when at last I headed home, as the problems were fundamentally not my own. With the founding of StageDirect and the construction of the CoHo Theater, I was constantly on call and never really able to stop the whirring of the gears. Amy knew she was marrying an intense, career-minded person when she took me to have and to hold, but she understandably expected my intensity and careerism would confer a certain stability and material comfort that were fading fast.

The two of us had done a fair job of identifying which of our assets we would not touch no matter what happened to StageDirect. We fared less well when it came to maintaining our lifestyle.

We were hardly extravagant even during the leafiest of my years at Ball Janik, but we usually found time for just the two of us to go to a concert, a play, or just down the road for a meal. I was the instigator of these outings, the one who would pore over the weekend arts and entertainment section and suggest this or that.

As I sunk into the throes of StageDirect, I became less inclined to be our entertainment director. I was preoccupied and dejected. I rationalized that as I saw so little of the kids during the week, staying at home on weekends and renting a video or playing a game was a way to stay connected to the family. I was also keenly aware of our plummeting income. Even though we had plenty of savings that we could have tapped had we chosen to, I had always prided myself on living within my means.

Perhaps some idealized wife would have transformed her personality, become the social aggressor, and decreed that we would make a date at least once a month even if we weren't making a goddamned dime. Perhaps some model of adaptability would have tried to become the interim breadwinner herself—notwithstanding an absence from the workforce of over a dozen years, two young children, and a husband who was rarely home. But this was neither fair nor realistic to expect of the woman I married. She had gone further than most spouses in permitting me to leave a stable law practice, invest six figures in StageDirect, and sign a personal guaranty for CoHo's line of credit. I couldn't have asked for much more.

But the fun was going out of our marriage. We stayed at home—in a charming but cramped starter house we would have sold several years ago had I not taken leave of my professional senses—and began to irritate the hell out of each other. The furrows of our rut were deepened by the fact that Amy had never taken to Portland. She came to view it as my town, my civic obsession, my non-stop networking orbit. She was very close to her mother (her father had died shortly after we left DC), who lived on the East Coast with the rest of Amy's family and rarely visited Portland because of the dreary weather. Even though Amy went back east for a month or more each summer with the kids, she felt disconnected, particularly as her mother neared eighty.

As several StageDirect opportunities fell by the wayside—in particular, PBS passing on the Arab-American show *Sajjil*—I began to realize that I could either stay where I was and watch my marriage and business go down the tubes, or I could strike out in a different direction. The logical destination was DC, where Amy and I had courted and where her family was centered. I thought of seeking a senior-level appointed position in the Bush administration but was concerned that the pickings might be slim at this point. Although the average tenure of a Washington political appointee is short, it seemed more likely that top slots would open up later in '03 or early in '04, as the first wave of politicos traded on their connections and cycled off into the private sector.

Then it struck me that I might have two bites at the DC apple. For years I had entertained thoughts of running for office myself. Like most behind-the-scenes political wannabes, I had nurtured unspoken thoughts as I labored on campaigns about how I could improve on the shortcomings of my candidates. The Holy Grail for Oregon Republicans was the First Congressional District, the seat lost by the party in the aftermath of Watergate and never regained. Every election cycle, Republicans chanted the mantra that this was a winnable race, and every time they nominated a candidate too far to the right to capture the suburban centrists who were the key to the district.

The incumbent, David Wu, had narrowly beaten my Bush campaign colleague Molly Bordonaro for an open seat in '98 and had shellacked a far-right state legislator in 2000. Wu was a lawyer with a glittering educational pedigree—including degrees from Stanford and Yale—but he was regarded in both Republican and Democratic circles as arrogant, aloof, and inept. He had alienated the important high-tech community in his district because of votes against free trade. He was sitting on a sizable pile of campaign cash, almost $1 million, but was still considered vulnerable against a well-financed opponent who could attract independents and moderates.

I was convinced I could be that opponent. I was confident that I could build a formidable fundraising team by drawing on my work for the President and Gordon Smith. I had worked effectively with social conservatives for years, and my pro-choice, keep government out of the bedroom positions would help me pull votes from the center. I was battle-hardened through toiling on a host of campaigns, and my service to others had left me with a host of uncashed chits that would translate into finance committee members, endorsements, and volunteers.

The economic disaster that had befallen Oregon also gave me a compelling platform on which to run: investing in an educational infrastructure in the Portland metropolitan area that would be the basis for rebuilding the region's shattered economy. The tech crash had been calamitous for the First Congressional District, home to a fragile enclave of companies known as the "Silicon Forest." Portland's lack of a first-rate university left the local technology sector beholden to investment by outsiders, especially California companies like Intel—who could pull the plug at any time. I loved Portland State University, but it would require a comprehensive public and private partnership and a major infusion of resources to make it a vehicle for locally spearheaded growth. With my background in emerging companies, venture capital, and higher education, I thought I could make the case that I was best suited to lead such an initiative.

Oregon was in dire straits. It had led the nation in unemployment for two years running, with a higher rate in the Portland area than in the rural parts of the state. Tax revenues had declined precipitously, leading to a funding crisis in the public schools that prompted the middle class to begin abandoning the school system. One of Portland's draws had been the opportunity to live in a lovely neighborhood right in the city and send our children to the local public school, but we were now concerned whether we would be compromising our kids' futures if we didn't pull them out of the system. It was tempting to walk away from a place that no longer offered the same economic and educational prospects as when we had moved there a dozen years earlier, but I saw a congressional campaign as a chance to make a stand for my adopted state while pointing my family in the direction of DC.

I had a slight problem: I did not live in the district. However, I had worked in the district since moving to Portland, and perhaps more importantly, I had been instrumental in building a new theater and founding a small (albeit struggling) business that were both located in the district. I wasn't sure how my involvement in theater would cut politically, but I hoped that it would smooth some of the rough edges that Democrats and independents associated with Republicans.

My idea was to lease our current home, rent a townhouse in Northwest Portland near the theater, continue trying to reverse the fortunes of StageDirect as I built up a campaign team, and see if I could head off a primary challenge from the right by getting into the race early. If I were not able to gain the traction I'd hoped for or faced too tough a primary opponent, I could always pull out and hope that some plum positions in the administration had opened up. If I made it through the primary, I could either pull off an upset, unseat Wu and become a congressman; or be rewarded by the party for my valiant effort against tough odds with an even better DC job than I would have been able to achieve otherwise.

The major risk in two of these three scenarios was President Bush not winning reelection, but he was enjoying near-record popularity and the smart money was betting on a second term.

My wife was weary of my grandiose schemes, but even she had to admit it seemed like a rational plan and represented our best shot for getting back to Washington. It built on all I had done in the community and in politics. It would mean up to another year and a half of living on reduced means, but I pledged that we would sink only nominal amounts of personal money into both StageDirect and the political campaign, and a lease on our current home should cover the rent on a townhouse in the district, with some money to spare. The elementary school in Northwest Portland was one of the strongest in the system, which gave us some comfort regarding the kids' education.

I would not be turning my back on StageDirect. I would still be able to devote a substantial amount of time to the business during '03 and could play an advisory role thereafter. Our best hope at this stage was that our new agent, DLT, would be able to develop broadcast opportunities for us, but the key player in that arena would be Jeff, who was consulting for StageDirect in exchange for the use of our camera and editing equipment. We would become a video production company, leaving distribution in the hands of others. We could hire a capable entertainment lawyer to negotiate the requisite contracts. I would chair the board and be engaged in major decisions, but it did not seem crucial that I continue to manage the day-to-day operations of the company.

CoHo was also reaching a point where it could stand on its own. Our first season in the new theater had been a huge success thanks to *Spinning Into Butter*, and the second season was off to a promising start. We had paid down a large chunk of our debt and were operating solidly in the black. We would need to hire a full-time staff person if I were no longer there, but we had an excellent candidate for the job who was already on our board and the chances of securing a grant to support hiring an employee looked good. Additionally, if I became a congressman, CoHo's profile in town would go way up, which couldn't hurt.

It would be a damned shame if StageDirect or CoHo couldn't make it without me, but salvaging my marriage was more important. I knew that in some way I was continuing to indulge myself by harboring dreams of political glory and was well aware that running a political campaign was not a recipe for spending more time with my family. But I was convinced that what we really lacked in our relationship was a sense of direction, and that by replacing our current aimless drift with a plan and a timetable, we would go a long way to repairing the damage wrought by my adventures in the arts. I also knew I would have a blast throwing myself into a political campaign and hoped that a sunnier outlook on my part would rub off on my family.

I laid this scheme on my old friend Dan Lavey over beers in the paneled bar of the Arlington Club. Dan and I had stayed in close touch through my StageDirect travails, and I'd shared with him copies of *Poona* and several of our other productions, knowing they would appeal to his offbeat sense of humor. He was not surprised to hear of my change in direction, but had not expected me to propose a run in the First Congressional District. As he mused on it, however, he warmed to the prospect. He shared the view that Wu was beatable and saw no heavyweights on the Republican side clamoring to get into the race. It would require a heavy-duty fundraising effort, but he thought I was capable of pulling it off with the right help. There was no question in either of our minds that "the right help" meant his wife Lori, Gordon Smith's chief fundraising consultant, who had recently left the CoHo board because their first child was due later that spring. Lori was still planning on working several campaigns in this election cycle, and she had not committed to anyone for this race. He suggested that I begin laying out a fundraising plan and schedule a meeting with her.

I took to this with a vengeance. This was turf I knew involving people who respected me, not the alien world of Hollywood that had treated me with such contempt—when they took any notice of me at all. I made a list of seasoned, motivated finance committee members. I planned fundraisers targeting Silicon Forest, homebuilders, forest products, lawyers, young professionals, and other key constituencies, each with designated event chairs. I even outlined events in Chicago, where one of my high school classmates was now a congressman; Silicon Valley, where I thought I could enlist the support of my old mentor Tom Campbell; DC, where Ball Janik had a government relations office; and possibly in New York with the Republican Leadership Council, the moderate crusaders whose meeting I had attended with Craig Berkman. I thought I could raise $250,000 by the end of the year, which would make me credible, though no juggernaut.

Over lunch, Lori agreed to come on board. I would pay her a consulting fee for an initial assessment period of several months, after which I would make a decision whether to go forward. She and Dan would schedule meetings for me in DC with Greg Walden (Oregon's lone Republican congressman), the National Republican Congressional Committee staff, and Gordon Smith. Lori would also help me begin to make the rounds of major Portland donors. Dan had strongly recommended the campaign consulting firm of Kieran Mahoney and Greg Strimple, who had done great work for Gordon. During Gordon's first campaign, I had seen Mahoney in action—an intense, high-revving New Yorker in a roomful of laid-back Oregonians—and thought we would get along fine. Lori suggested I meet with Mahoney and Strimple when I headed back to DC. Lori and I scheduled another meeting with Dan where she would lay out a plan for this exploratory period, and I left the lunch with a sense of anticipation I had not felt in a long time.

Shortly afterwards John Easton—Gordon's chief of staff—was back in Portland, and I joined him and Dan for dinner. John was an old hand in Oregon Republican circles whom I'd known for years. He had a thatch of ginger hair and a mischievous grin that brought to mind Tom Sawyer. His brother, Mike, was a high school English teacher in a Portland suburb who had been part of CoHo's high school outreach program from its early days. I considered John—whose wife was Louisiana Senator John Breaux's chief aide—a savvy political operator and a straight shooter. He was encouraging of my run against Wu, but not effusively so. Wu would enjoy all the advantages of incumbency, and the Democrats were determined not to give up any further ground in the House. Gordon would do all he could to help, although I could not depend on an endorsement in a contested primary. We had a few drinks and Dan and John—who were fraternity brothers from the University of Oregon—got a kick out of referring to me as "Congressman." They also teased me, with some justification, for using a congressional race to escape the place I was seeking to represent.

When I walked into my meeting with Lori and Dan a few days later—check for her consulting fee in hand—I knew from their sagging body language that something was amiss. Dan didn't mince words. He'd sent my bio on to the consultants Mahoney and Strimple, who were impressed with my credentials. Then one of them accessed the StageDirect website and saw our video page and trailer for *Poona the Fuckdog*. He quickly picked up the phone and told Dan that with this production on my record I had no prayer of winning a congressional race. If I didn't have a social conservative primary opponent when I got into the race, I soon would once the conservatives got wind of *Poona*. The usual array of religious groups would join the chorus, and I would spend the entire campaign on the defensive, trying to refute what would be irrefutable to these folks.

I was floored. I'd understood that in a hard-fought campaign I would have to place some of the more provocative StageDirect productions in the context of my overall record as a theater producer, but I'd never even remotely considered *Poona* as grounds for automatic disqualification. Nor had Dan and Lori, who had seen the video themselves and thought it was hillarious. I protested that this was social satire, not obscenity or pornography (with no nudity whatsoever), that had been favorably reviewed by unimpeachable publications like the *New York Times*, the *New Yorker*, and the *Chicago Tribune*.

Dan conceded the force of my argument, but said that while R ratings were fine in the entertainment world, electoral politics was fundamentally a PG affair. It all came down to the three or four issues that would form the dialogue of the campaign, and as an unknown challenger I could not afford for one of these to be a play with a naughty word in the title and a Fairy God Phallus as a character. His counsel to me was to forget about running for office and move on. Lori glumly nodded her agreement and said that this would likely spook donors who might have no problem with the play itself but wouldn't want a candidate perceived to have baggage.

I put on as brave a face as I could, told them I had no interest in embarking on a wild goose chase, thanked them for their candor (and for not taking my check), gathered up my meticulous finance committee list and fundraising event outline, and staggered out the door. I drove back to my office at the theater and just sat there, sick and numb. I was at an age where I felt I still had not foreclosed any major options in life. Up until that moment, I could have "grown up to be President." Now a massive door had slammed shut in my face, and the well-appointed rooms beyond that I had always considered to be within my reach would be forever denied.

It was not that I'd had a childhood fixation on higher office, a sense of birthright that was now being snatched away from me. In fact, I'd grown up with a decided contempt for politicians and had always considered myself more of a technocratic, high-level appointment type. But I'd been around the game for years now and thought I could play with the big boys if I had a mind to. Well, now I did have a mind to, and they would have no truck with me.

The fact that StageDirect was foundering obviously didn't help my state of mind. It was obvious that if I'd just stayed at the law firm and not sullied my record with these flaky theater videos, my slate would be clean and all options still open to me. Not to mention that my marital state would be a whole lot merrier.

This funk lasted about a day. One of the advantages of housing StageDirect in the CoHo Theater was that I was reminded every day that I came to work of why I had gone into this business in the first place. All I had to do was wander out of my office into the theater to drink a draft from the pure spring of live performance—ninety-nine seats arrayed within an actor's breath of this gem of a performance space, stage lights deployed at all angles on the grid overhead, unadorned set poised for the coming weekend's audience—and forget for a moment about the fetid pools in which I was flailing. Sam Gregory's *Child of Pleasure* had closed that weekend, and I was still cresting on the wave of good feeling that came of nurturing a budding talent and finding acceptance for his writing. I was unashamed of any of the work StageDirect or CoHo had produced, and if the campaign consultants of the world cast me aside because of *Poona the Fuckdog,* well, they could go fuck themselves. It was a badge of honor that the experts deemed me a man of too many moving parts to be a cog in the political wheel.

## AMONG FRIENDS

I was thankful to have been found unworthy before I'd tossed my hat in the ring so I didn't end up spending grueling months of fundraising and campaigning only to have to bow out gracelessly in the heat of the battle. It would have been an uphill fight anyway, and even if I'd won, I would then have faced the grind of raising a family in DC and tending to a constituency 3,000 miles away. Additionally, John and Dan's teasing about escaping from Oregon was spot-on: if it were wise for the sake of my family to leave Portland, I should do it honestly, not in the guise of a bid for Congress.

Which brought me back to Plan B: to pursue a senior appointive position in the administration. I had no idea what might be available midway through the President's term, but I saw little reason to hold off on exploring my options. This was the course of action my wife and I had agreed upon, and she would view it as a betrayal if I were now to suggest staying in Portland to see what happened with StageDirect. I could accept Ball Janik's invitation to return to the practice of law on a part-time basis while keeping an eye on StageDirect, but that made sense only if we were committed to staying in Portland, which we clearly weren't. And if we were going to make a move, it made sense to do it by the summer so that the kids would be in their new home by the start of the school year.

When I had first signed on with the Bush campaign, I thought I would go for a national-security related job such as the Assistant Secretary for International Narcotics slot in the State Department. But that all seemed very long ago. Through CoHo and StageDirect, I had dedicated myself to the arts. I felt at home among artists, not like the moonlighting lawyer-poseur of yore. Outside of my family, I took the greatest satisfaction in presenting a finely crafted work of performing art. It was clear to me that if I were going back into government, I had to pursue a position with the National Endowment for the Arts (NEA).

Following that chance encounter with the husband of the interim NEA chair at the Smith family wedding, I had done a little research on the agency. I knew that it had been founded, along with the National Endowment for the Humanities, in the sixties during the Johnson administration. I knew that its budget at one time had reached almost $200 million before being slashed to half that amount in the mid-nineties. I knew that about two-thirds of its grants were made directly to artists and arts organizations, with the remaining third allocated through partnerships with state and local arts agencies. I knew that clashes with Congress over controversial projects it had funded in the late-eighties—including Robert Mapplethorpe's erotic photography and Andres Serrano's notorious *Piss Christ*—had led to significant restrictions on grants to individual artists and that the overwhelming majority of the agency's funding now went to organizations.

I also now knew I wanted to work there. I went on the NEA website and found to my delight that both the General Counsel and the Deputy Chairman for Grants & Awards positions were held by acting officials. In the federal bureaucracy, an acting designation generally meant that the job was intended for a political appointee but the seat was being kept warm by a career civil servant pending an appointment. I was prepared to try for either job, but the Grants & Awards position sounded fantastic. It appeared to offer the opportunity to set national arts policy, interact directly with top-flight artists and institutions, and assess how organizations had developed their base of support and determine if and how the federal government should help build on that base. The position seemed like a natural extension of all that I had been doing with CoHo for years: inviting artists to submit proposals for collaboration; evaluating the submissions based on artistic merit, team caliber, budgetary responsibility, and overall feasibility; and working in tandem with those selected to make their dreams a reality. It would give me a national platform to promote the mission I had undertaken with StageDirect: expanding the audience for the arts.

This job could also open any number of doors after I left government. As it stood, I was a former law firm partner in a middling city who had co-founded an up-and-coming small non-profit theater company and started a pioneering but floundering theater video start-up. Even with my Stanford and Williams credentials, such a résumé probably wouldn't get me that far in the major league arts world. But with several years of administering the NEA's grants program under my belt, I might have the chance to take my career in directions I couldn't have imagined before— perhaps directing a major arts-oriented foundation or running a national-caliber theater company.

Within a week of my gut-wrenching banishment from the ranks of congressional candidates, I was on the phone to John

Easton and Dan Lavey to see whether these positions were within reach. I soon learned that my timing was perfect and why these plum jobs were still open: when Eileen Mason took over as interim NEA Chairman following the death of the President's initial appointee—a conductor and composer named Michael Hammond—she was reluctant to recommend any additional political appointments to the White House knowing that the new Chairman would want to assemble his or her own team. She put career NEA staffers in these positions on an interim basis and waited for the appointment of the new Chairman. And waited. It took almost a year before the President settled on Dana Gioia as the replacement for Michael Hammond. Gioia had come on board a few months before and was just now turning his attention to filling these key slots. It appeared that no serious candidates had yet emerged for the Deputy Chairman for Grants & Awards or General Counsel positions and that I stood a good chance of landing one or the other.

I was also heartened by what I had read about Dana Gioia. He appeared to have trumped me by a healthy margin in his ability to straddle the bourgeois and bohemian worlds. He had earned undergraduate and MBA degrees from Stanford and had worked for fifteen years in New York as an executive for General Foods, eventually rising to Vice President of Marketing. But he had also taken a master's degree in comparative literature from Harvard and was an acclaimed poet, literary anthologist, and cultural critic. He seemed almost a latter-day Wallace Stevens—the insurance company executive who became one of the giants of twentieth-century American poetry—although as an artist, Gioia practiced in public what Stevens kept largely private. I was hopeful that Gioia would feel a kinship with another corporate type turned man of the arts, not to mention a fellow Stanford alumnus.

John Easton and Dan jumped on my candidacy immediately. Dan worked through Arthur Mason to establish an informal pipeline to Eileen Mason, who had now returned to her original post as NEA Senior Deputy Chairman, the number two person in the agency. The word that came back from Arthur Mason was that if I were enthusiastic about the Deputy Chairman's job, I should go for it, with the General Counsel spot as a back-up.

As Gordon Smith's chief of staff, John worked through official channels. He arranged for Gordon to send a glowing letter on my behalf to the head of the White House Personnel Office. My own mother could not have improved on Gordon's testimonial. He sang the praises of my "extensive and impressive résumé" and "unique and diverse background," citing my "passion for the arts" and "determination to continually develop opportunities within the artistic community" as making me "an ideal choice for this position." Gordon made special reference to my work with CoHo and StageDirect, which he described as "a unique company, which specializes in capturing contemporary theater on digital video," and said that I had "acquired an intimate understanding of the management aspects of theater production and the significant role that grants play in facilitating opportunities within the artistic community." The coup de grace was an understated sentence inserted toward the end of the letter: "Gary's name may also be familiar, as he served as George W. Bush's 2000 campaign Oregon Victory Finance Chair."

Of course, no one in White House Personnel had ever heard of me, but they had now. Gordon had recently miffed the White House by displaying his trademark independence and voting against a controversial measure that would allow drilling for oil in the Arctic National Wildlife Refuge, but he was still a well-regarded Republican Senator who had just decisively won reelection. If Gordon was high on a prospective appointee, particularly in an area of the government not exactly besieged by Republican office-seekers, the administration would pay attention.

And they did. John and Dan began to hear encouraging signals coming out of both the NEA and the White House. The mythical constituency "everyone" was said to like my résumé and to be struck by my combination of artistic pedigree and campaign credentials. Gordon followed up his letter by inviting Dana Gioia, Eileen Mason, and the NEA's political liaison, Ann Guthrie Hingston, to a get-acquainted meeting in his office where he gave a strong plug for my candidacy. John, Dan, and Molly Bordonaro all placed calls on my behalf to David Thomas, the staffer in Karl Rove's political office who was responsible for Oregon and a number of other western states.

Shortly after Gordon's meeting with Dana Gioia, I received a call from Ann Hingston. She was upbeat and told me that Gioia was anxious to meet me. He was going to be coming to Portland for a conference in early June and wondered whether I might be able to interview with him then. As it happened, my marriage-shunning brother had chosen that week to end his bachelorhood, so I had to beg off. We agreed that I would fly back to Washington in late May (on my nickel, incidentally) to meet with the Chairman and the appropriate people in White House Personnel. She was effusive about the energy that Gioia was bringing to the NEA and his determination to lead the agency out of the shell into which it had withdrawn following the devastating budget cuts of the mid-nineties.

Curiously, Hingston also asked if I had read *Leaving Town Alive: Confessions of An Arts Warrior* by former NEA Chairman John Frohnmayer. I knew Frohnmayer was an Oregon lawyer who had been appointed by the first President Bush and then forced out of office in the midst of controversy, but I had never read his book. I promised to pick up a copy before my interview in DC.

After a humbling stretch being a nobody going nowhere, it was comforting and flattering to once again be among friends and be considered a person with prospects. I took nothing for granted, however. In case the NEA job did not pan out, I assembled a non-profit oriented résumé, visited the Chronicle of Philanthropy and other websites that post arts-related jobs, and registered with a number of executive search firms that specialized in non-profit placements.

I also had earnest discussions with John, Dan, and Molly Bordonaro about *Poona the Fuckdog*. Thanks to its tainting of my short-lived congressional career, I had gone from viewing *Poona* as one of the chief assets in StageDirect's video library to the potential bane of my existence. It was hard to imagine that a play favorably reviewed by major national publications and of unquestionable artistic merit would be a concern with respect to a job in the nation's flagship arts agency, but then I had never thought it would stand in the way of running for office. After the rude jolt I had just received, I did not want any further nasty surprises, either for my family or for those working to secure my appointment.

The consensus of my backers—all savvy political operators— was that *Poona* should not pose a problem for my NEA candidacy. Seeking a high-level appointment, they said, was very different from running for office, where there are opponents who have a vested interest in rattling every possible skeleton in your closet. Appointments requiring Senate advice and consent—such as judicial nominations in the post-Bork era—could precipitate ugly political clashes, but the Deputy Chairman's post was not subject to Senate confirmation.

More importantly, they said, I was applying to an arts agency accustomed by its very nature to dealing with provocative content. This was not the sanitized, PG-rated world of political campaigns. And, as Molly noted, it was not as if I were hawking a crucifix in urine, a la Serrano. *Poona*, however saucy its bedtime stories for grown-ups might be, was a far cry from the works that had put social conservatives up in arms.

Their counsel was to let the NEA and the White House get to know me: my Williams and Stanford credentials, my background as an accomplished corporate lawyer, my extensive work in the community, my service in government, my longstanding involvement in Republican politics, and my commitment to non-profit theater. They would then understand the context in which I had launched StageDirect and produced Poona and the rest of our theater video library, which should defuse any concerns. Once the administration appeared to have reached a level of comfort with me, I should make them aware of any potentially controversial productions before my appointment was announced, so that they would not be caught off guard if questions should surface.

This struck me as a sound approach and a fair balancing of ambition and disclosure. Of course I wanted the job. It seemed like an ideal position for my talents and experience, it moved us near family, it offered a springboard for a new career in the arts, and it paid a healthy salary.

I did not want to be tiptoeing around, however, constantly looking over my shoulder and fearful of being outed as a producer of provocative theater. I was proud of what my companies had produced and was prepared to tell anyone about StageDirect and its work. It was not as if our shows were some dark secret, in any case. Our productions had been widely reported in the press and were, of course, offered on our website (although I had made the decision not to feature *Poona* on our site and video home pages when we were courting WGBH to handle our home video distribution, as *Poona* did not fit their profile and would not have been part of that package).

I prepared for my DC interviews by looking into the backgrounds of the NEA officials who would be my primary points of contact: Ann Hingston and Eileen Mason. Through our phone calls and e-mails, I sensed Hingston was a bloodless political minder placed in the agency to make sure it did not end up on the wrong side of the conservatives who had made its life miserable during the first Bush administration. This impression was borne out by my research, which showed that her connections on the right were more impressive than her artistic credentials. Most recently she had served as national program director for Best Friends, an organization founded by conservative icon William Bennett's wife Elayne that promoted sexual abstinence among low-income girls. I had no objection to the program, but it was not clear to me how it qualified her for a senior position at the NEA. She had mentioned in passing about returning to government to complete her federal retirement vesting, which seemed indicative of her level of passion for the arts. She had headed the post-election transition at the agency, which demonstrated that, politically, she was viewed as a safe pair of hands by the White House.

Eileen Mason was a seasoned Washington bureaucrat, but her arts background similarly did not overwhelm. Her principal qualification for the Senior Deputy Chairmanship (and interim Chairmanship) at the NEA seemed to be over twenty years as an administrator and manager with the U.S. Nuclear Regulatory Commission and Federal Energy Regulatory Commission. She had served on the board of the Arts and Humanities Council of Montgomery County in Maryland and, as an amateur violinist, had been a musical advisory panelist for the Maryland State Arts Council.

I was taken aback by the thin artistic resumés of the agency's senior brass but viewed their lack of hands-on experience in founding and building arts organizations as an opportunity. I brought something to the NEA's management team that was not currently represented: namely a grassroots, in-the-trenches background that I felt would make me an astute judge of grants applications and a valuable resource for the organizations we were funding.

I also read John Frohnmayer's book, which reinforced my conviction that I had the right pedigree for this job. Frohnmayer came from a distinguished family of Oregon lawyers with strong connections to Senator Mark Hatfield. Hatfield was a long-time friend of the first President Bush and was instrumental in securing the NEA chairmanship for Frohnmayer. Frohnmayer came across as a gentleman and professional of the first rank: bright, able, hard working, principled, and well-read. He also struck me as stupendously ill-qualified to head the NEA. Bush's appointment of Frohnmayer as NEA chairman didn't quite rate in political ineptitude with his selection of Dan Quayle as Vice President, but it wasn't far behind. Evidently Bush chose this Oregon trial lawyer because the President thought Frohnmayer, who hailed from the agrarian southern part of the state and had once studied theology, would appeal to rural social conservatives. In fact, he was a metropolitan social liberal who had little but contempt for religious conservatives.

Frohnmayer's background in the arts was similar to Eileen Mason's: he was an amateur singer who had served on the Oregon Arts Commission but appeared to have little direct experience dealing with artists. He had almost no partisan political background whatsoever. The Frohnmayer family were notorious in Oregon for considering themselves above the seamy fray of politics, and John certainly fit that reputation. In his book, he seemed to take pride in having avoided Republican political involvement.

Frohnmayer admittedly faced a set of challenges at the NEA that would have tested the mettle of the most gifted arts maven/politico. He was under siege by both the artistic community who reviled him for revisiting prior grant decisions, and by right-wing trogylodytes who wanted to do away with federal funding of the arts altogether. But Frohnmayer lacked the arts vocabulary to put suspicious arts organizations at ease and the political vocabulary to inspire confidence in unsympathetic fellow Republicans (or conservative Democrats). He had no meaningful life experience to call on in either context and it showed—painfully.

I had no illusions about the political pressures I would face as Deputy Chairman for Grants & Awards. This was a highly political appointment, and I would be operating in a highly political environment. Just as the overwhelming percentage of CIA operations raised no red flags, I assumed that the vast majority of NEA grant applications were routine, ordinary course matters. But it would be my handling of that handful of possible stinkbombs that would shape whatever legacy I would leave at the agency. I expected the Ann Hingstons of the world would be out to kill any project that might ruffle the feathers of social conservatives. I also anticipated that an arts community deeply distrustful of the President would be looking for any opportunity to claim the administration was playing politics with the grants process. It would be a delicate task, but I thought I was well suited by virtue of my interaction with artists through CoHo and StageDirect, my history of partisan engagement, and even my scars from Iran/Contra to balance the competing pressures fairly and deal effectively with both constituencies.

I understood that though a senior official, I would be a subordinate and that the ultimate decision-makers were the Chairman and the National Council on the Arts that advised him. It was not for me to decide, but to cull out those applications that were deserving of greater scrutiny and present them to my superiors. The key, I knew from my time in the bureaucracy, was in how the tough cases were presented up the line; it was here that I thought I could make an impact. I had a record of championing innovative, provocative, fresh, and unique works of art, and I had no intention of stopping now. I planned to advocate for grants supporting high-caliber art that challenged its audience—even if it might raise some hackles politically. I thought I had the communication skills as a well-trained lawyer to sway a few of the critical handful of decisions in favor of the pioneering artist.

I also believed I could help the President. Bush had won a hairs-breadth victory in the 2000 election, and he would need to expand his base to hold on to office in '04. Presidential elections are decided on economic and national security issues, not arts policy. On the margin, however, the arts represent a relatively inexpensive means of reaching out to independent voters and softening the hard edges of the stony Republican profile. Ever since the dark days of the Frohnmayer era, steely-eyed GOP professionals had viewed the NEA as a downside-only proposition, with no prospect of winning over the liberal artistic community and the always-looming risk of antagonizing the conservative base. I may have been naïve, but I felt that a more aggressive and adventurous approach to arts funding, if properly presented, could help pick up some pivotal swing voters.

CoHo opened *Memoir*, its final show of the season, the weekend before I left for my interviews. The memoirist in John Murrell's lovely two-handed play is Sarah Bernhardt, who defied the virulent anti-Semitism of her era to become the Steam Age's most celebrated actress. Though I had read the script several times, I was surprised as I watched the opening performances at how powerfully Sarah's ambivalence about her Jewish identity resonated with me. Baptized and placed in a convent by her mother—who favored her blonde, beautiful, and non-Semitic-featured sister—Sarah nonetheless retained a strong sense of her Jewish origins. She conquered both the ascendant bourgeoisie and declining aristocracy of the time, yet maintained a bohemian otherness that seemed bound up in her Jewishness. The audience loved the performance of the two Equity actors playing Sarah and her long-suffering secretary in the intimacy of our beautiful new theater, and as I headed east for Washington I felt more like a bona fide theater producer picking up the cudgels of politics than a political hack dabbling in the arts.

# WASHINGTON (NEARLY) II

The NEA is headquartered in the cavernous Old Post Office Building on Pennsylvania Avenue, kitty-corner from my former stomping grounds at Covington & Burling. I arrived a few minutes before my scheduled time and was soon joined in the Chairman's anteroom by Ann Hingston and Eileen Mason. My impressions from afar were borne out in person. Hingston—blonde and angular—came across as a tight-lipped, humorless politico whose antennae were in a perpetual state of agitation. Mason was a compact technocrat whose brisk efficiency was tempered by a genuine charm. Both wore standard-issue Republican female-of-ficeholder outfits that looked like the height of Junior League fashion some fifteen years ago.

They ushered me into Dana Gioia's office. I wasn't sure whether he would incline in dress toward the well-pressed executive or the disheveled poet, but it was clear as I shook his hand that General Foods had won that battle. His gleaming white shirt was impressively starched and his suit pants impeccably creased. He wasted no time on small talk. With a boyish alacrity that reminded me of the Stanford Law professor who had hit me with the first-ever question posed to my section, he launched into a Socratic-style interrogation. He took me through the mission and history of both StageDirect and CoHo Productions. I stressed that StageDirect was not looking for established, conventional shows but for plays that were fresh and original. He asked for examples of our work and I promised to send him some. I made clear, without dwelling on specifics, that both StageDirect and CoHo were targeted at grownups, not fun for the whole family. CoHo had produced a promotional piece for our '03/'04 season that I had brought along from Portland. When he saw that our season included *Loot*—a riotous piece by the irreverent British playwright Joe Orton—he role-played a conservative congressman conducting an inquisition as to why such plays had any place in the world of federally funded arts. Gioia worked me over pretty well, but it was evident that he appreciated Orton and was just engaging in devil's advocacy.

Throughout this initial fusillade, Mason and Hingston—seated on opposite sides of a conference table with Gioia at the head—were completely silent. Then the Chairman's body language shifted in a manner suggesting that I had successfully run the gauntlet, and the conversation turned to the position for which I was being considered. Mason threw out several examples of ostensibly problematic grants that had not been flagged by the staff for review by the brass. The message was plain: my job was to make sure that nothing remotely controversial issued from the NEA grants pipeline without being run through the filter of senior management. I was neither surprised nor offended by this display, although it was not subtle.

I was a little surprised, though not offended, by what followed next. My interview with White House Personnel was set for that afternoon with two women, Andrea McDaniel and Elizabeth Hogan. It appeared that Gioia and his lieutenants had reached a level of comfort with me and wanted things to go well with the White House. Gioia said I should mention to McDaniel if I had been to church on Sunday, as that would sit well with her. Hingston and Mason chuckled in agreement. It was doubtless intended as a light-hearted, just-among-us-Christians remark. I had been passing for a Christian my whole adult life, and now did not seem the time to come out of the religious closet. I said nothing, and the session soon came to a close.

The White House interview was not—of course—at the White House, but in one of the low-slung executive outbuildings that have mushroomed under the imperial presidency fostered by both parties. McDaniel and Hogan both proved to be junior staffers—barely thirty, if that. McDaniel came across as a small-town Southern fundamentalist, exquisitely polite but hardened in her world view. Hogan, who appeared to be the senior official of the two, was more urbane and cosmopolitan. Dan, John, and Molly had evidently pulled all the right strings, as the interview was a love-fest focusing on the work I had done for the President through the Victory campaign in Oregon. They wanted to make sure I would be a team player for the President, and I demonstrated how I had shown my allegiance in the field when it counted. They let me know they had been trying to fill this position for a long time and how excited they were for a Bush appointee to take office. They both said how pleased they were to find someone with both the necessary political and arts background. The comparatively little time we spent discussing the arts was devoted to Hogan's aspiring actress sister and to one of the plays CoHo had chosen for our upcoming season, the Irish hit *Stones in his Pockets*, which Hogan had seen and enjoyed.

As we came to the end of the session, Hogan asked me what sounded like the standard last question on their checklist: was there anything in my background that could prove embarrassing to the President? I said they should be aware of two things. I discussed my low-level involvement with the Iran/Contra scandal, but expressed my conviction that I had done nothing wrong. I then said that as a principal of both CoHo and StageDirect I had produced theater for adults, with some productions that featured nudity and bad language, including profanity in the title. Hogan replied, "So what you're saying is that you've produced material that would be R-rated, but not X?" I said, "Exactly." That appeared to be all they needed to hear, and Hogan escorted me to the elevator with an encouraging smile.

I made my way to Gordon Smith's office on Capitol Hill, weary but satisfied. Gioia had put me through my paces, but I thought I had acquitted myself well. I felt I had shown that this odd coupling of arts and politics on my résumé was, in fact, a happy and even formidable co-existence. The Chairman's "church on Sunday" remark was a little off-putting, but it seemed harmless enough. And from the perspective of disclosure, I had clearly laid out both the mission of StageDirect and the risqué content of some of our productions.

It had still been an ordeal, however, and it was reassuring to see the friendly faces of Gordon and John as they greeted me in the Senator's office. Almost immediately after I came through the door, Gordon started teasing me about *Poona the Fuckdog*. My jaw dropped. While Gordon has a keen sense of humor, he is also a fairly strait-laced Mormon. He said with a hearty laugh that *Poona* sounded hilarious and that he thought StageDirect should shoot for a national tour. All the *Poona*-related tension that had been knotting my system since the collapse of my congressional campaign vanished at a stroke. If a Republican Senator is making fun of me over this production to my face, how big of a concern could it be? I reviewed the day's proceedings, and John promised to call Eileen Mason and the White House for word on my performance. I then walked Gordon and John over to the site of their annual office photo just north of the Capitol, with the *Poona* banter continuing most of the way.

John and I had agreed to meet for dinner that evening. He was very bullish on my prospects. He talked about what a pleasure it was to advocate for a well-qualified candidate who deserved the position he was seeking, in contrast to the many hacks and hangers-on who constantly pestered Gordon's office to push their candidacy for jobs they had no business pursuing. He consoled me over my abortive First Congressional District campaign and said it was Oregon's loss. I couldn't help pouring out the platform on which I would have run before such a sympathetic audience. It was therapeutic for me; he played along beautifully.

We also talked about Gioia's interest in viewing some Stage-Direct videos. We considered sending him all of StageDirect's titles—including *Poona*—but concluded this would serve little purpose, as he would never watch them all anyway, and from the vantage point of disclosure it could look as if we were trying to bury *Poona* in a stack of other titles. We decided it made sense to give him a contrast between a more arts-oriented title like *The Haint* and a more commercially-minded production like *Mass Murder*, together with an explanation of the StageDirect selection process and how it might differ from my work at the NEA. I was comfortable with this approach and called Amy in Portland to ask her to overnight copies of both these videos so I could drop them off while I was still in the area.

I took advantage of being on the East Coast to make a day trip to New York for a meeting with StageDirect's agent, DLT Entertainment. I had never laid eyes on these people, and after the fiasco with our previous agent, I wanted to get a sense of who was representing us (although I was mindful that the face-to-face scrutiny to which I had subjected ICM to in Los Angeles had yielded precisely nothing). I had managed to set up a meeting at DLT's office with the head of the theatrical division of the entertainment conglomerate Clear Channel regarding a possible joint venture, which I thought might help get DLT's attention. I also wanted to confirm, before disclosing my DC plans, that Jeff could be the point person on broadcast projects without the need for my active participation. I came away convinced that he could, which left my conscience clear about going forward with the NEA opportunity.

My mother had taught me from an early age to err on the side of sending thank you notes, and I followed maternal protocol in thanking Eileen Mason, Ann Hingston, Elizabeth Hogan, and Andrea McDaniel. I mentioned that I would be staying with family in the area for a few days (I had free accommodations at my mother-in-law's and thought I might as well check out the local real estate market), and Mason invited me to lunch a few blocks from the NEA. I took this to be a good sign—as was Elizabeth Hogan's reply, in which said she was "very optimistic" about my chances. The purpose of the lunch soon became evident: I would be reporting to Mason, and she wanted to make sure I was under no illusions regarding the chain of command. She mentioned that someone else had been appointed to my position shortly after she took office, but that Mason had let her go when this appointee proved not to be a team player. Mason was as gracious as ever, but the message was as unsubtle as the directive in the Gioia interview about running even the most remotely controversial grant applications up the flagpole.

*The Haint* and *Mass Murder* arrived at my mother-in-law's from Portland, and I packaged them up for Gioia with a note that read as follows:

*Enclosed are VHS screening copies of two videos produced by Stage-Direct. At the risk of appearing defensive, I want to make clear that the standards used to select productions for StageDirect are not those I would apply in reviewing grants for the NEA. StageDirect is a for-profit enterprise with a duty to maximize the return to its investors. Having said that, I consider The Haint a wonderful example of Southern storytelling and a truly virtuoso performance by Troy Mink. Mass Murder, while at times compelling, is not as impressive artistically, but has a strong marketing "hook" because of its portrayal of notorious serial killers.*

I also included a copy of the *Wall Street Journal* article and mentioned that StageDirect had been profiled and our titles reviewed in a number of national publications, including the *Los Angeles Times, Library Journal, Booklist,* and *USA Today.*

I returned to Portland to a chorus of favorable reviews, both of my performance in Washington and for CoHo's production of *Memoir.* John, Dan, and Molly all reported that I had made a very positive impression at the NEA and the White House. Several days after my return, Ann Hingston called to say that I was the choice of the Chairman and that now all the agency needed was a sign off from the White House, which appeared imminent. She followed up with an e-mail verifying my salary and setting possible start dates in June so that I could be introduced at the next National Council on the Arts meeting in early July. Amy and I had originally planned to move at the end of the summer, but figured that I could stay with her mother and shuttle back and forth as we made the transition. We hired a realtor and prepared to put our house on the market.

We also sat down with the kids, now nine and seven, and explained that we would be leaving Portland. This was hard news for them to swallow, as the children on the block had come to form a merry and close-knit crew. This was the only neighborhood they had known, but they took some comfort in learning they would be near their grandmother in the Washington area.

I also visited with my fellow board members at CoHo Productions. I had been preparing them for my possible departure for some time, starting with a spring retreat focused on leadership transition. We had applied to a charitable trust formed by the parents of a friend of mine for a major matching grant to hire one of our board members as a full-time managing director. We would not find out the trust's decision until later in the summer, but preliminary indications were encouraging. I was convinced that with a staff person in place and my continued involvement on the board (albeit from afar), we had the ability to not just survive but prosper. Our first two seasons in the new theater had been a solid success, we had further reduced our construction debt (although I was still on the hook as a personal guarantor), our subscriber base had risen to about 300, and we were set to open our '03/'04 season with O'Neill's classic *A Moon for the Misbegotten*, featuring three outstanding Equity actors. I had committed to call on our program advertisers over the summer for renewals so that we would enter the new season with a healthy stream of advertising revenue.

As I prepared to head to my brother's wedding in the Midwest, Dan Lavey (who still got a kick out of calling me "Congressman") got word that the White House political shop headed by Karl Rove had signed off on my candidacy. Now all that remained was for the White House Personnel office to process my paperwork and officially advise the NEA. It seemed clear that all relevant players had reached a level of comfort with me, so I planned to call John Easton after I arrived at my parents' home in Chicago to confirm that this was the appropriate time—prior to any public announcement of my appointment as we had discussed—to provide a description of all the shows StageDirect and CoHo had produced.

Then I received a panicked call from my wife as I sat down to dinner with my parents the day before we were to drive up to Wisconsin for the wedding. A bizarre letter from Dana Gioia had arrived at our house thanking me for meeting with him and for the submission of *The Haint* and *Mass Murder*, but informing me that there were no positions available at the NEA. I was dumfounded. It appeared to be a form rejection letter, yet there were the specific references to my interview and the StageDirect videos. Amy was frantic. Based on what we had heard unofficially, we had told our Portland realtor to proceed with an open house the following week. There was no time to lose in selling our home in Oregon if we didn't want to end up owning two houses simultaneously—we were committed to having the kids in place in the DC area before the start of school and the Portland real estate market had cooled considerably. She asked whether we should call the realtor and tell him to hold off.

I figured this had to be a terrible mistake. Everything I had heard since my return from Washington had been favorable, and it seemed inconceivable that all the intelligence gathered by John, Dan, and Molly—not to mention my own communications with Ann Hingston—would be so wildly off base. Still, I'd been riding an impressive streak of bad luck, so I couldn't rule out anything at this stage.

I wasn't able to reach Ann Hingston until late the following morning. She expressed great surprise at the letter, but as the consummate political underling was not prepared to officially allay my concerns until she had spoken with the Chairman. Gioia was then en route to Portland for the conference I was missing because of the wedding. I had been the picture of poise with my poor wife (and told her by all means to proceed with the open house), but I was on tenterhooks until I finally heard back from Hingston late in the day with word that Gioia's secretary had misunderstood his instructions and sent out an erroneous letter. My heartbeat returned to something approaching normal, but I decided at that point to hold off on providing the description of the StageDirect and CoHo shows until I knew with certainty (though still prior to any public announcement) that the job was truly mine.

At the wedding, I escorted my daughter, as Amy had decided to stay in Portland with our son because of his year-end dance recital as well as the upcoming open house. It was our first major daddy-daughter excursion, and we had a ball. She was still a little downcast because of the upcoming separation from her friends, but she knew she still had the long months of a Portland summer before her. My brother was the male equivalent of radiant, and good-naturedly put up with our teasing that because the Chief Justice of the Wisconsin Supreme Court officiated at the ceremony, there could be no appeal. The usual exultation of a wedding was heightened by the performance that weekend of our beloved Cubs, who took two out of three from the Yankees in an epic series that marked the Bronx Bombers' first appearance at Wrigley Field since the days of Ruth and Gehrig.

The call from Washington came on a Monday, the day after we returned from the weekend's festivities. The job was mine. Hingston said that her call represented the official offer, as it was not agency practice for political appointees to be issued written offer letters. My parents toasted me with some bubbly that was conveniently on ice, and Amy and I rejoiced long distance. I called our realtor in DC and told him to go ahead with an offer on a Bethesda townhouse I had found the weekend after my interview. To my amazement, Amy had allowed her mother to act as proxy and did not insist on flying back to see the house herself, though she scrutinized every millimeter of the online tour photos.

After I put my daughter to bed that evening, I sat alone in a quiet corner of my parents' home and reflected on the grand plans

I had hatched and discarded. I had gone to DC at twenty-five a brash bachelor set on international CIA intrigue and had left five years later a married man bound for the provinces. For a decade in Portland I had remained unswervingly on track: building a practice, plugging myself into the community, becoming a player in politics, setting the stage for a high-level return to government, all the while keeping a hand in the artistic game. Then, on the cusp of realizing everything I had strived for, I had torched my master plan and yielded to the passion for theater that had gradually overtaken me. The construction of the CoHo Theater had been an unqualified success, but StageDirect had provided my first bitter taste of hubris. I had rebounded with the bold stroke of launching a bid for Congress, only to find my aspirations dashed by a slightly naughty theater video.

But it had turned out all right in the end. I had not compromised on anything fundamental to me—my artistic integrity, my political principles, my unwillingness to remain in a job that no longer excited me—and I had been rewarded with a high-echelon position that could not have been better designed for me if I'd drawn it up myself. The wounds suffered by my marriage were soon to heal with the return to my wife's hometown and the stability of a steady job. StageDirect's remorseless draining of my bank account—including almost nine months without a paycheck—was about to come to a close. And all this was topped with the lustrous promise of a fascinating career in the arts after my government service was done.

I flew back to Portland with my daughter on Tuesday and was able, because of the time change, to spend a few hours in the office digging out from a week's absence. I spoke with a number of my CoHo and StageDirect compatriots to share the good news from Washington. I received a call from someone named Ann Puderbaugh in the communications office at the NEA wanting to set up a time to go over a press release she was preparing on my appointment. We set a time for the following day.

That Wednesday morning, an e-mail arrived from Ann Hingston alerting me to a call I would receive from the NEA legal staff about ethics and relations with arts organizations. Shortly after receiving the email, I had the call with Puderbaugh, which was unexceptional. She just wanted to ensure she was accurately describing my background. She mentioned that she was familiar with the StageDirect mission and the company's six productions, as she had just visited our website. I checked with her on the likely timing of the press release. She said it could go out any time during the next two to three weeks. I mentioned that there were people I wanted to contact personally before there was a public announcement so that they heard the news from me, not by reading it in the newspaper. I asked for at least a week to make those calls. The timing was fine with her, although she cautioned me that the agency was prickly about people in the media or the arts community learning of an appointment in advance of the NEA's announcement. I assured her I would be contacting friends and business associates outside of these NEA constituencies.

After I hung up with Puderbaugh, I called John Easton and Dan Lavey. We agreed that with the arrival of the official word and the agency's beginning work on a press release, now was the time to provide particulars of the various StageDirect and CoHo productions to the NEA. The consensus was that I should call Eileen Mason and have a discussion with her first, followed by a written description of the various productions. As it was already nearing the end of the Washington business day, I decided to place the call to Mason the following morning.

As I headed home that Wednesday evening, I turned on my cell phone, which I generally left off while in the office. On my voicemail was a very peculiar message from Ann Hingston saying that she needed to speak to me right away about something that had arisen that might affect my position. Her language was stilted and evasive and it cut me to the quick. What in the hell had gone wrong? Had the White House reversed course? Were there budgetary problems? Was it *Poona*? The wording of Hingston's message suggested more of an institutional issue than something related to me personally, but it was impossible to know. I tried to reach her on her office phone and then on her cell phone, each without success. I drove home, hands shaky on the wheel, and resumed my frantic calling from our family room. Unable to reach her, I tried Dan at home to see if he had heard anything. He hadn't. I debated whether to try to reach Hingston at home. In addition to all the other steps we'd taken based on the NEA offer, we had an offer pending on the Bethesda townhouse that could be accepted by the seller at any time. I managed to locate Hingston's number through directory assistance and got her answering machine. I heard nothing that evening, which made for a restless night.

The NEA left me to twist in the breeze until just after lunch the following day, when Hingston finally called me at the office. She informed me in an officious tone that the NEA had chosen to withdraw my offer. Almost choking with mingled rage and despair, I spluttered out, "Why?" She would give me no explanation. My voice shaking, I practically hissed "You make me an unconditional, official offer. You know that I have acted on that offer, including making an offer on a house. And now you just suddenly withdraw it without even giving me the courtesy of an explanation?" This was greeted with a sanctimonious repetition of the party line. I ended the call.

Shattered, numb, despairing, forsaken: none of those withering words could do justice to my state of collapse as I sprawled at the desk of my failing company, alone in the little theater that was a monument to my passion for the arts—a passion that had seemingly ruined my life. My saving grace had vaporized. There would be no glorious denouement to my personal drama of marital unhappiness, unfulfilled entrepreneurial visions, and mounting bills. I had no more grand plans.

I went about the mortifying task of calling my wife, my parents, my CoHo and StageDirect colleagues, and my political backers to let them know the disastrous news. They offered what solace they could, but there was no comfort to be had. On top of all my devastated prospects, I feared that the NEA would unofficially put out word—however groundless it might be—that they had pulled the offer because of alleged concealment of my background in the arts and that the reputation for integrity I had built over an entire career would be destroyed.

Sometime during this ordeal, I picked up a telephone message featuring an unfamiliar voice. The woman identified herself as an official at Wolf Trap, an amphitheatre outside of Washington that played host to many symphony and popular concerts. She was calling to say that she had been referred to me as the new NEA grants chair by Dana Gioia and that she would love to discuss an application they were intending to submit. At first I sat stunned, wondering whether the agency had made yet another terrible mistake following the erroneous form letter. Then I burst into thunderous laughter. It was priceless, particularly in light of the lecture I had received from the NEA public relations flak the previous day about not jumping the gun on a public announcement. The fact that this woman was calling from DC only made the irony more delicious. I wrung as much out of that laugh as I could. My only other smile that day followed word that the seller of the townhouse in Bethesda had chosen to counter our offer, so were able to wriggle free of that transaction unscathed.

My supporters pledged to find out what they could about the withdrawal of the offer. In the meantime, years of childhood training in good manners held sway. The day after the bomb dropped, I sent an e-mail to Eileen Mason passing on the message from the errant Wolf Trap favor-currier. I took the opportunity to express dismay at the turn of events and sought to confirm that no one had impugned my integrity in the process. She smoothly thanked me for the message and assured me that she had heard no discussion of my integrity within the agency. You would have thought from the mannerly tone of the exchange that one of us had spilled soup on the other's clothing and was offering up the name of a dry cleaner to rectify the clumsiness.

That afternoon I received a sympathy call from Gordon Smith. He did not come to be a United States Senator for nothing: he was equal parts empathetic, indignant, and optimistic. He said he could not imagine what Amy and I must be going through, that I was a tremendous candidate, that it was the administration's loss, and that he held out hope he could land me another position in Bush's second term. He was classy, gracious, and reassuring. I was still too shell-shocked to do anything but stutter out a few words of thanks for his support and his thoughtfulness in making the call.

Shortly afterward, reports started arriving from the front. John Easton learned that not only *Poona* but also *Straight* had played a major part in the NEA's decision to cut me loose. Dan Lavey reported that the administration had expressed frustration over my failure to disclose the existence of these titles earlier in the appointment process, but said—based on a candid conversation with White House staffer David Thomas—that the decision was ninety percent attributable to the content of the StageDirect productions and ten percent to disclosure-related concerns. Dan's take was that it would not have mattered when these productions were disclosed; I would have been toast at any point. This was consistent with what Mason herself had e-mailed me, that my integrity had not played a part in the agency's internal discussions.

Thomas, who was no longer worked in Karl Rove's office, also told Dan that the NEA—not the White House—had been chiefly responsible for the decision.

As this intelligence flowed in and the shock of losing what had been so firmly in my grasp wore off, my anger began to mount. I was incensed both by the spinelessness of the withdrawal and the gutless manner in which it had been communicated. Were these alleged champions of the arts so supine that they would sacrifice an appointee—whom they all agreed was extremely qualified—because of videos of two theater productions, both of unquestionable merit and national acclaim? Were they so obsessed with appeasing the administration's puritanical right-wing base that they would effectively practice censorship in their hiring decisions based on content that caustically explored the roots of homosexuality or satirically deployed profanity? And having made the cowardly decision to withdraw my offer, were they so callous as to chop off at the knees without the courtesy of an explanation someone who had labored loyally on behalf of Republican candidates for over two decades, especially in the President's own campaign?

In the midst of my pain and outrage, I understood that these were the reactions of an amateur. Somewhere some steely-eyed professional politicos in comfortable leather chairs had determined that they were prepared to risk nothing relating to the NEA that might raise a peep out of the right, even if it meant casting aside a well-qualified loyalist. And those same cold-blooded operators had decreed that in whacking this guy it was prudent not to let him know what hit him, because who knows what he might say or do.

I also recognized that as an amateur, I needed the help of professionals if I were going to fight back. I called John Easton at his office in DC and told him that he and I both knew this decision was not right. It was not right in substance, and it was not right in process. It was an affront to Republicans like Gordon Smith who understood that the purpose of the arts was not simply to amuse and entertain, but to enlighten and provoke. And it was in fact an affront to Gordon Smith himself, who had vigorously supported my appointment with full knowledge of all aspects of my background, including these very productions. In as many words I challenged John: what are you going to do about this?

It soon became clear that the answer was "not much." Perhaps the only thing that could have saved my candidacy was Gordon getting on the phone to Karl Rove and Dana Gioia and telling them that this was bullshit and that they would be well advised to reconsider. To my knowledge, he did not do this. I cannot say that he made a political miscalculation in letting the axe fall on me without protest. He was in hot water with the White House over his vote against drilling in the Arctic National Wildlife Refuge, and he needed to pick his spots for further confrontations. Religious conservatives in Oregon had teed off on Gordon in his '02 reelection campaign for pandering to liberals on various social issues, and some of them would have had a field day if he appeared to be advocating for the likes of *Poona the Fuckdog* and *Straight*. He may well have concluded that he could not overturn the administration's political judgment and that it would be folly to try.

Gordon Smith and his circle did a magnificent job of going to bat for me when it was easy to do so. It was easy because I was a manifestly qualified candidate who by any measure had paid his political dues. They surpassed all expectations in writing letters, arranging meetings, and working the phones when no real expenditure of political capital was required. No chits are truly being cashed to advance an office-seeker who stands to make everyone look good. But, with apologies for the mixed metaphors, when the chips were down and the bloom was off their fair-haired boy, they kept their powder dry.

I cannot fault them much. I was, after all, a grown-up with long political experience who had accepted the risk of seeking a political appointment on which there could be no guarantees. Their judgment as to the impact of the StageDirect productions was likely clouded by their familiarity with me: their knowledge from our years of working and socializing together that I was not some sleazy pornographer. I believe they were genuinely surprised by the administration's decision and were in no way complicit with the eventual outcome. They were supportive and caring throughout the entire process, including after the boom fell. But the fact remains that they stepped aside and did nothing to challenge the administration's cowardice when the shit hit the fan, despite all I had done for the party and for Gordon.

John Easton appeared to limit his efforts on my behalf to post-mortem calls to David Thomas. I told John that if it became clear the NEA position could not be salvaged—and without Gordon interceding, it was plain that it couldn't—I wanted to know where I stood with the administration overall. Was I a pariah across the board? After several weeks of John reporting that Thomas was sparingly returning his calls, my status was obvious: I was a dead man as far as Bush and company were concerned. I told John to cease and desist. He counseled patience, but Dan Lavey advised me to accept that I was damaged goods and move on. He said I should be thankful that at least I was not thrown from the train after starting the NEA job and moving my family across the country.

Dan was right, of course, but I was not in a thankful frame of mind. I had to console a wife whose visions of a renewed stability and a new life near her aging mother had been suddenly dashed. I had to explain to young children that the promised move near Grandmom—which they had shared with all their friends— would not take place, but that our house would remain on the market while we tried to sort out our next steps. I had to face the reality that we had psychologically left Portland, but physically remained there, without income. And I had to come to grips with the bitter recognition that my sandcastles of Washington glory had been washed away forever, and that for the first time in my adult life I found myself with no master plan.

## CAROLINA

My favorite writer of short fiction, Somerset Maugham, wrote a wonderful story called *The Alien Corn*, in which a wealthy Jewish family in early twentieth century England has gone to great lengths to conceal its origins. They change their name (from Bleikogel to—the fitting—Bland) and take up the life of landed British gentry, while maintaining a thriving business in London that has made their country estate possible. The apple of their eye is their elder son, who readily passes as a young English gentleman and has the looks and sporting prowess to cut a figure in fashionable circles, gaining a social distinction his parents could never hope to achieve. They indulge his youthful excesses while keeping a tight and sullen grip on the Semitic-featured younger son, who is kept out of view and groomed to run the family business.

But their pretensions to British aristocracy begin to unravel. The elder son develops a keen interest in the piano. He drops out of Oxford and London society in hopes of becoming a concert pianist. His parents are at their wits' end. The world of music is no place for an English gentleman, except as a patron. They bully and cajole in an effort to change their son's mind, but to no avail. He leaves England and becomes a bohemian on the Continent.

I have reflected often on Maugham's revealing tale in the time since the NEA debacle. Was I—a closeted Jew with an Anglicized name raised in the WASPy enclaves of Winnetka and Williams College—alien corn in the soil of the Republican Party? For many years I thought not. I felt at home, and even embraced, in the partisan circles in which I traveled. My talents were appreciated; my contributions were recognized. My defining political values—personal liberty and responsibility and skepticism of government—seemed rooted in Republican ideology.

Curiously, Ronald Reagan—whose spendthrift ways cut against my fiscally tight-fisted grain—gave comfort to me as a Republican Jew. His administration attracted legions of conservative intellectuals, including many neo-conservative Jews, who sought to re-make the conceptual landscape of Washington. As a grassroots activist who then left the Beltway for provincial Portland, I did not readily identify with these lofty think-tank theorists, but it was reassuring to see Jews in such high places within the GOP.

Of course I was aware of being a distinct minority. There were precious few Jews, declared or otherwise, around me in Oregon Republican circles. Every once in a while an anti-Semitic remark would issue from the mouth of a fellow activist—perhaps after a few drinks had lowered the PC guard—and no one would object, least of all me. But I was not ashamed of taking the road less traveled, and I was contemptuous of the great mass of Jews who flocked, reflexively and in lockstep, to the Democratic Party.

The absence of Jews in Republican politics also presented me with opportunities. My stereotypical verbal facility earned me a reputation as a formidable speaker and eloquent master of ceremonies, both of which aided my advancement through the Republican ranks. On occasion my cleverness landed me in slightly distasteful roles—like playing Morrie Amsterdam to Gordon Smith's Dick Van Dyke—but on balance, being a lone Jew among the Gentiles served me in good stead.

I don't know that I ever attributed my passion for theater to my Jewish ancestry, but on some level I acknowledged a linkage. I was proud of the Jews' legacy of artistic achievement and thankful that I was endowed with at least some of that creative spark. But Jews are hardly alone in their devotion to the arts, and the Jewish obsession with professional achievement means that many gifted artists forsake the arts for law or medicine and only display their talents in office party skits or upon retirement.

No, what I came to regard as uniquely Jewish in myself was a certain cosmopolitan perspective that seems to make Jews more accepting of the unconventional in society. I lack the credentials to offer a scholarly explanation, but two thousand years of diaspora—of adapting to disparate environments all over the world, of surviving prejudice and oppression—appear to have conferred on Jews a cultural tolerance and openness that is less characteristic of peoples who have enjoyed a more stable and grounded history. Perhaps it was because Jews never had the opportunity to develop a landed aristocracy and were compelled to ply mercantile or financial trades that brought them into contact with both the high and low elements of society and of cultures around the globe. Perhaps it was because of the clustering of Jews in more urban areas, away from the insularity of agrarian life. Perhaps, in America, it was because of a sense that the country's social conventions were dictated by WASP elites—not of the Jews' making—and thus more open to question. Whatever the explanation, I have found Jews to be more worldly in their outlook, more prepared to embrace diverse and unorthodox views, and less judgmental of those whose world view or lifestyle does not comport with traditional norms.

I don't mean to suggest that the Jewish community in the US is not bourgeois. Jews have been as keen as any immigrants to America to amass wealth and all its social-climbing trappings and have been remarkably successful in doing so. And it's not to say that Judaism is without a fundamentalist fringe that is as doctrinaire and inward-looking as any of the world's religions. But my own sense of Jewish identity was rooted in a cosmopolitan outlook that shaped my values, my friendships, and my career.

Above all else, this cosmopolitanism informed my approach to the arts. I viewed theater as an unblinking beam of light trained on the human condition—taking life as it is found, however strange or foreign, without prejudice or predisposition. I did not shy away from the controversial or the contrarian, the odd or the offbeat, just because the reality portrayed was alien to my own. I did not seek in the performing arts a reinforcement of my own comfort zone, but an exploration of dimensions not necessarily "dreamt of in my philosophy."

Time and again over the past twenty years, I had the opportunity turn away from this window onto otherness, to yield to the warm caresses of convention and all the material pleasures she could lavish upon me. And time and again—as a Stanford law student performing Brecht in sterile lecture halls, a CIA lawyer moonlighting on the fringe stages of the nation's capital, a Covington & Burling associate honing a script penned in the sun-splashed south of Spain and on the banks of the Nile, a Ball Janik partner wandering with CoHo through the desert of makeshift venues, and finally a roll-the-dice and go-where-no-one-has tread-before theater video entrepreneur—I rebuffed her advances and insisted on a place in my life for the unconventionality of the artistic world. Whether my insistent embrace of the arts was attributable to the Williams grad's eternal preservation of options, a chronic inability to mature, or an enduring poseur complex I really cannot say. Whatever the motivation, I followed the dictates of my nature, and as I look back I sense the cosmopolitanism of the unacknowledged Jew refusing to relinquish his roots.

For some twenty years, the cosmopolitan happily co-existed with the Republican. This was not by accident, of course. I chose to pursue my politics in environments that I suspected would be hospitable to my ways. I ran in a crowd of educated, informed, intellectually curious men and women who were passionate about a brand of Republicanism that did not exclude artistic creativity. Many were religious, many were pro-life, and many would deem themselves social conservatives, but they attended and lauded CoHo plays that were unfamiliar and at times unsettling. Senator Gordon Smith was our icon, a paragon of enlightened conservatism who—atop a bedrock of religious conviction—managed to cultivate political fields of tolerance and openness.

I supported George W. Bush in 2000 because I believed he was cut from this same Republican cloth. I did not distrust him because of his born-again religious profile or his pro-life stance. On the contrary, I felt these made him a more sensible choice than his father had been to lead a party that—with the mass defection of the South from the Democratic Party—had undeniably become more conservative. I thought it essential that our presidential candidate have credibility with those on the right who controlled our congressional delegation and numerous state parties. I recognized that Oregon was no microcosm of the nation nor of the Republican Party, and I had no interest in trying to remake either in Oregon's image. We were not going back to the days of Nelson

Rockefeller or Robert Taft, and it was critical that we nominate a candidate who could unify the party against the Al Gore-led rump of Clintonism.

The first President Bush had failed to win reelection in '92 for a host of reasons, but primarily, in my view, because he lacked a core identity that resonated either with the Republican faithful or the persuadable swing voters. His patrician roots—hopelessly tangled somewhere between Kennybunkport and Midland—conferred a certain noblesse oblige that led him to oblige everyone while convincing no one—fiscal hawks, pro-lifers, name your constituency—that he was really one of them. I believed George W. Bush, because of the Texas makeover the next Bush generation had undergone, had the stuff to overcome the family legacy and build an identity that was unimpeachably conservative yet informed by a value system honed for generations on the playing fields of Andover and Yale.

In other words, I expected that a second-generation President Bush would govern as an enlightened conservative, guided by a Texas populism that was tempered by a family history of Eastern Establishmentarianism. He would not pander to the right as his father had because he would not have to: he was one of them. Yet he would not hesitate to display the compassion that his campaign so ballyhooed and, yes, the cosmopolitanism that was his heritage.

Perhaps this was too much to expect of any politician. Perhaps I conveniently overweighted the Eastern elite element of George W. Bush's make-up because, like any political apostle, I tended to project my own aspirations and sensibilities on to the candidate at the expense of his actual experience and personality. Perhaps I should have discounted the endorsements of Gordon Smith and others of similar political stripe as expedient jumps onto a front-running bandwagon, rather than a clear-eyed assessment that this was a candidate of like mind.

But whatever my blind spots might have been, I was betrayed by this man. There is no question that he presented himself to the nation as a unifier, a consensus-seeker rather than an ideological zealot, and a leader prepared to reach out to heal the yawning divides in this country. His administration's decision to withdraw its offer to me as the Deputy Chairman for Grants & Awards at the National Endowment for the Arts is admittedly no declaration of war or landmark tax cut, but it speaks volumes as to who George W. Bush truly is and how he has actually governed. He will do nothing—nothing—that will antagonize the social conservative wing of the Republican Party. I will give him credit for not pandering to social conservatives, because pandering suggests an aspect of pretending to be something that you're not. This President Bush is in foursquare alignment with social conservatives and thus has no need to pander.

He and Karl Rove have made a cynical calculation that there is no reason to upset "the base" on social or cultural issues, as voters will ultimately cast their ballots on whether they feel secure regarding the homeland and the economy. Why bother to risk antagonizing the true believers when there is so little to gain? In their view, there is no political upside associated with an agency like the NEA. All that might come out of the NEA of any political consequence is some provocative piece of pointy-headed twaddle that will have the right-wingers up in arms.

I doubt the White House was so crass as to lay this out explicitly to Dana Gioia when he accepted the chairmanship, but I'm sure the message was clear: avoid controversy at all costs. Entertain and divert, but do not dare or provoke. The agency followed this script admirably when it laid out its first major initiative under its new Chairman: touring productions of Shakespeare. Shakespeare is the finest dramatist in the English language, but it is scarcely breaking new ground to make the Bard's plays the opening act of the Bush/Gioia NEA. And God knows it won't offend even the most knuckle-dragging of reactionaries.

The White House staffer, David Thomas, told my supporters in Oregon that it was the NEA that made the decision to pull my offer, not the White House. But that is a distinction without a difference. The NEA may well have made the call, but they did so because they had a firm grasp on the political context in which they were operating. The mob boss does not need to give express orders to his capos on who needs to be hit; they catch his drift. This does not, however, absolve the NEA from the utter fecklessness they displayed in letting me go.

No doubt the administration, if they deign to take notice of this matter at all, will say that it was a minor personnel action and had no bearing on policy. They either will probably not comment publicly on the reasons for their decision, but privately they will put out that I was not forthcoming during the review of my candidacy or will manufacture some other skeleton in my closet. My conscience is clear. I hid nothing from these people. I answered their questions forthrightly. I believed my supporters when they told me that disclosure was a non-issue here and that the administration would have sawed off my branch whenever my connection with Straight and Poona came to light.

As much as I deplore the cynical calculations of this administration, I'll give George Bush this: I believe much of the evident lack of cosmopolitanism in this man is genuine. With all due apologies to a town I have never visited and know only through press accounts, he appears to be very much a product of Midland, Texas and has done a commendable job of nullifying his Eastern Seaboard cultural inheritance. He appears curious about other cultures only to the extent he considers them a threat to the national security of the United States. He appears curious about ways of life that are not his own only to the extent these represent perceived political opportunity, such as his shameless efforts to court the Hispanic vote.

And it is for that reason that I, a cosmopolitan Jew, would have indeed been alien corn in the administration of George W. Bush and why I said at the outset of this memoir that I believe they did me a favor by showing me the door before I even entered the room. For months after they withdrew the offer I was despondent over all that I had lost: the status of a high-level appointment, the security of a comfortable paycheck after a long period without income, the glamour of hobnobbing with prominent artists, the prospect of a promising career post-government, and a fashionable exit from the stage of Portland, Oregon. I despaired of regaining the confidence of my wife, who had been awaiting a return to stability near her family in DC. I had the sickening sense of having thrown away over a dozen years of my life in a provincial rat race of civic and political networking that had failed me miserably in my hour of need.

As I bottomed out emotionally, I had no choice but to confront the fact that a choice I thought I would never have to make had been made for me. I had operated for two decades under the belief that I could play leadership roles in both the arts and Republican politics. I had achieved distinction on both fields of play without feeling compromised or conflicted. And I probably could have continued to successfully straddle both worlds had I been content to limit my horizons to Oregon.

But I was an ambitious man, and I aspired to play on the national scene. It was not enough for me to polish the little gem that was CoHo Productions; I aimed to pioneer the dissemination of theater to a vastly larger audience by means of digital video. It was not enough for me to be a mover and shaker in the Oregon GOP; I craved a senior administration appointment.

My ambition brought me a rude bust in the chops in both arenas: StageDirect struggled trying to cut through the big-dollar, mass-market, formula-fed, star-vehicle thicket of Hollywood. I was sent packing by the Bush gang before I entered his culturally constricted, politically craven, and artistically vapid administration.

The NEA debacle forced me to the painful recognition that I could not pull off this wondrous Renaissance Man act, that I would not be afforded the privilege of hopping back and forth between two yellow brick roads. I could be a creative person and play in the arts, or I could be a political person and play with the Republicans. It was either Door Number 1 or Door Number 2, and after months of bitter grieving and halting recovery, I found that George W. Bush had actually made the right choice for me.

I realized that the greatest fulfillment for me had come not in practicing the rituals of politics: it came in fitful bursts of energy and vision into a coherent whole that I could call my own play, in marshalling the resources to present the great gifts of a Sam Gregory or a Troy Mink or a David Schmader to an appreciative audience, and in forging partnerships with artists that found a market for their art without dilution or adulteration. Politics had brought great fellowship, the rush of competition, the thrill of victory, praise from my peers, and clients for my legal practice—but it did not move me. It was not my calling, it was not my passion, and it was not (to reach back to my college philosophy days) an end in itself.

I believe I would have acquitted myself well as the Deputy Chairman for Grants & Awards, but at some level I would have been prostituting myself. Being a part of this administration would at some point have forced me to betray what I knew was right and good as an artist and thus betray my own nature. I would have had to suppress my cosmopolitanism among the incurious, my desire to dare among the conformists, and yes, my Jewishness among the Christians.

I understand the gravity of this last remark, which is not intended to label the Bush administration as anti-Semitic in the sense of discriminatory practices or ethnic slurs. They would no doubt trot out the many high-profile Jews who have served in this government, from Paul Wolfowitz to Ari Fleischer. But my own experience with the NEA and my observation of so many other actions, big and small, by Bush and his team—from the decision during the 2000 campaign to speak at Bob Jones University, to the appointment of John Ashcroft (a smart, educated, competent zealot), to the right's usurpation of the faith-based initiatives program, to the marketing of Harriet Miers for the Supreme Court based on her born-again bona fides—lead me to believe that at the core of this administration is a rigid fundamentalist Christianity to which cosmopolitan Jews are thoroughly alien.

Jewish neo-conservatives found a comfortable home in the Reagan administration, which while occasionally pandering to religious conservatives was basically secular—led as it was by a former Hollywood actor who rarely went to church. Jewish neo-conservatives also had a prominent place in the first Bush administration, which was presided over by an Eastern Establishment patrician for whom religion was institutional rather than evangelical.

But I suspect Jewish neo-conservatives in this administration feel like strangers in a strange land, and I suspect that they practice some level of cultural self-censorship in the workplace. I suspect they can only be themselves once they have left the office. Perhaps for the apparatchiks at the Department of Defense, the remaking of the map of the Middle East is worth it. But for me, an artist who would have been a key player in the federal government's funding of the arts, it would have struck to the very heart of who I have found myself to be.

I have come to recognize that for me, it is best to leave politics to the professionals. In that arena I am an amateur—perhaps a gifted amateur—but an amateur all the same. I have never been able to cast aside an idealism that I must now class as naïveté. I persist in believing it is not only culturally beneficial but politically advantageous for Republicans to demonstrate a spirit of adventure in the arts, as it represents a relatively inexpensive means of reaching out to independents and moderate Democrats who are inclined to view Republicans as heartless, soulless, and artless. But George W. Bush and Karl Rove have proved that it is sounder politics to govern like Jesse Helms—slavishly catering to the religious conservative base while counting on fear and insecurity and bringing home the old bacon to carry the day. The lesson they took away from the 2000 campaign is that all you need to win the election is a simple majority in the Electoral College and that, with as much unmitigated loathing as that election unleashed on the other side of the aisle, it made no sense to pursue a politics of broad coalitions and grand compromises. I never thought I would yearn for the days of Bill Clinton—whose economy with the truth was much more objectionable to me than his handling of the actual economy—yet he had the courage to play against partisan type on issues from welfare reform to balancing the budget, and it seemed to serve him in good political stead. But the professionals probably reckon those were different times.

So I have left politics behind. I have not, however, chosen to forswear the Republican Party. I have too many fond memories, too many good friends (although a few less after publication of this memoir, I suspect), too many common causes, too many Dorchester Tent Shows, and too many campaigns won and lost. I continue to believe that my fundamental values of personal liberty and responsibility and skepticism of government are Republican values though—as I just noted—I am chronically naïve. I have no interest in grousing about how the religious right has hijacked the party of Lincoln or about the disappearance of the Rockefellers and the Percys and the Hatfields. I count many friends in the ranks of social conservatives, who have geographically and demographically broadened the base of a formerly Eastern elitist party. I applaud their attention to the role of morality in public (and private) life, to the disintegration of the traditional family, to a focus on the fundamentals in public education. I know that there are many enlightened conservatives like Gordon Smith all over this country who make one proud to be a Republican. In my view, it is George W. Bush who has forsaken the promise of his administration, who has turned his back on his pledges of unity and healing, who has exploited rather than sought to bridge cultural divides, and who has led me to deem myself a non-practicing Republican.

The cultural gap I speak of is vast. I believe David Brooks is correct in asserting that the old-line, prep school, Ivy League blue-blooded WASP bourgeois order—founded on family and tradition and epitomized by the first President Bush—has largely given way to a multi-ethnic meritocracy—founded on education and achievement—that is prepared to embrace bohemianism, at least in some diluted, mass-merchandised, sixties nostalgia-fulfilling form. But, as Brooks has also written, the effect of this tectonic shift in our national power structure has been felt mainly in the so-called "blue" state elites on either coast, bypassing a huge swathe in the middle of the country which was never truly under the sway of the old WASP order in the first place. It is, of course, an over-simplification, but this "red" zone rejects even the modest bohemianism of the coastal elites as an assault on traditional values and established social convention.

I had not expected George W. Bush to be a full-bore bohemian any more than I had based my sales projections for StageDirect on large-scale video purchasing in Wichita or Paducah. But uniquely positioned as he was—with one foot in the blue world of Andover and Yale and the other in the red world of Midland—I had hoped that he might be an enlightened agent of cultural unity and that I might have the opportunity to deploy the arts in the service of that unifying effort. Ah well…

Amy and I have chosen to settle in her mother's ancestral region of the Carolinas, near—but not on top of—her family. I am aware of the irony in relocating to a Bible Belt state following a government appointment that foundered on the shoals of fundamentalism, but perhaps it lends credence to my assertion that I am uncomfortable not with religious conservatives in general but with the Bush administration in particular. In any case, we found we could not stay in Portland. Amy yearned for the East Coast, and my life in Oregon was so bound up in Republican politics that it was evident I needed a clean break. We flirted briefly with heading to DC anyway (psychologically we had already moved into that Bethesda townhouse), but decided that it would be too hurtful to relocate so close to the source of my woes. The comparatively inexpensive housing prices in the Carolinas enabled us to buy a larger home with the equity from the sale of our Portland house, which gave us a nice cushion with which to face the lingering uncertainty and instability. Our marriage has not fully recovered from the strains of the past several years, but I am hopeful that it will.

I am resolved that the arts will continue to play a pivotal part in my life. I remain active on the board of CoHo Productions, which recently opened its tenth season and its fifth in the CoHo Theater. Although the life of an arts non-profit is never stable, CoHo has paid off its theater-construction debt, exercised an option to extend its lease, and qualified for a line of credit on its own. I am working to launch a new theater festival in North Carolina that is dedicated to Southern plays and playwrights. Before tackling this memoir, I wrote a brief account of my days as a paperboy for the *Chicago Tribune* that proved a therapeutic retreat into my childhood in the aftermath of the NEA trauma, and I have recently completed a novel that revolves around a black box theater in Portland. There is more writing to come.

I am a father and a husband, and my family responsibilities will take precedence over any artistic aspirations. I am not so far lapsed from the bourgeois, nor so completely given over to the bohemian, to just resign my family to a life of penury. But I will always stake out a place in my life for the creative, even if it's writing for a mere hour each day before the rest of the family is awake or after they have gone to bed. I must.

In *The Alien Corn*, the Jewish son who turns his back on the comfortable life of a young English gentleman for a marginal existence devoted to music finds that he is an artistic mediocrity. I am keenly aware that I might meet a similar fate. I know I had the leadership ability, the push and drive, the organizational bent, and the oratorical flair to excel in the political world, just as the wayward son had the looks and the sportsman's skills to make a mark in London society. I still think about what might have been if I had never embarked on this odyssey in theater that led me from acting to *Bodyhold* to CoHo to StageDirect and ultimately to the productions of *Straight* and *Poona the Fuckdog* that did in my Republican career. But it was not in my nature—nor in that wayward son's—to make another choice. I am prepared to accept the consequences, which may well mean forsaking some measure of glory and distinction in an arena where I possessed considerable talent in favor of obscurity and rejection in a field where I may find I possess little. I might have lost the perfect job, but at least I have not hidden my light under a Bush.

# AUTHOR ACKNOWLEDGEMENTS

I am grateful for the unflagging enthusiasm and editorial agility of Kathryn Juergens; the steady hand of Dennis Stovall; the insightful comments of Ann Cole, Jim McDermott, and Jeff Meyers; the reassuring voice of Roger Cole; the commitment of the team at Ooligan; and the support and encouragement of Catherine Crawford Bradford, Kathy McCleary, Bill Powers, Amy Kinney Ruff, David Schmader, Marguerite Scott, Susan Terris, the Bridgeport Alehouse Literary Society, and the board of CoHo Productions. Above all, I thank Amy for her loving indulgence.

Gary D. Cole was raised in the suburbs of Chicago. He is a graduate of Williams College and Stanford Law School, where he acted in numerous theater productions. Cole served as a lawyer at the Central Intelligence Agency before writing a play based loosely on his Agency experience. After joining a Portland, Oregon, law firm, Cole founded a professional theater company, CoHo Productions, and became active in Republican politics. In 2000, he served as Finance Chair for the Bush Republican Victory campaign in Oregon and also launched StageDirect, a company that captures contemporary theater on digital video.

In 2003, Cole was appointed by the Bush administration to head the $60 million annual grants program at the National Endowment for the Arts. The administration later withdrew his appointment. Cole now resides with his wife and two children in Raleigh, North Carolina.

# PRESS ACKNOWLEDGEMENTS

Ooligan Press takes its name from a Native American word for the common smelt or candlefish, a source of wealth for millennia on the Northwest Coast and arguably the orgin of the word "Oregon." Ooligan is a general trade press rooted in the rich literary life of Portland and the Pacific Northwest. Founded in 2001, it is also a teaching press in the Department of English at Portland State University. Besides publishing books that honor cultural and natural diversity, it is dedicated to teaching the art and craft of publishing. The press is staffed by students pursuing master's degrees in an academic curriculum and integrated apprenticeship program under the guidance of a core faculty of publishing professionals. By publishing real books in real markets, students combine theory with practice; the press and the classroom become one.

The following Portland State University students completed the primary edit, design, and market effort for *Artless: The Odyssey of a Republican Cultural Creative.*

Workgroup Members:

Project manager: Kathryn Juergens
Cover design: Laura Howe and John Kimball
Interior design: Laura Howe and Tara Paluck
Back copy: Bo Björn Johnson
Acquisitions: Deborah Jayne and Kevin Vandehey
Editor: Kathryn Juergens
Copyediting: Bo Björn Johnson and Aime Shelton
Proofreading: Andrea Deeken and Bo Björn Johnson
Marketing: Andrea Deeken, Rich Geller, Laura Howe, Bo Björn Johnson, Kathryn Juergens Tara Paluck, and Ruth Scovill

Others who helped with *Artless: The Odyssey of a Republican Cultural Creative:*

Susan Applegate
Lake Boggan
Jaime Burbach
Karli Clift
Nancy D'Inzillo
Dirk DeVries
Brittany Ferry
Kelley (Kate) Jacquez
Deborah Jayne
Karen Kirtley
Emily Léger
Amy Lin
Peggy Lindquist
Jonah Loeb
Bo Mandoe
Rex Marshall
Adreanne Mispelon

Meredith Norwich
Paulette Rees-Denis
Chris Ross
Danae Samson
Kelley Schaefer-Levi
Jill Shellabarger
Corey Simpson
Karthik Sridhar
Dennis Stovall
Tracy Swensen
Robin Weage
Jason Weeks

# CONTINUE THE ODYSSEY

Want to learn more about Gary D. Cole and his political odyssey? Explore enhanced and supplemental book features at www.enhancedbooks.com by registering at www.enhancedbooks.com.

This feature may not be available indefinitely. See the registration information on the copyright page.

For the most up-to-date information on books from Ooligan Press and about the graduate publishing program at Portland State University, turn your browser to www.publishing.pdx.edu.

# ORDERING INFORMATION

All Ooligan titles can be ordered directly from the publisher or from your favorite bookseller in the United States, Canada, and online.

Ooligan Press
PO Box 751
Portland, OR 97207-0751
www.publishing.pdx.edu

# COLOPHON

This manuscript was set in ITC Berkeley Oldstype Std. Chapter headings are set in Engravers LT Std with running heads in Didot LT Std. It was printed on 60# white offset book sheet. The cover is 10 pt. C1S.

It was produced in Adobe® InDesign® CS2 with graphic work from Adobe® Photoshop® CS2.